MW01625442

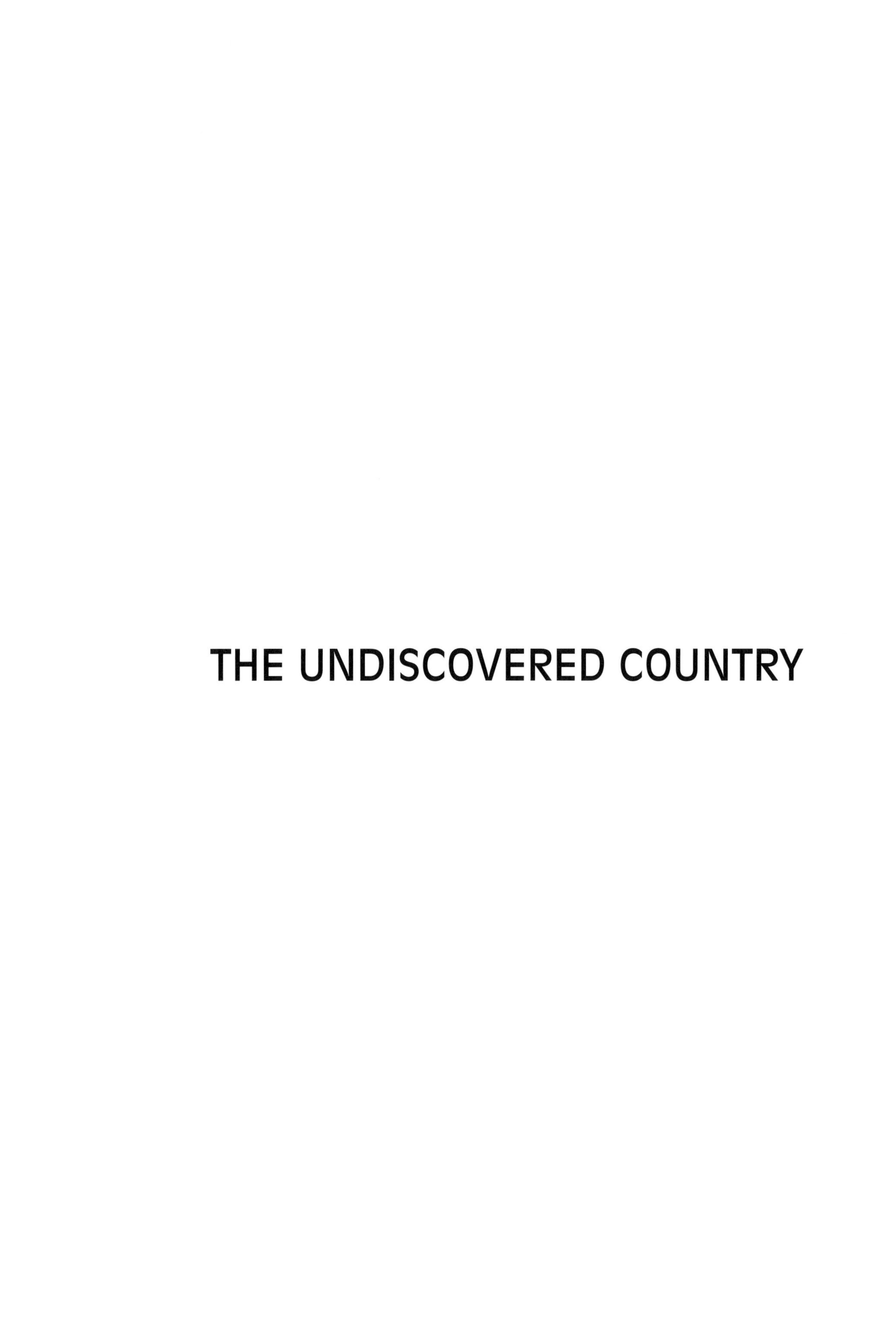

THE UNDISCOVERED COUNTRY

THE UNDISCOVERED COUNTRY

Russell Ferguson

Hammer Museum
University of California, Los Angeles

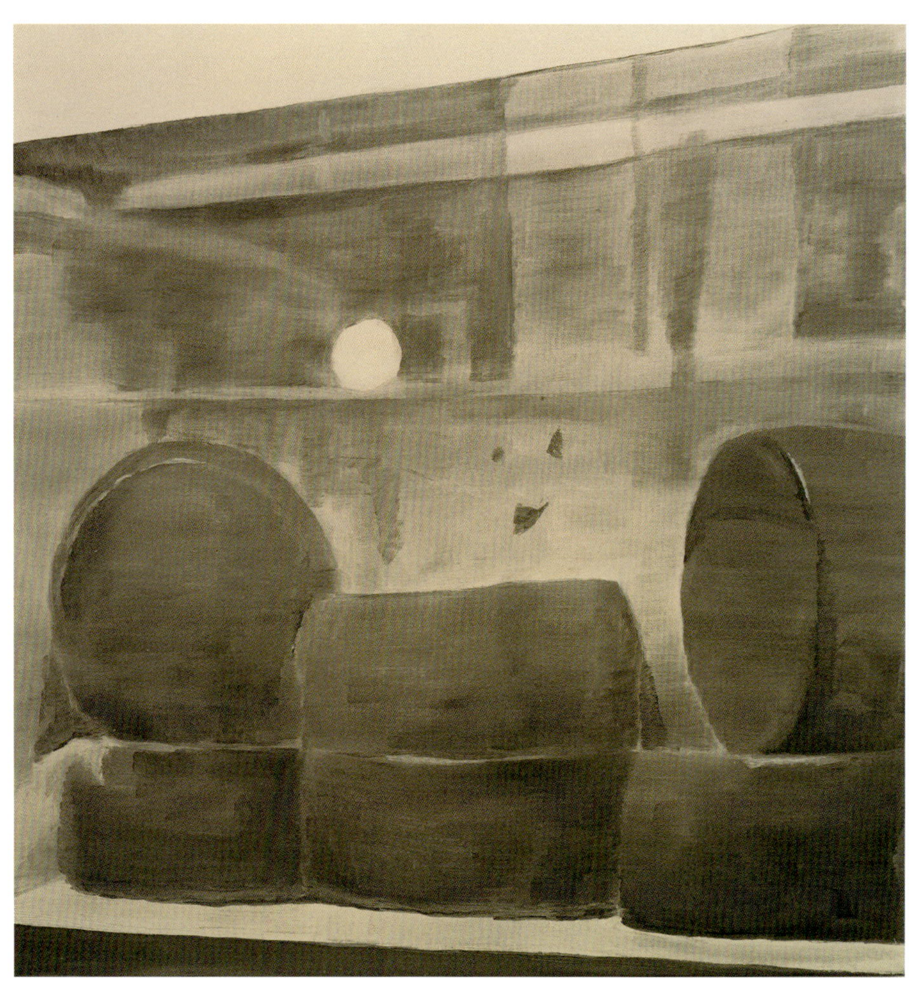

Luc Tuymans
Cheese, 1995

DIRECTOR'S FOREWORD

Painting is both the most revered and most contested of artistic media. Its death has been announced time and time again without, in the end, seeming to affect the continuing vitality of the medium.

"The Undiscovered Country," an exhibition covering work created between the mid-1960s to the present, examines the effect—aesthetically and philosophically—of both photography and abstraction on painting's ability effectively to represent the world around us. Organized by Chief Curator Russell Ferguson, the exhibition reflects the Hammer's commitment to examining works by young artists within the context of work by their more established colleagues, in the process questioning established art historical narratives and exploring the roads less traveled.

We are deeply grateful to the Warhol Foundation for joining us in this venture. Their generosity and their commitment to innovative scholarship have been crucial to making this exhibition possible. My sincere gratitude goes also to Eileen Harris-Norton and the Peter Norton Family Foundation, Beth Swofford, Maria Hummer and Bob Tuttle, David Teiger, Gail and Stanley Hollander, and The Broad Art Foundation.

And finally, I thank the staff of the museum for their dedication to the exhibition, and especially Russell Ferguson, whose wide-ranging and eclectic vision is at the heart of this project.

Ann Philbin

INTRODUCTION AND ACKNOWLEDGMENTS

This book occupies a potentially contradictory place in relation to the exhibition that it accompanies. In the exhibition, the argument of the project will be made almost entirely visually. Sixty paintings will be juxtaposed, at their real scale, in a set of galleries, without a great deal of verbal explanation. In the book the paintings appear as reproductions, of course, but I also provide a text that—in a further potential contradiction—attempts to articulate a conception of painting that is at least in part predicated precisely on its *resistance* to language. The book, therefore, runs a certain risk of standing in opposition to the exhibition. My hope, however, is that, taken together, the two might stand as complementary, rather than contradictory.

At the same time, however, both the exhibition and the book do actively embrace contradiction. When I say that the works resist language, for example, I certainly do not mean that the artists who made them are in any way ignorant or naïve about the difficult questions of representation around which the exhibition is structured. One of the initial motives that prompted me to undertake this project, in fact, was frustration at a surprisingly persistent critical position that tacitly exempts painters from the broader ramifications of their practice, focusing instead on rapturous evaluations of this or that piece of brushwork or on a virtually anecdotal response to the work's context. In this ahistorical approach, the old masters are presumed to constitute an unbroken and unproblematic lineage for young painters. Such positions are, I believe, less common among serious painters themselves, who tend to be quite aware of the burden they willingly pick up each time they address a blank canvas.

The text that follows cites many examples of the ongoing frustration felt by a wide-ranging group of painters in the face of this burden, the struggle to continue with painting, and what relevance such a practice can still have today. I ascribe this ongoing crisis of confidence to the successful challenge to painting's command of depiction that emerged with the invention of photography. In my view, photography introduced a fundamental break in the course of painting that has resulted in repeated crises for painting—and for individual painters—ever since.

Yet the real anguish evidenced in the statements of artists quoted in the text is itself partly contradictory, in that it goes hand in hand with the continuing—and equally evident—*pleasure* in painting that all the artists included here have also felt. This pleasure is perhaps the key sustaining factor that makes it possible to continue painting in spite of everything that militates against doing so. As Lukas Duwenhögger has put it, they work on in the midst of a "chaos of connections."

Out of the struggle with this chaos, I have attempted to draw out some (by no means exclusive) lines of development that seem to me to offer continuing possibilities for painting. The painters whose work I have selected manifest a wide range of approaches. They avoid, however, for the most part, the linearity of a flat, graphic style that denies the importance of painterly qualities. And they also owe little allegiance to the hectic expressionism that equates wild gesture with authentic emotion. They seem to me nevertheless to have found a place to work in which an acknowledgment of painting's history and the various challenges to its representational authority can be balanced with the production of works that still offer ways of seeing accessible only through painting.

The exhibition would not have been possible without the help of an enormous number of people, and I extend my deepest gratitude to all of those whose efforts have contributed to this project.

My heartfelt thanks go to the lenders of the exhibition, listed separately following these acknowledgments. Museums lent works that are among the most important in their collections, and many private individuals were willing to give up paintings that are an intimate part of their daily lives. Without their tremendous generosity the exhibition would not have been possible.

"The Undiscovered Country" has been very generously supported by the exhibition's funders. A substantial grant from The Andy Warhol Foundation for the Visual Arts was a valued vote of confidence in the project. I am also deeply grateful to Eileen Harris-Norton and the Peter Norton Family Foundation; Beth Swofford; Maria Hummer and Bob Tuttle; David Teiger; Gail and Stanley Hollander, and The Broad Art Foundation.

At the Hammer Museum, our director, Ann Philbin, has been an enthusiastic supporter of the exhibition from the moment I proposed it, and brought several specific works to my attention. I am very grateful for her unstinting backing. Curatorial assistant Aimee Chang worked on every detail of the exhibition and this publication, which could not have been realized without her endless daily attention to countless issues great and small. Our discussions concerning the content of the exhibition and the book were also extremely helpful to me.

Jennifer Wells, director of development, was tireless in her efforts to secure support for the exhibition, as were her staff: Sarah Sullivan, Stacen Berg, and Andrew Kaiser. My thanks also go to Lisa Whitney, chief financial officer, whose help has gone well beyond financial issues. Our registrars Portland McCormick, Grace Murakami, and Julie Dickover handled the complex shipping of paintings from all over the United States and Europe. Mitch Browning and Steven Putz were responsible for the installation. Sarah Stifler, head of public programs, has been enthusiastic in setting up a stimulating series of lectures and panel discussions. My thanks go also to Cassandra Coblentz, head of academic initiatives. Steffen Böddeker, communications director, expertly coordinated the press and publicity for the show, along with Melissa Goldberg, and with the help of Cynthia Wornham and Domenic Morea of Ruder Finn. Our intern Matthew Thompson was also very helpful. The entire staff of the museum were supportive of this project, and I would also like to thank George Barker, Ken Booker, Cindy Burlingham, Paul Butler, Jennifer Cox, Claudine Dixon, James Elaine, Andrea Gomez, Mo McGee, Michael Nauyok, Catherine O'Brien, David Paley, Paulette Parker, Becky Perez, Carolyn Peter, David Rodes, Roberto Salazar, Maggie Sarkissian, Mary Ann Sears, and Laura Young.

This book has been designed by Lorraine Wild and Stuart Smith. As usual working with them was a pleasure, and I am thrilled with the results. The copy editor was Jane Hyun, who made many useful suggestions on the text, and corrected many details throughout the book with her accustomed skill and thoroughness. Many of the ideas expressed in the book were first discussed with Karin Higa, and her helpful and thought-provoking comments on the text were a great help to me in attempting to clarify the ideas in it.

I am also deeply grateful to the following people and organizations whose enthusiasm and assistance were invaluable: Matt Aberle; Lily Asalde-Brewster; Kim Schoenstadt, Brienne Arrington, and Jen Liu, assistants to John Baldessari; Jean M. Bickley; Rachel Zur and Tanya Bonakdar of Tanya Bonakdar Gallery, New York; Lacy Boughn; Susan Brewer; Joanne Heyler, Juliana Hanner, and Jeannine Guido at The Broad Foundation; Corrina Durland, Laura Mitterand and Gavin Brown of Gavin Brown's enterprise, New York; Daniel Buchholz, Christopher Müller, and Katharina Forero of Galerie Daniel Buchholz, Cologne; Tracy Cannon; Regina Fiorito and Gisela Capitain of Galerie Gisela Capitain, Cologne; May Castleberry; Mark Coetzee; Lynne Cooke; Madeleine Richardson of the Crex Collection; Alexandra Nyerges and Tuliza Fleming of the Dayton Art Insitute; Elizabeth Dee and Joseph Wolin of Elizabeth Dee Gallery, New York; Sarah Decker; Andrea Feldman Falcione; Suzanne Feldman; Douglas Fogle; Mark Francis; Jaime Frankfurt; Stephen Friedman and Karin Eklund of Stephen Friedman Gallery, London; Alison Gingeras; Barbara Gladstone, Rosalie Benitez, and Kelly Kyst of Barbara Gladstone Gallery, New York; Lissa McClure and Marian Goodman of Marian Goodman Gallery, New York; Brad Grossman; Madeleine Grynsztejn; Kati Haack; Richard Hawkins; Ned Rifkin, Kerry Brougher and Amy Stack of the Hirshhorn Museum and Sculpture Garden; George Horner; Daniel Hug; Konoi Keith; Kourosh Larizadeh; Eric Litke; Karyn Lovegrove and Tim Buggs of Karyn Lovegrove Gallery, Los Angeles; Katalin Néray of the Ludwig Museum, Budapest—Museum of Contemporary Art; Kris Kuramitsu, Gwen Hill, and Kelly Barrie at the Peter Norton Family Foundation; Anders Bergstrom of McKee Gallery, New York; Allie Card of Metro Pictures, New York; Victoria Miro and Nina Øverli of Victoria Miro Gallery, London; Shirley Morales and Kevin McSpadden; Robert Fitzpatrick and Elizabeth A. T. Smith of the Museum of Contemporary Art, Chicago; Jeremy Strick, Paul Schimmel, Ann Goldstein, Michael Darling, and Karen Hanus of The Museum of Contemporary Art, Los Angeles; Amber Noland; Vlasta Odell; Christiaan Braun of the Over Holland Collection; Trudy Kramer of the Parrish Art Museum; Faustino Quintanilla; Shaun Caley Regen and Lisa Overduin of Regen Projects, Los Angeles; Jill and Dennis Roach; Kippy Stroud; Richard

Telles and Deborah Hede of Richard Telles Fine Art, Los Angeles; Brian Butler and Alexis Johnson of 1301PE, Los Angeles; Michael Toledo; James Welling; Rebecca Wilson; Ealan Wingate; Angela Choon, Bellatrix Cochran-Hubert, Hanna Schouwink; Amy Baumann, Amie Robinson, Matt Siegle, and David Zwirner of David Zwirner, New York.

In conclusion, I must thank, more than anyone else, the artists. Many have been more than generous, not just in making works available for the exhibition but in providing information and insight into their own works and into painting in general. The time spent in their studios has been the greatest privilege, and pleasure, of working on this project.

Russell Ferguson

LENDERS TO THE EXHIBITION

Charles Asprey, London
John Baldessari
Brian Biel
Paul Brach and Miriam Schapiro
The Brant Foundation, Greenwich, Connecticut
Eli and Edythe L. Broad Collection, Los Angeles
Melva Bucksbaum and Raymond Learsy
Cabinet Gallery, London
Janice and Mickey Cartin
Vija Celmins
Elizabeth Cunnick and Peter Freeman, New York
The Dayton Art Institute
Mari Eastman
Thomas Eggerer
Galerie Daniel Buchholz, Cologne
Collections of Eileen Harris-Norton and Peter Norton, Santa Monica
Alan Hergott and Curt Shepard
Hirshhorn Museum and Sculpture Garden, Smithsonian Institution, Washington, D.C.
Stanley and Gail Hollander
Hort Family Collection, New York
Craig and Lynn Jacobson
Thomas Lawson
Ludwig Museum Budapest—Museum of Contemporary Art
Tracy and Gary Mezzatesta
Museum of Contemporary Art, Chicago
The Museum of Contemporary Art, Los Angeles
Ovitz Family Collection, Los Angeles
Laura Owens
The Parrish Art Museum, Southampton, New York
QCC Art Gallery, The City University of New York
Jack and Joan Quinn, Beverly Hills
Rubell Family Collection, Miami
Keith and Kathy Sachs
Saint Louis Art Museum
Tony Shafrazi
Jose Noe Suro, Guadalajara
Jamie and Steve Tisch
Dean Valentine and Amy Adelson, Los Angeles
David and Monica Zwirner

Private Collections

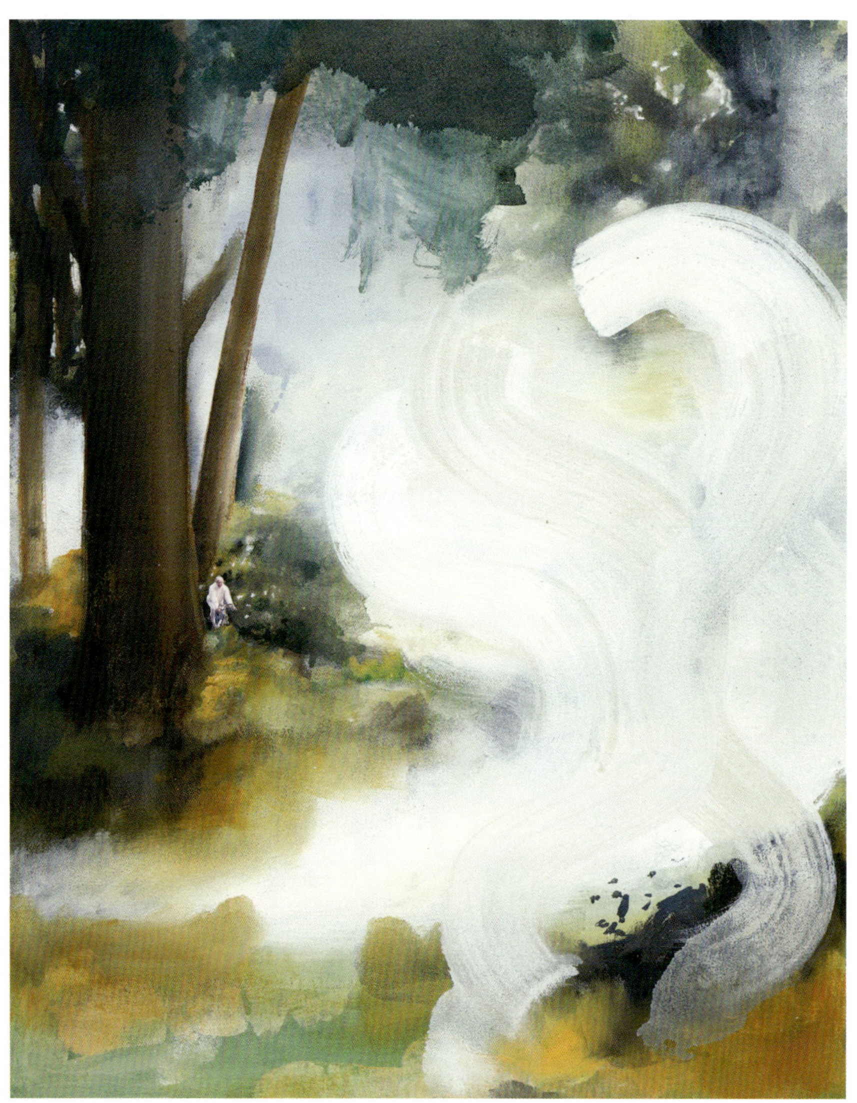

Jochen Klein
#39, 1996

the dread of something after death,
The undiscovered country, from whose bourn
No traveler returns, puzzles the will

Shakespeare, *Hamlet*, III, i, 78–80

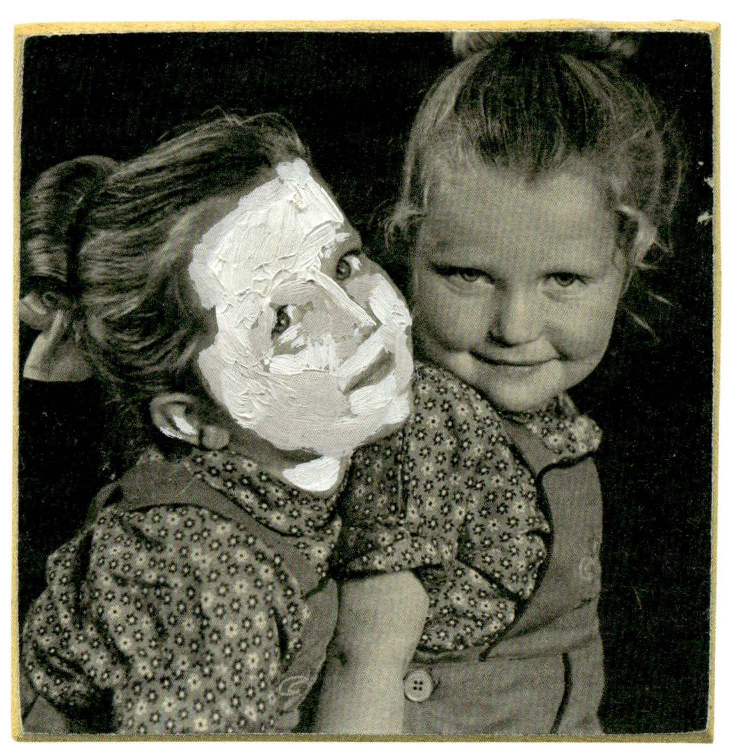

THE UNDISCOVERED COUNTRY

NOTHING LEFT TO SAY

The academic painter Paul Delaroche is believed to have been the first of many to announce, after seeing a daguerreotype in 1839, that "From today, painting is dead."[1] Photography's pictorial capacity threatened many of painting's most fundamental functions. Most of all, photography precipitated the long, ongoing crisis of painting by challenging its capacity to *represent*. A hundred and fifty years later, Gerhard Richter echoed Delaroche's response, this time with the benefit of hindsight: "There's almost nothing left to say about photography because it's so obvious that photography has taken away one important part of painting: the function of portraying, depicting."[2] Richter's simple yet ambiguous "nothing left to say" suggests the scale of the problem for painting. If photography really has taken over the primary role in representation, *is* there in fact anything left to be said? How can painting contribute to representation now? Complicating the situation further, painters who want to *depict* have to deal not only with the dominance of photography in the capacity to represent, but also with a whole tradition of abstract painting that moved on from representation altogether.

Gerhard Richter
Untitled, 1964

Richter's careful, obsessive obliteration of a child's face in a printed photograph (*Untitled*, 1964) is both an expression of the futility of painting and evidence of its persistence. The thick, creamy paint insists on its own materiality in defiance of the greater representative power of the photograph. "Painting was my attempt to explore what painting is still able and permitted to do," Richter said. "It was also the sheer obstinacy of carrying on painting, even though nothing seemed to come of it."[3] The pure painterly impulse struggles with its limits, and with the continuing desire to make recognizable images.

For painting, the steady usurpation by photography of its authority in representation created a new and increasing need for an *articulation* of the importance of painting. As Yve-Alain Bois has written, "industrialization meant much more for painting than the invention of photography and the incorporation of the mechanical into the artist's process.... It also meant a threat of the collapse of art's special

1 Delaroche, quoted in Helmut and Alison Gernsheim, *A History of Photography* (London: Thames and Hudson, 1969), 70.

2 Richter, interview with Jonas Storsve (1991), in *The Daily Practice of Painting: Writings and Interviews 1962–1993*, ed. Hans-Ulrich Obrist, trans. David Britt (Cambridge: The MIT Press, 1995), 227.

3 Richter, interview with Wolfgang Pehnt (1984), in ibid., 114.

status into a fetish or a commodity. It is in reaction to this threat that the historicism and essentialism of modernism was developed."[4] To this day many painters retain a profoundly ambivalent relationship to the medium that has been so successful in challenging their historic role.[5] Painters, of course, made use of photography from the very beginning, whether they concealed their use of it, like Ingres, or championed it, like Delacroix.[6] Even an artist as painterly and as apparently un-photographic in his approach as Fairfield Porter made use of photographs as studies in the way that earlier artists would have used a sketchbook.

For many younger contemporary painters, the photograph is so imbricated in the visual that the challenge has perhaps become less *whether* to deal with it than *how*. The question now is how to make a painting that is something other than a painted rendering of a photograph; how to transform a source image into something beyond illustration. But for many artists, including painters, the question of which medium commands the greatest representational authority has largely been settled. As Kerry James Marshall has bluntly put it, "In the hierarchy of representational approaches, from drawing to painting to photography, photographs, even low-quality ones, have a greater truth-telling capacity than drawn and painted images."[7] The assumption is that painting must now look elsewhere for its raison d'être. The goal cannot be to supplant photography, but rather to go beyond it somehow.

LIKE A HOUSE PAINTER

Ambitious painters recognized early on that photography had irrevocably changed the terms of their art. One of the driving forces behind Impressionism was the need to respond to photography's claim of authority in representation. Impressionism sought out effects beyond the reach of photography. Color was paramount. A loose painterliness replaced the earlier emphasis on correct drawing, and ephemeral

4 Bois, "Painting: The Task of Mourning," in *Painting as Model* (Cambridge: The MIT Press, 1990), 233.

5 Marcel Duchamp, in a 1922 letter to Alfred Stieglitz, expressed an elegantly hostile ambiguity that continues to resonate: "You know exactly how I feel about photography. I would like to see it make people despise painting until something else will make photography unbearable." *The Writings of Marcel Duchamp* (New York: Da Capo, 1989), 165.

6 Ingres is reported to have said that photography was "admirable but one must not admit it." Quoted by Van Deren Coke in *The Painter and the Photograph* (Albuquerque: University of New Mexico Press, 1964), 8. This publication gives numerous specific examples of paintings and their photographic sources, including works by Delacroix, Manet, Cézanne, Gauguin, Picasso, and many others.

7 Marshall, "Notes on Career and Work," in *Kerry James Marshall* (New York: Abrams, 2000), 122.

atmospheric effects eclipsed elaborately worked-out compositions. An "impression" would now suffice. The retreat from representational authority had begun, as had the search for an alternative site of authority and autonomy. This turning away from the mimetic, specifically the literalness of the photographic, has been powerful ever since; it stands always alongside the parallel embrace of the photograph. Cubism, for example, can be seen as the investigation of a non-photographic system of representation that could encompass both time and movement. In both Impressionism and Cubism, artists made use of a brushstroke that was becoming increasingly autonomous, parallel to rather than entirely within representation. This ambivalent mark has proven central to representational painting ever since,[8] and has in fact become the cornerstone of an approach to painting that neither denies the authority of photography nor surrenders to it. It insists on the parallel authority of the act of depicting and the act of painting.

As early as the 1860s, artists were demonstrating an increasing indifference to finish. The painter was not to be looked on merely as a craftsman but as an intellectual who would offer a distinctive way of looking at the world in the broadest sense, a way that might or might not offer a polished image. Painters began to abandon the traditional final stage of making a painting: varnishing. Instead of the even tone produced by varnishing, they welcomed the varied tactility of the painted surface and even the roughness of the canvas itself. The most frequent objection to advanced painting in the late nineteenth century was precisely that the work was "unfinished." To many viewers, what was now offered as a completed work appeared to be no more than a study. One reason that the oil sketches of Constable and Corot seem so modern to our eyes, in fact, is precisely this unfinished quality. Such sketches remained essentially private, however. The Impressionists insisted that their paintings be recognized as

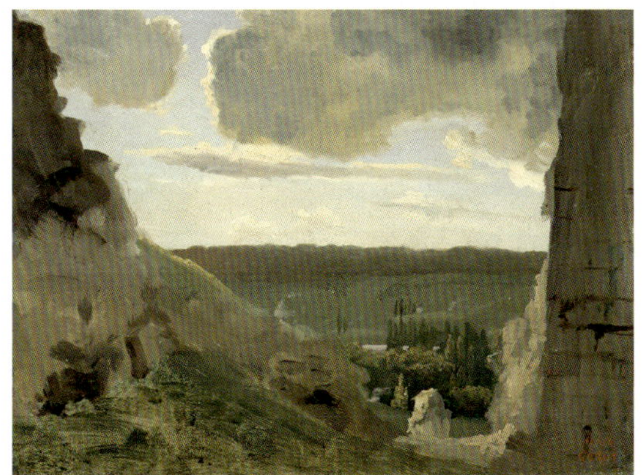

Jean-Baptiste-Camille Corot
Study of Medieval Ruins,
1829–34

8 Of course, this tendency can be traced even further back, in the rendering of water, fabric, clouds, etc. in Western painting, and in the treatment of landscape more broadly in classical Chinese painting. See Hubert Damisch, *A Theory of /Cloud/: Toward a History of Painting*, trans. Janet Lloyd (Stanford: Stanford University Press, 2002).

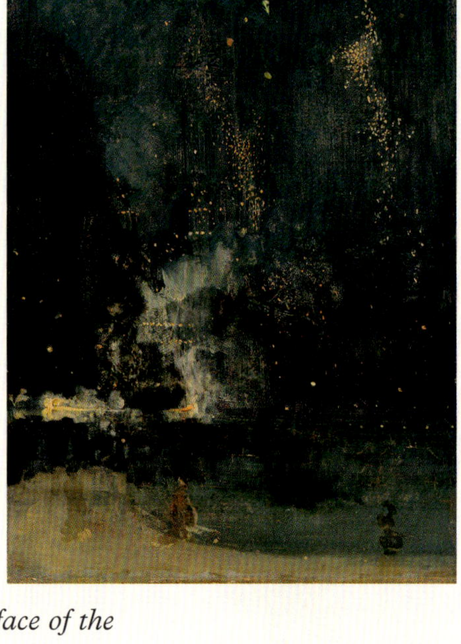

finished works, worthy of public exhibition. "Manet believes he is making paintings, but in reality he only brushes in sketches," said one critic.[9] Another offered sarcastic encouragement: "Let's thin out some Veronese green in a big pot and go at it like a house painter. Let's put the colors on flat without bothering at all about breaking them up."[10] Whistler was famously accused by John Ruskin of "flinging a pot of paint in the public's face."[11]

In the late work of Cézanne, the aesthetic of the unfinished achieved a decisive resolution, in part through a certain *lack* of resolution, the grain of the canvas support more than ever retaining its own presence within the depiction. As Hubert Damisch has described:

> *In the gaps, in what is lacking in the image, the canvas itself manifests its material nature, while the attention paid to the flat surface of the picture wins out, once and for all, over endeavors to create an illusion of depth. It is through this shift from an* image, *offered to the imagination, to a* picture, *offered as such to the spectator's perception, even more than through the deconstruction of the traditional space that made that shift possible, that Cézanne's work at the turn of the twentieth century marks a* break.[12]

The retreat from highly finished representation became its own kind of tradition. A deliberate de-skilling, an explicit rejection of conventional technique, is now one of the key ways for painters to represent the world without chasing in vain after photography. With photography in command of specificity, advanced painting seeks ambiguity. This offers a double appeal: on one hand offering the indeterminate space of fleeting visual registration, and of memory; on the other recognizing the autonomy and even arbitrariness of the painted surface itself. In an apparent paradox, a self-consciously flat, even apparently clumsy method of applying paint has became a favorite tool of the most sophisticated artists. Showy representational effects are disdained as academic, in favor of a direct technique that emphasizes formal structure, composition, and color relationships.

James Abbott McNeill Whistler
Nocturne in Black and Gold, the Falling Rocket, c.1875

Fairfield Porter
Six O'Clock, 1964

9 Albert Wolff, *Figaro*, 1869. Quoted in George Heard Hamilton, *Manet and his Critics* (New Haven: Yale University Press, 1954), 139.

10 Louis Leroy, *Charivari*, 1869. Quoted in ibid., 133.

11 Ruskin, quoted in Andrew MacLaren Young, et al., *The Paintings of James McNeill Whistler* (New Haven: Yale University Press, 1980), 98.

12 Damisch, *A Theory of /Cloud/*, 226–27.

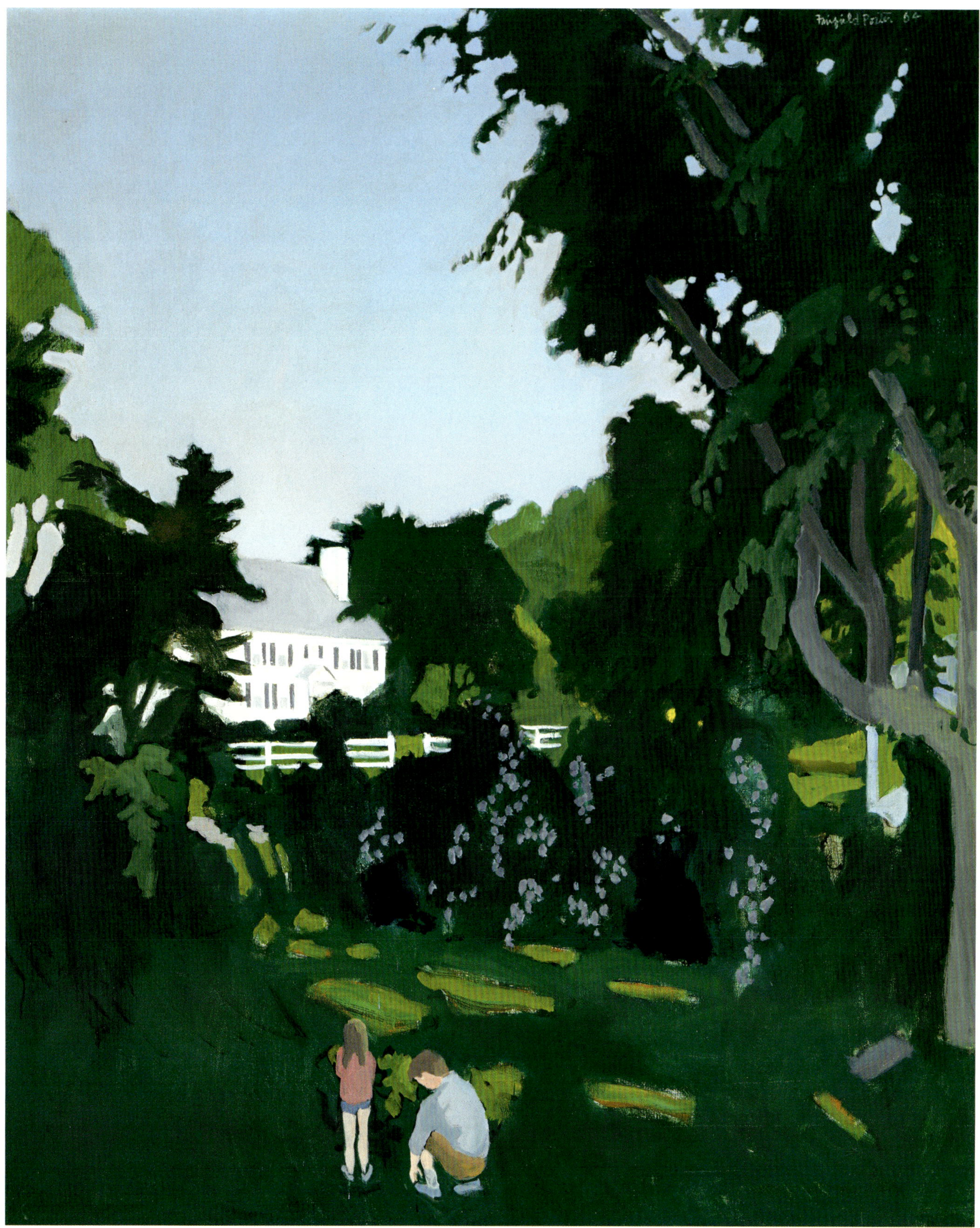
Fairfield Porter 64

Porter's paintings of the 1960s are paradigmatic of this way of working, without directly echoing the work of earlier painters. They avoid the potential traps of both academic mimeticism and strident expressionism. In paintings such as *Six O'Clock* (1964) or *Amherst Campus No. 1* (1969), leaves, figures, cars, and patches of light are all rendered with an absolutely straightforward, deceptively flat application of paint. The representational element in Porter's work is always unequivocal, but without any concomitant sense that the result needs to be highly finished. His painting is also profoundly anti-hierarchical. A college parking lot is as valid a motif as any more picturesque or romantic landscape. In his *Self-Portrait* (1968), the studio furniture is evidently as important as the figure of the artist himself. The result is a kind of realism that is always, self-consciously, a painting. Individual strokes and patches of paint have the same value in the composition as they would were the painting completely abstract.

Much of the most significant contemporary painting today seems in this way both straightforward and almost unfinished, quiet but persistent. Compositions are often casual. Color moves in and out of naturalism. The result is a painterly ambiguity that holds the viewer in suspension between the inescapable history of the medium and the immediate physical presence of the work, between the pull of memory and the constantly renewing present.

Fairfield Porter
Amherst Campus No. 1, 1969

Painting has access to a quite literal depth that remains unavailable to photography. Paint on canvas, with all its tactile variations between staining and impasto and the varieties of underpainting and glazes, responds to light in a fundamentally different way than the more purely two-dimensional surface of a photograph. And this response is itself constantly in flux, as the surrounding conditions of light continue to change. The play between illusionistic depth created through composition and another depth created through the physical presence of the paint itself remains a crucial area in which painting retains an autonomy still unchallenged by other media. This protean quality is very familiar to painters themselves. As Philip Guston put it, "I do have a faith that it is possible to make a living thing, not a diagram of what I have been thinking: to posit with paint something living, something that changes each day."[13] Equally, Laura Owens has said that "It's odd to think of paintings as static, they are so much more. They don't move like film

13 Guston, "Faith, Hope, and Impossibility," in *Philip Guston: Retrospective* (New York: Thames and Hudson; and Fort Worth: Modern Art Museum, 2003), 95.

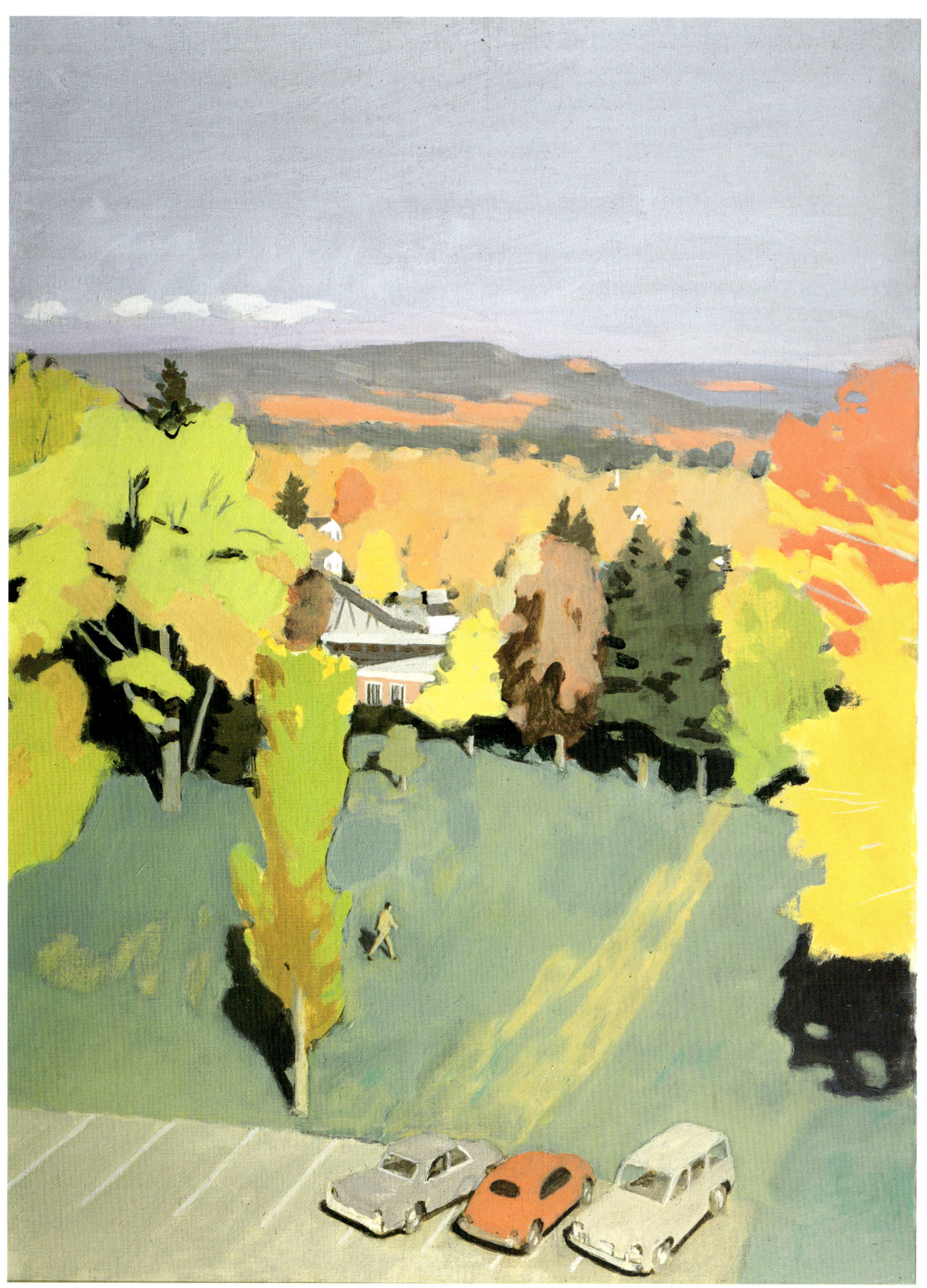

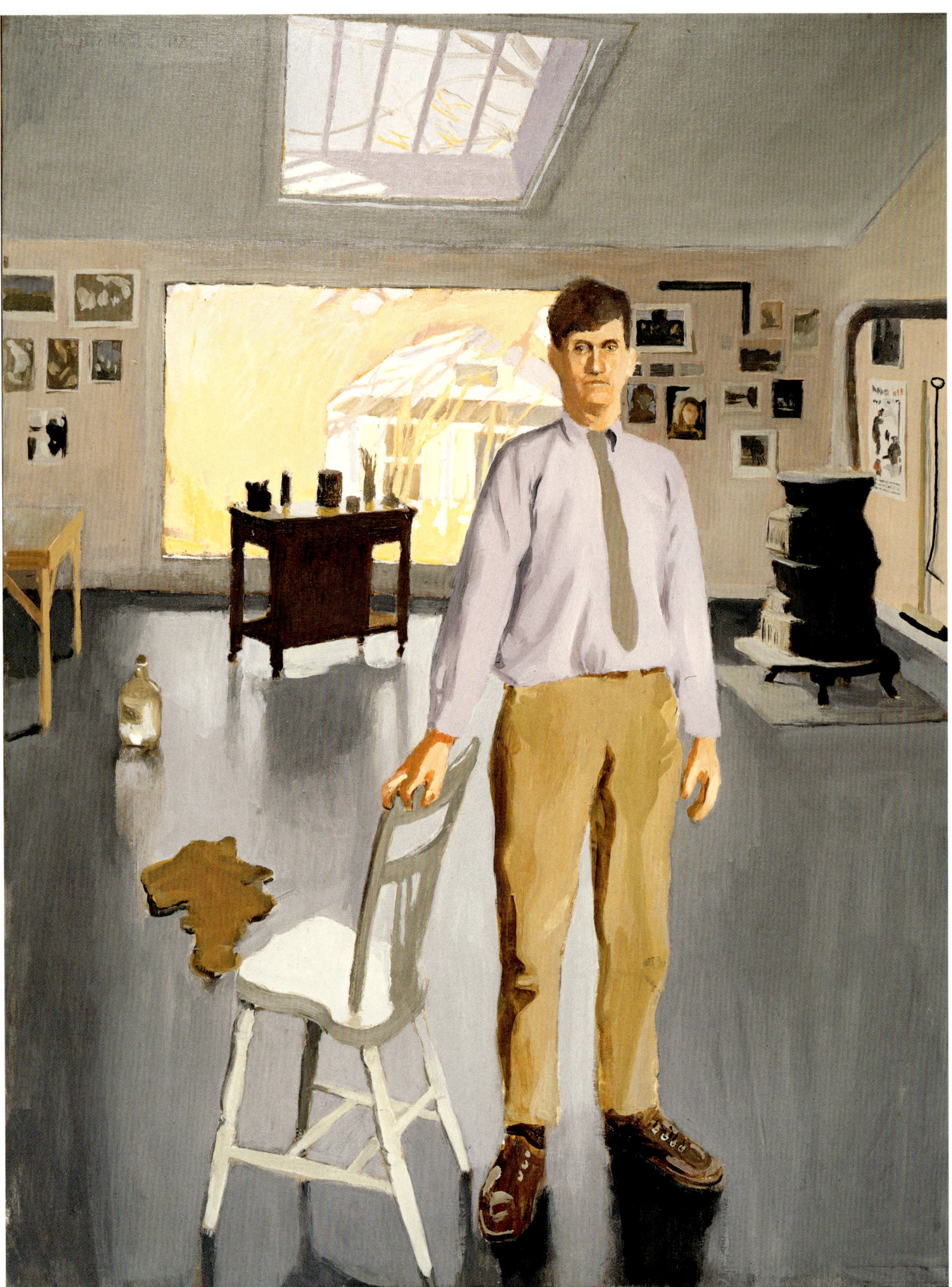

but seem to have a lot more movement than photography. Maybe it is potential movement, something like breath."[14] For Peter Doig, "Good painting is often about that moment when things are changing and therefore in motion, albeit not literally."[15] All three stress a certain fluidity in painting, a quality that can find the transitory within the fixed plane of the work.

Painting is not indexical. There is no automatic one-to-one relationship between what is depicted and the depiction itself, as there is in photography. This tension between the image and the action that creates it is one of the key elements that continue to generate a viable space for painting. For Charles Sheeler, active by the 1930s as both a painter and a photographer, "Photography is nature seen with the eyes outward, painting from the eyes inward."[16] The only link between the nominal motif and the painting itself is the artist, who controls the relationship between the subject and the physicality of the painting. At the point at which the represented image meets the materiality of the painted surface, representation *always* breaks down. In a painting such as Luc Tuymans's *Backyard* (2002), for example, the motif is quite clear: as the title indicates, it is a backyard. Yet at the same time the trees and grass that make up the bulk of the image are rendered in an overtly brushy manner that constantly restates the physicality of the paint and the trace of the artist's hand. The viewer is inexorably reminded of the materiality of the work.

Fairfield Porter
Self-Portrait, 1968

A photograph nearly always presents its image as a section of a broader landscape that continues indefinitely in all directions. "A photograph has edges, the world does not," as Stephen Shore put it.[17] The abrupt edge of a photograph, the sharp cut that it makes across a visual field, had an immediate impact on the composition of paintings. Degas is widely recognized as being among the first to replicate the more or less arbitrary quality of the edge of a photograph in his paintings, in a decisive break from compositional tradition. Peter Galassi has outlined a number of historical precedents for Degas's work, arguing that photography itself was inconceivable without the move away from single-point perspective that artists had already begun to explore. For Galassi, "it is not Degas's work that needs explaining but the invention of photography," which would not have been possible without an "accumulation of pictorial experiment."[18] The invention of photography,

14 Owens, in *Cavepainting* (Santa Monica: Santa Monica Museum of Art, 2002), 22.
15 Doig, in ibid., 22.
16 Sheeler, in Frederick Wight, *Charles Sheeler* (Los Angeles: UCLA Art Galleries, 1954), 26.
17 Shore, *The Nature of Photographs* (Baltimore: Johns Hopkins University Press, 1998), 28.
18 Galassi, *Before Photography: Painting and the Invention of Photography* (New York: The Museum of Modern Art, 1981), 17, 18.

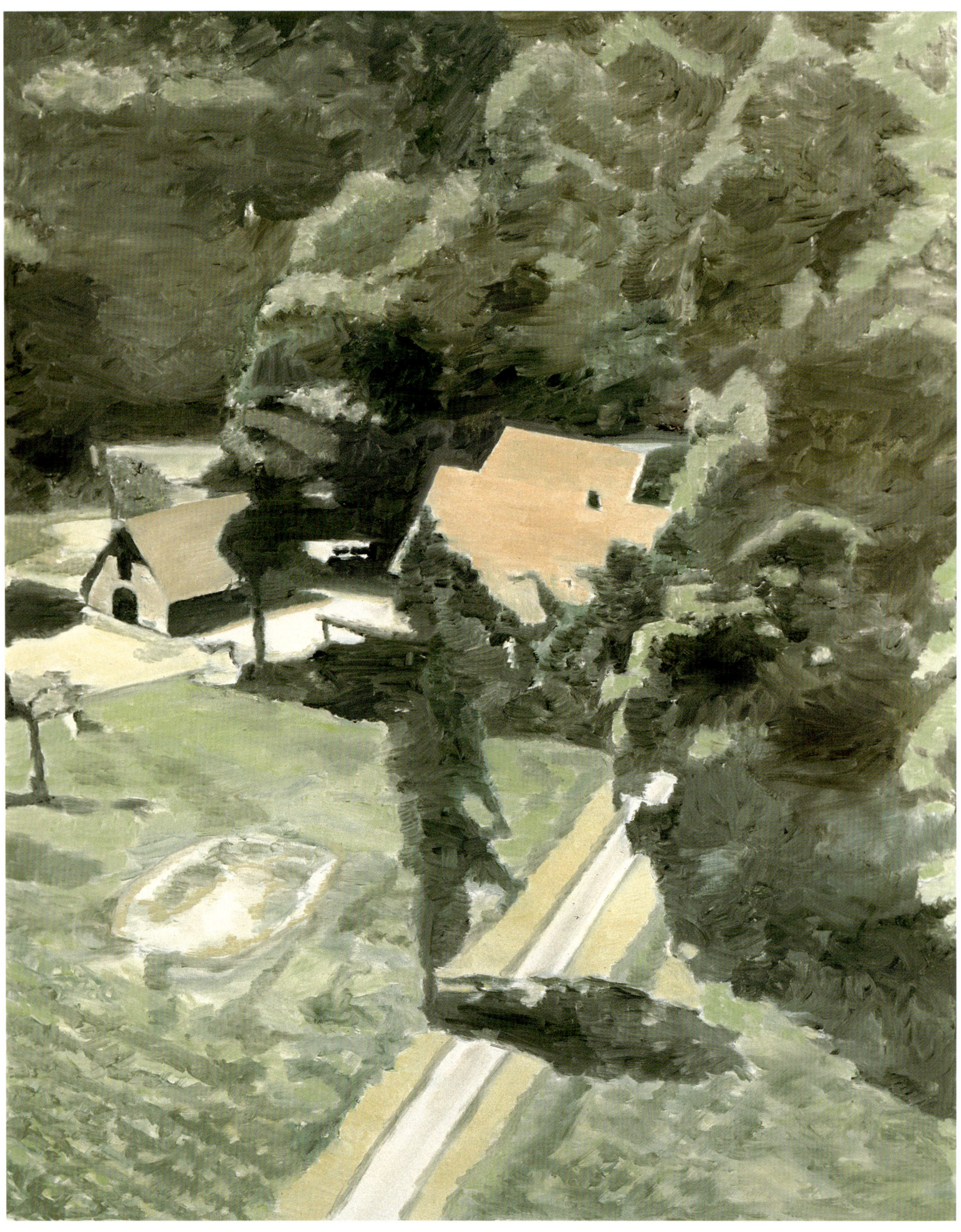

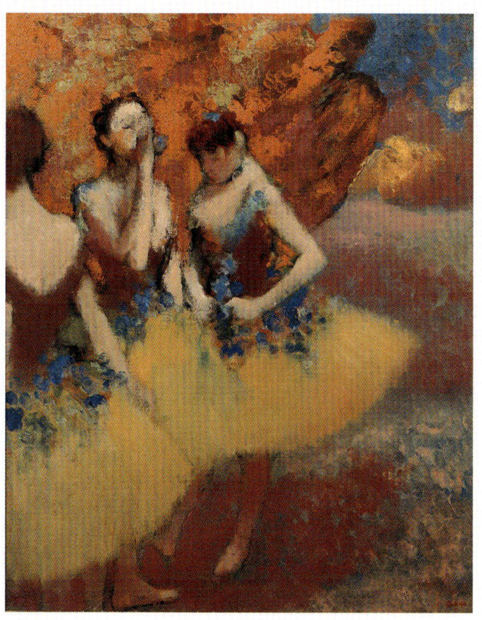

nevertheless, indubitably accelerated such experiment. Until this point, the primary goal of composition had still been to contain the entire work unequivocally between the edges of the canvas. Paintings, in which each element is imagined and rendered by the artist, exist in this sense half way between the photograph and the world. Paintings have edges, but the relationship of the painting and its subject to those edges is far less arbitrary than in most photographs.

Although painters learned to see the attraction of new kinds of composition, the issue of the edge never really went away, and indeed it became one of the great questions of abstraction. Even in representational painting, there is really no such thing as a truly "found" composition, since the whole surface is built up slowly, progressively, element by element. Painters have to work with angles and relationships that they fully determine, and each decision contributes to a constructed composition no matter how much the artist might try to resist it. Even an image truncated by the edge of the canvas has been cut at that precise point as the result of a conscious process. Each element is inevitably part of a composed structure.

Luc Tuymans
Backyard, 2002

Edgar Degas
Three Dancers in Yellow Skirts, c.1891

THE MEDIUM THAT REQUIRES THE GREATEST AMOUNT OF FAITH

By 1936, Walter Benjamin had already recognized:

> *The nineteenth-century dispute as to the artistic value of painting versus photography today seems devious and confused. This does not diminish its importance, however; if anything, it underlines it. The dispute was in fact the symptom of a historical transformation the universal impact of which was not realized by either of the rivals. When the age of mechanical reproduction separated art from its basis in cult, the semblance of its autonomy disappeared forever.*[19]

Philip Guston
White Painting I, 1951

Philip Guston
Untitled, 1975

Despite this increasing separation of painting from cult value, its defenders have relentlessly continued to make use of a quasi-religious vocabulary of faith. Rudi Fuchs's hymn of praise to Anselm Kiefer could be taken as typical of this trope, if also perhaps as its limit: "Painting is salvation," he wrote. "The painter is a guardian-angel carrying the palette in blessing over the world."[20]

The same appeal to faith can be found, however, more seriously in the statements of a number of artists who were tenaciously wrestling with the very viability of painting. In 1965 Guston defended his work, at that time fully abstract, in an essay explicitly titled "Faith, Hope, and Impossibility."[21] Only a few years later, when Guston admitted to himself that he had in fact lost faith in abstraction, the passion with which he rejected it was characteristic of a true believer turned apostate: "American Abstract art is a lie, a sham, a cover-up for a poverty of spirit."[22] When representation returned to his work, it was in landscapes of sickly pink, littered with old boots and trash, populated by the Ku Klux Klan and other nightmarish figures. When Guston first showed these new paintings in 1970, the shocked audiences who had admired his earlier work perceived his change of direction in equally religious terms. Peter Schjeldahl remembers that he thought the new paintings were a "profanation,"[23] as perhaps, in part,

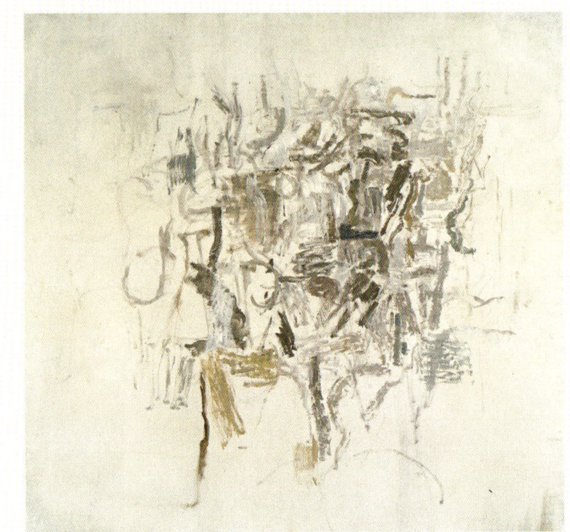

19 Benjamin, "The Work of Art in the Age of Mechanical Reproduction," in *Illuminations* (New York: Schocken, 1978), 226.
20 Fuchs, in *Anselm Kiefer* (Venice: Bienale, 1980), 62.
21 Reprinted in *Philip Guston: Retrospective*, 93–95.
22 Guston, quoted in Musa Mayer, *Night Studio: A Memoir of Philip Guston* (London: Thames and Hudson, 1991), 170.
23 Schjeldahl, "Philip Guston" (1984), in *Hydrogen Jukebox* (Berkeley: University of California Press, 1991), 227.

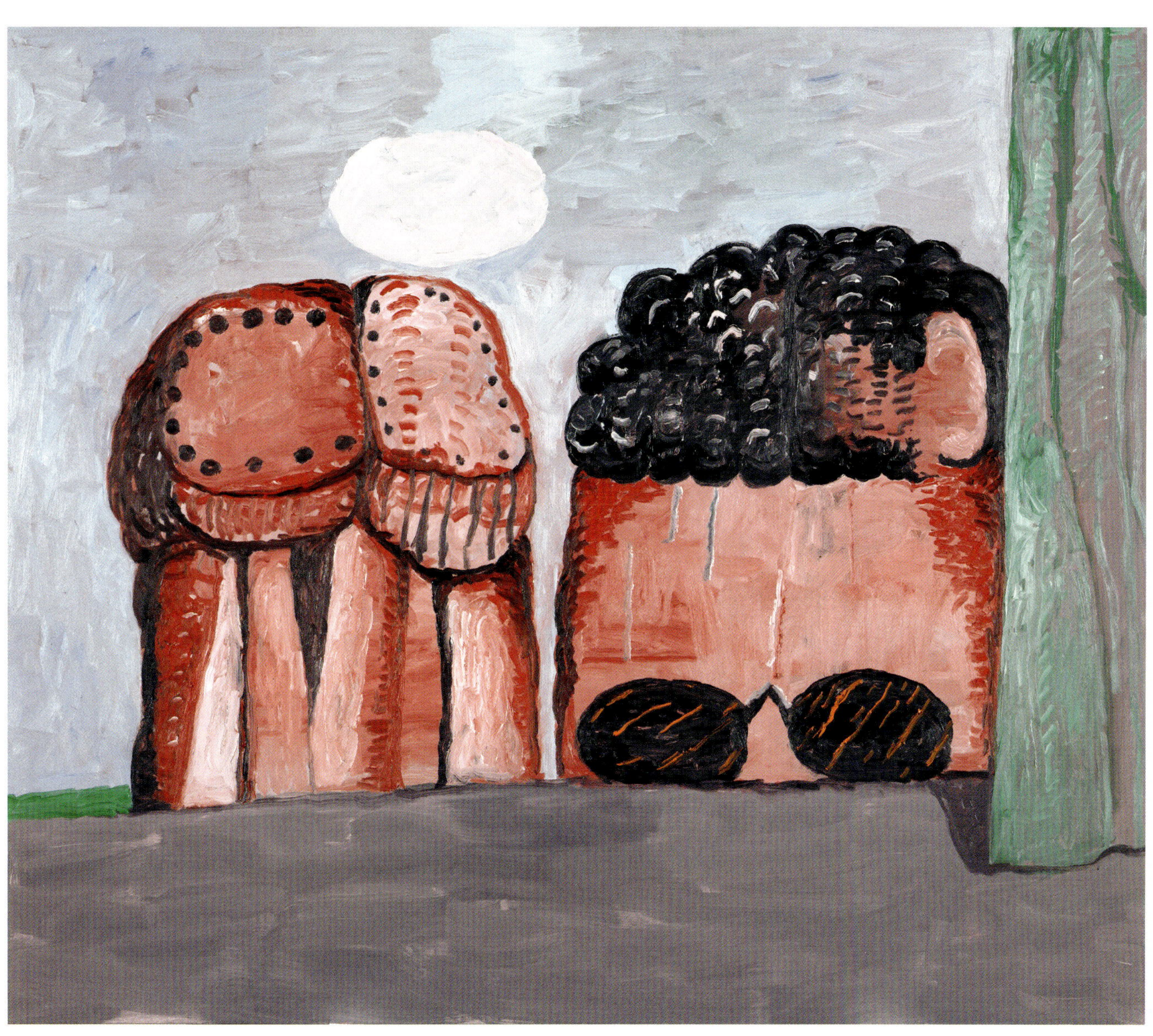

they were meant to be. Guston was not merely abandoning pure abstraction, but abandoning it in favor of a repulsive world only just redeemed by his painting.

Painting can appeal to faith in the long history of the medium itself, something that in photography always seems a little precious, dependent as it is on the precision of its recording of a precise moment. Owens draws freely from Chinese painting, Impressionism, embroidery, the rococo, and any other source, high or allegedly low, to fuel her paintings. Doig's lumpy yet gigantically scaled artist alone in a mountain landscape retains some vestige of a longstanding Romantic tradition. Richter can paint an *Annunciation After Titian* (1973) with as much or as little conviction as he paints a set of color chips or a *Waterfall* (1997). For him, "A painting of color chips is no different from a little green landscape. Both reflect the same fundamental attitude. The attitude alone is decisive."[24] To reach that point, however, he wrestled with crises of faith comparable to those of Guston. "All the utopias are shattered, everything goes down the drain, the wonderful time of painting is over," he has said. "There are examples where I have tried to reincarnate Titian and others, but of course it didn't work out. I wanted to paint the Annunciation for myself."[25] This despair for the present state of painting, and for his own capacity to paint, can extend beyond any particular work: "We have lost all faith, everything that creates meaning. Incapable of faith, hopeless to the utmost degree, we roam across a toxic waste dump."[26] No matter how arbitrary the field of painting can appear to be, the appeal to faith in order to redeem it never seems very far away.

Gerhard Richter
Annunciation After Titian, 1973

following pages:
Gerhard Richter
Waterfall, 1997

Peter Doig
Figure in Mountain Landscape (I love you big dummy), 1999

24 Richter (1976), quoted by Benjamin H. D. Buchloh, in "Readymade, Photography, and Painting in the Painting of Gerhard Richter" (1977), in *Neo-Avantgarde and Culture Industry: Essays on European and American Art from 1955 to 1975* (Cambridge: The MIT Press, 2000), 388.

25 Richter, interview with Robert Storr, in Storr, *Gerhard Richter: Doubt and Belief in Painting* (New York: The Museum of Modern Art, 2003), 172. This ongoing anxiety also informs the title chosen by Storr for his book.

26 Richter, "Notes, 1988," in *The Daily Practice of Painting*, 171–72.

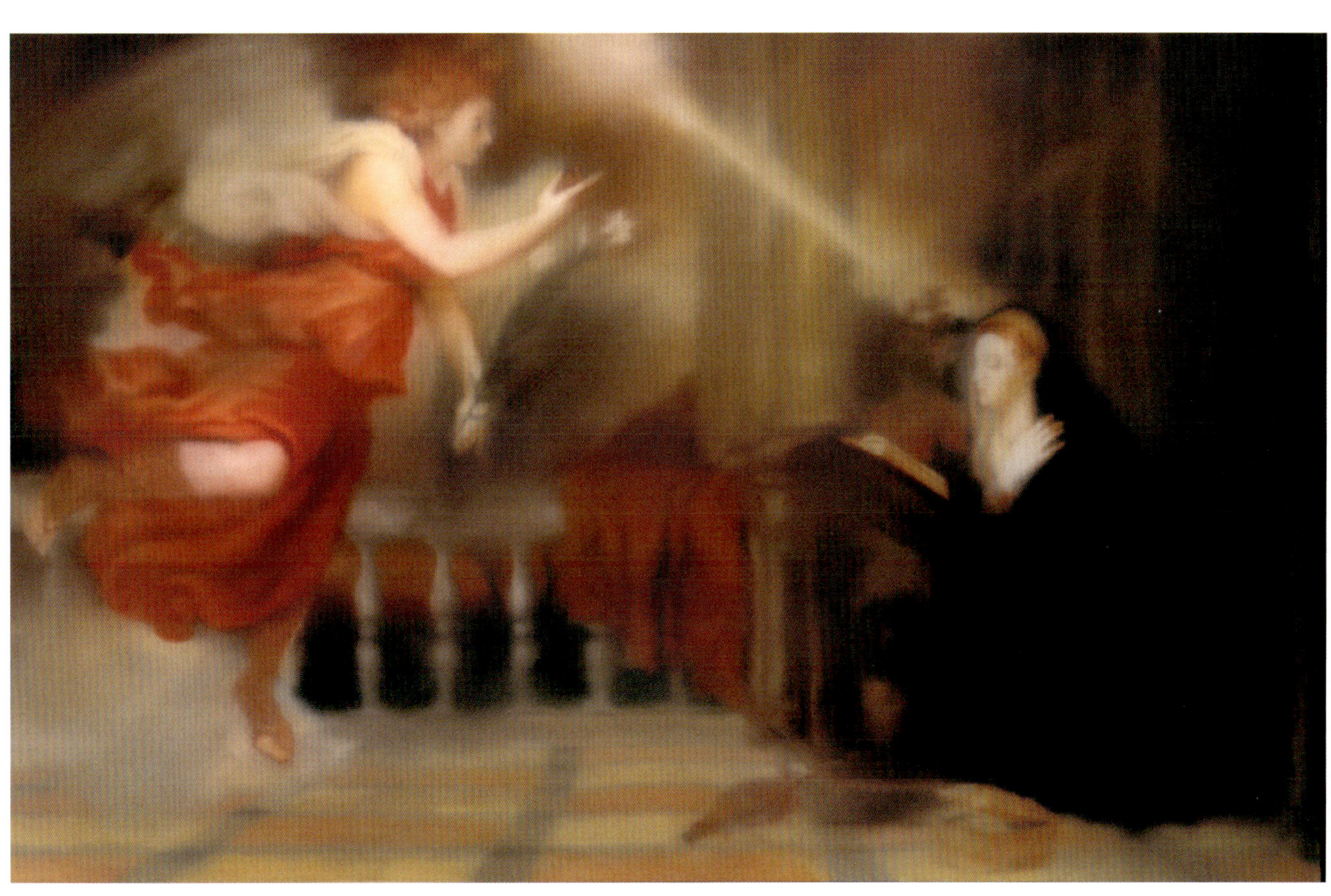

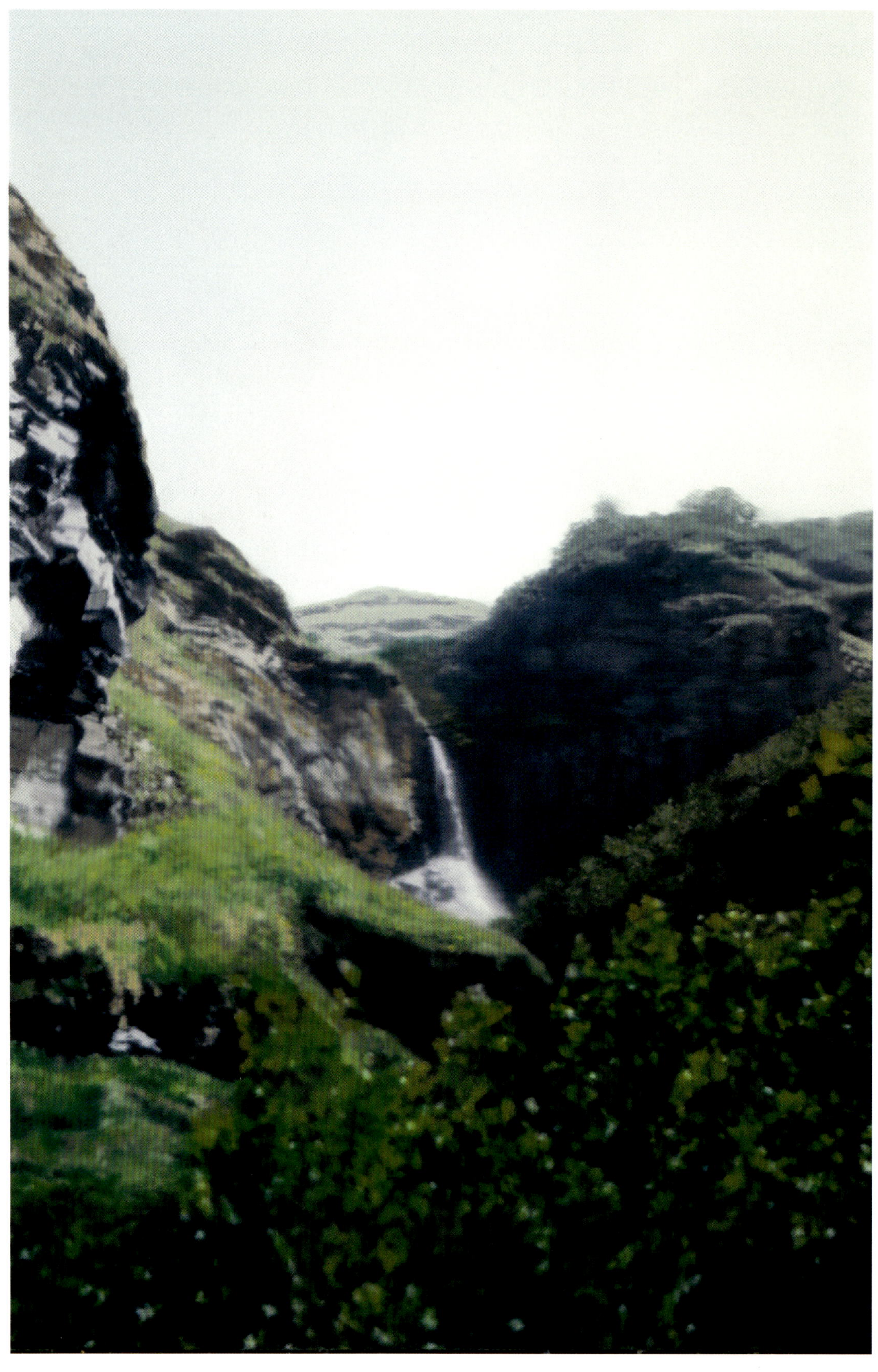

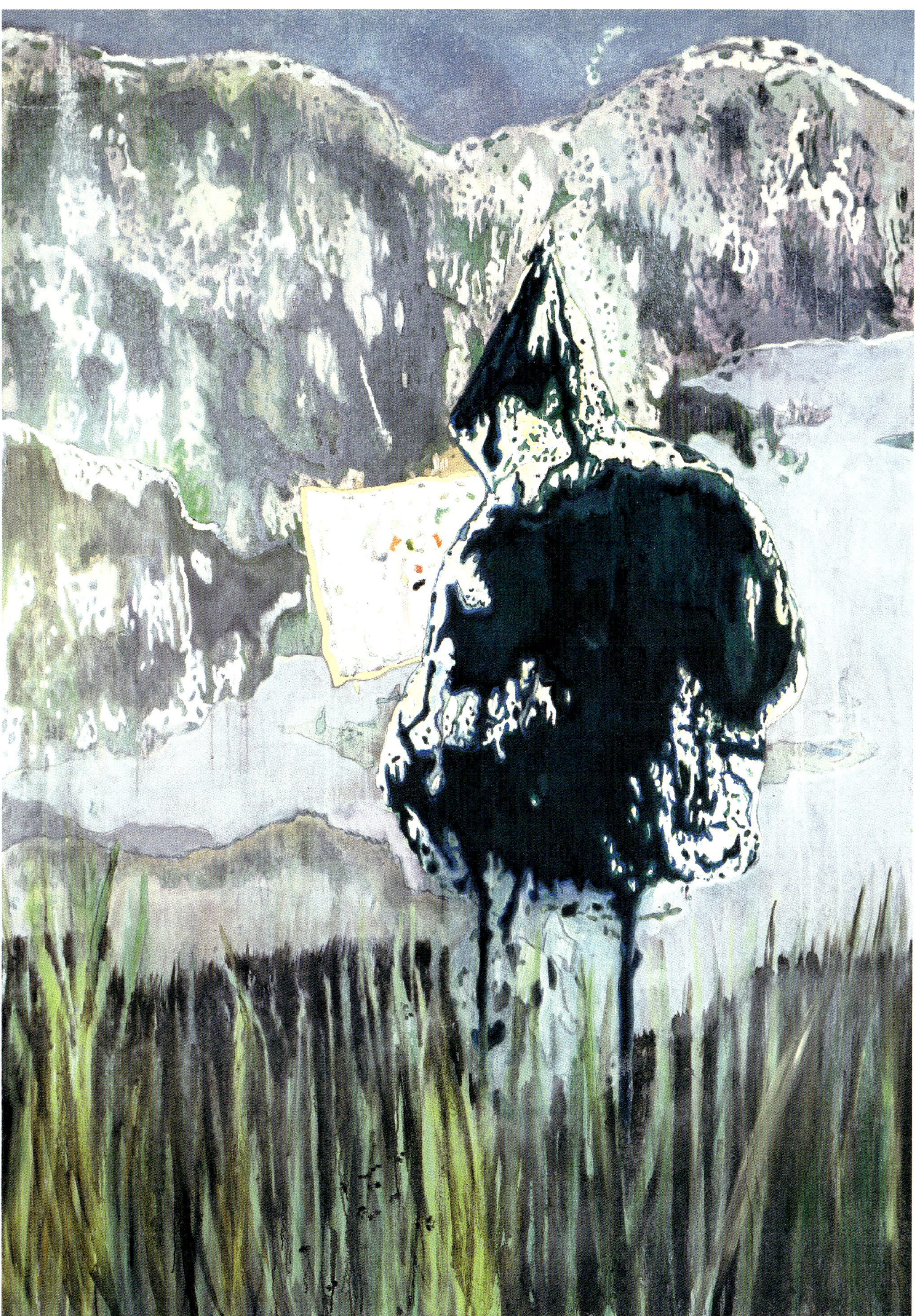

Even in the early 1980s, when a new generation of artists and critics were questioning the validity of painting in general, the explicit resort to faith among its defenders recurred. Thomas Lawson, for example, in his influential essay "Last Exit: Painting," sought to justify painting in precisely such terms:

> *It seems at this point, when there is a growing lack of faith in the ability of artists to continue as anything more than plagiaristic stylists, that a recognition of this state of affairs can only be expressed through the medium that requires the greatest amount of faith.*
>
> *For it is this question of faith that is central. We are living in an age of skepticism and as a result the practice of art is inevitably crippled by the suspension of belief.*[27]

CHAOS OF CONNECTIONS

Painting now seems always in crisis, always in need of some appeal to a higher power to keep it alive, yet always somehow able in the end to summon up one more breath, to keep going like Vladimir and Estragon, if not Lazarus. As Douglas Fogle has written, "we barely flinch when it miraculously rises from the dead again and again."[28]

"Yet has the end come?" Bois asked in 1986:

> *To say no (painting is still alive, just look at the galleries) is undoubtedly an act of denial, for it has never been more evident that most paintings one sees have abandoned the task that historically belonged to modern painting (that, precisely, of working through the end of painting) and are simply artifacts created for the market and by the market (absolutely interchangeable artifacts created by interchangeable producers). To say yes, however, that the end has come, is to give in to a historicist conception of history as both linear and total (i.e., one cannot paint after Duchamp, Rodchenko, Mondrian; their work has rendered paintings unnecessary; or: one cannot paint anymore in the era of the mass media, computer games, and the simulacrum).*[29]

27 Lawson, "Last Exit: Painting" (1981), in Brian Wallis, ed., *Art After Modernism* (New York: New Museum; and Boston: Godine, 1984), 164.

28 Fogle, "The Trouble With Painting," in *Painting at the Edge of the World* (Minneapolis: Walker Art Center, 2001), 14.

29 Bois, "Painting: The Task of Mourning," in *Painting as Model*, 241.

So the end is always *about* to come, always just around the corner. But for Tuymans, as for many artists today, "The question of whether painting is dead or alive is anything but interesting.... Painting is a way of thinking and constitutes an enormous archetypal pattern which artists constantly fall back upon."[30] The constantly announced death of the medium only redirects our attention to the life after death. As Hamlet proclaimed:

the dread of something after death,
The undiscovered country, from whose bourn
No traveler returns, puzzles the will.[31]

The odor of conquest that lingers around a phrase such as "the undiscovered country" is by no means irrelevant. Shakespeare's metaphor, written at the Elizabethan dawn of modern imperialism, suggests for us not only the empty canvas before which the painter must stake his or her own individual claim, and not only the uncharted territory into which painting found itself after its so-called death. It also evokes the sense of privilege and entitlement that still adheres to this most canonical of media, which has made it unappealing to many artists, especially those who do not identify themselves with positions of authority. Despite its increasingly common crises of confidence and even of identity, painting still periodically lays claim to a kind of divine right of kings, a claim that is routinely supported in the art market. There is a persistent reactionary rhetoric that simply dismisses all other media as irrelevant, indeed inferior. As Benjamin Buchloh has defined it:

The key terms of this ideological backlash are the idealization of the perennial monuments of art history and its masters, the attempt to establish a new aesthetic orthodoxy, and the demand for respect for the cultural tradition. It is endemic to the syndrome of authoritarianism that it appeal to and affirm the "eternal" or ancient systems of order (the law of the tribe, the authority of history, the paternal principle of the master, etc.).[32]

30 Tuymans, in Vincent Geyskens, "Interview with Narcisse Tordoir and Luc Tuymans," in *Trouble Spot. Painting* (Antwerp: NICC and MUHKA, 1999), 122.

31 Shakespeare, *Hamlet*, III, i, 78–80.

32 Buchloh, "Figures of Authority, Ciphers of Regression: Notes on the Return of Representation in European Painting," in Benjamin H. D. Buchloh, Serge Guilbaut, and David Solkin, eds., *Modernism and Modernity* (Halifax: Press of the Nova Scotia College of Art and Design, 1983), 85.

One of the key issues for painters now, in fact, is how to make meaningful work without relying on such implicit appeals to dubious authority. Even the rigor of those like Buchloh, who have articulated so well the authoritarian underpinnings of the rhetoric around painting, can become in turn an orthodoxy. Buchloh himself has recognized this possibility in his acknowledgment of "a set of assumptions in which a latent resentment against contemporary culture at large could be linked with a leftist prejudice against any form of aesthetic deviance and transgression that did not comply with the prescribed patterns of the political models of critique and theoretical transformation."[33] The other side of the conservative embrace of painting is the "progressive" dismissal of it out of hand. Perhaps the issue in question is less the death of painting than the death of painting's ability to play a significant part in the public sphere. The same question could no doubt be raised about art in general, yet it is a particular concern for painting, given the historic status of the medium.

In postwar Germany, more than elsewhere in Europe, it had been abstraction that stood for the utopian aspirations to autonomy of an avant-garde still wrestling with the aftermath of the Nazi era. As Buchloh has written:

> *While it has been firmly established that one of the epistemic specifics of modernist painting had been to prohibit any representation of the historical and to dismantle any referentiality to the material world, it continues to surprise us how vehemently this quest for visual autonomy and self-referentiality was reestablished immediately after the most cataclysmic destruction in European history.*[34]

Any return to images begged the question of what those images might be. In this context, Richter's decision simultaneously to engage with representation and abstraction can perhaps be seen as a way of inoculating representation from a historical context that threatened to overwhelm it. But in pushing back into representation at all, Richter nevertheless ran the risk of uncovering things that neither he nor his audience necessarily wanted to see. In 1965 he painted *Uncle*

33 Buchloh, introduction to *Neo-Avantgarde and Culture Industry*, xxv–xxvi.

34 Buchloh, "Plenty or Nothing: From Yves Klein's *Le Vide* to Arman's *Le Plein*" (1998), in *Neo-Avantgarde and Culture Industry*, 260.

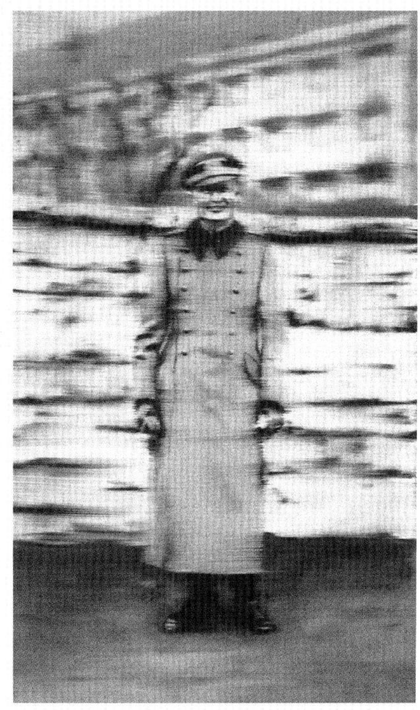

Gerhard Richter
Uncle Rudi, 1965

Rudi in a Nazi uniform. The private family snapshot was inevitably conflated with the burden of history, the image blurred like a hazy but persistent memory.

Photography derives some of its power from the abrupt juxtaposition of the past (caught in the instant of the shutter release) and the present (the response of a viewer to that image). Painting, however, slides more ambiguously between the past and present. As many painters have remarked, a painting from whatever era is always as present at any given moment as it was in the year it was painted. It is always now. For John Berger, "Paintings are prophecies received from the past, prophecies about *what the spectator is seeing in front of the painting at that moment.*"[35] Since a painting lacks the indexical relationship to the past that a photograph carries, it is more evidently an object in its own right, something that exists decisively in the present, even if it simultaneously refers to the past. Even "a little green landscape" contains some of this ambiguity, representing in the most conventional way yet at the same time keeping representation at arm's length. As Richter has written, "Of course, my landscapes are not only beautiful or nostalgic, with a Romantic or classical suggestion of lost Paradises, but above all 'untruthful.'"[36]

Lukas Duwenhögger is explicit in articulating the difficulty he experienced in approaching representational painting:

> *I can remember my situation at the [Düsseldorf] academy in the eighties. For me the problem of the connection between figurative painting and fascism was so strikingly obvious that for years I avoided painting. It was in a certain sense too close to that area for me. To take it up later in spite of this was a quite conscious decision to confront this kind of stigmatization: I didn't want to act as if this chaos of connections didn't exist.*[37]

35 Berger, "Painting and Time" (1979), in *The Sense of Sight* (New York: Pantheon, 1985), 206–07.

36 Richter, "Notes, 1986," in *The Daily Practice of Painting*, 124.

37 Duwenhögger, in the press release for the exhibition "I and My Chimney" at Galerie Buchholz, Cologne, July 2003.

In the exhibition "Oh, Boy, It's a Girl: Feminismen in der Kunst" at the Kunstverein, Munich, in 1994, Thomas Eggerer and Jochen Klein showed collaborative work dealing with their intervention at a public toilet in a park that was a center of gay cruising in the city. They had installed a plaque that read "Leave a Message." For them at that point, although both had trained as painters at the Munich Academy of Fine Arts and continued to paint, painting's tradition of "mastery" seemed incapable of dealing with the issues of gay identity that were at the forefront of their thinking. Painting, and especially the rhetoric of mastery that surrounded it, seemed almost like "the enemy medium."[38] In the same exhibition, however, Duwenhögger showed a number of relatively small paintings that suggested to Eggerer and Klein some unexplored possibilities. The modest scale of the work in itself seemed to imply a rejection of the macho grandiosity associated with ambitious painting. The motifs were theatrical, even camp: explorations of coded male homosexuality that for American viewers evoke the equally stylized and unclassifiable work of Paul Cadmus.

Lukas Duwenhögger
Choreographie für 3 Männer, 2 Besen und Signalband
(Choreography for three men, two brooms, and warning tape), 1994

For strict adherents of "institutional critique," paintings—any paintings—could not escape being primarily commodities, but Duwenhögger demonstrated that it was possible to paint without automatically buying into the hierarchical assumptions that painting has historically dragged in its wake. The "chaos of connections," and indeed of contradictions, need not result in a flat rejection of painting altogether. Such a rejection might even be seen as a kind of negative acceptance of its presumed status.

WE MOURN OUR LOSS

As Duwenhögger indicated, however, one cannot separate representation from its subject matter. If a painter is in fact going to represent, *what* will he or she represent? Regardless of style, the question of subject remains unavoidable. From the French Revolution on, it had been history painting that constituted painting's greatest claim to significance. It was in history painting that the artist had the opportunity

38 Eggerer, telephone conversation with the author, 3 June 2004. Both Eggerer and Klein later became members of Group Material, whose practice specifically rejected the hierarchical distinction between painting and other forms of representation and cultural production.

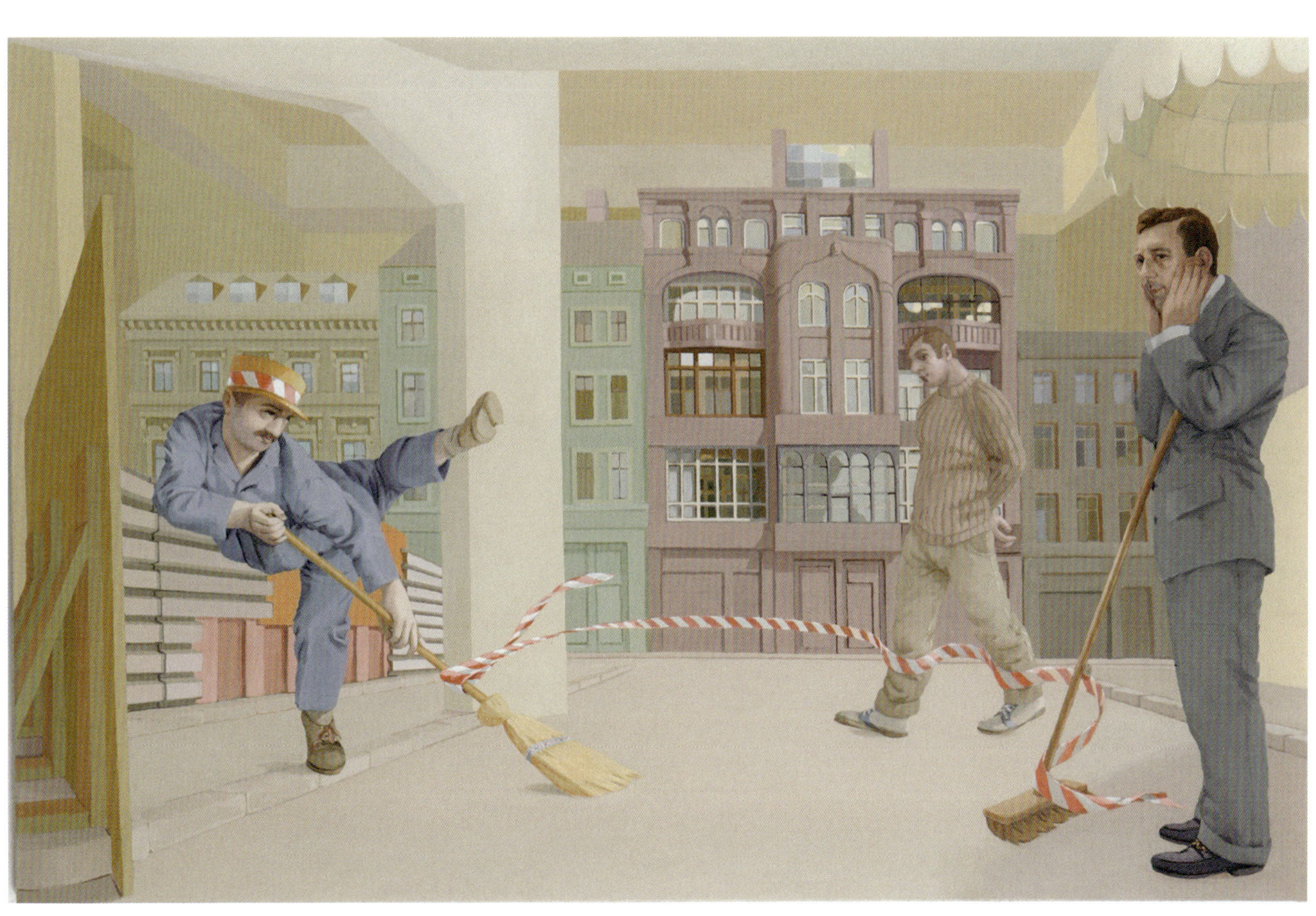

to bring together mastery of composition, intellectual rigor, and even the possibility of shaping the course of public events. Among the paradigmatic examples of this long tradition are David's *The Oath of the Horatii* (1784), Delacroix's *Liberty Leading the People* (1830), and (already in retreat from the heroic) Manet's *Execution of the Emperor Maximilian* (1867). How could that position be maintained without a fundamental primacy in representation?

In his series of paintings *October 18, 1977* (1988), Richter returned, more than twenty years after *Uncle Rudi*, to a kind of history painting. Like Manet, he focused on a moment of defeat. The paintings, a cycle of fifteen, all grisaille, derive from newspaper photographs and private snapshots pertaining to the urban guerrillas of the Red Army Faction. Each painting works in concert with the others, yet in the end the power of the series comes less from the images of dead bodies than from more "domestic" details, such as the bookshelves and record player in the cell of one of the group's leaders, Andreas Baader. The grisaille, the blurring of the images, and the apparently arbitrary selection of motifs—some images are essentially repeated, others seem almost trivial—combine to create just enough distance for the viewer to stay with the difficult images in a way that would be almost impossible with the photographs themselves. As Richter said of these works, "the photograph provokes horror, and the painting—with the same motif—something more like grief."[39] The series balances direct address to public events with an indirect quality that now seems to be the necessary leverage that painting needs to take on such issues.

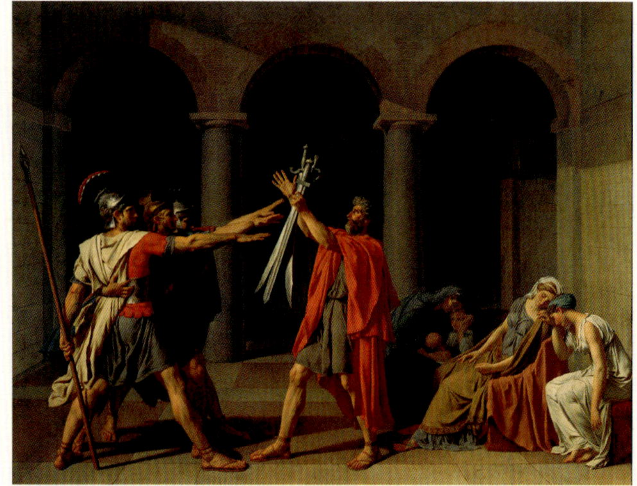

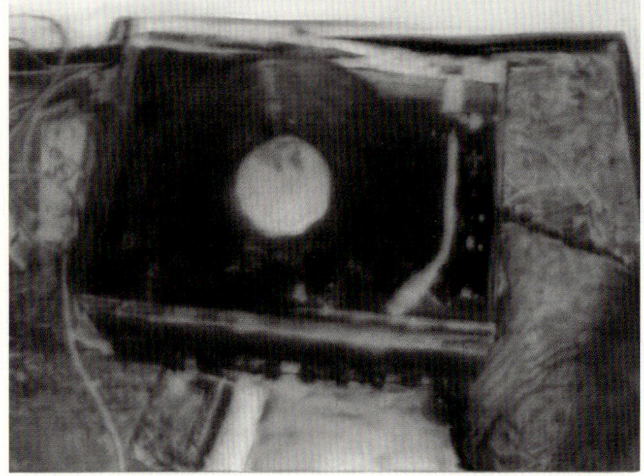

39 Richter, interview with Jan Thorn Prikker (1989), in *The Daily Practice of Painting*, 189. See also Robert Storr, *Gerhard Richter: October 18, 1977* (New York: The Museum of Modern Art, 2000).

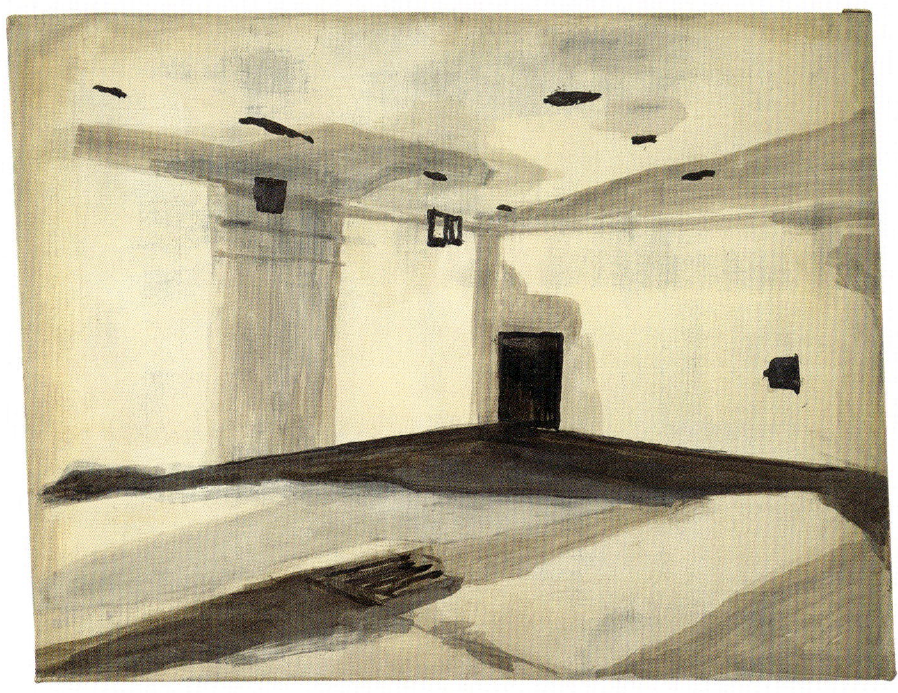

"To write poetry after Auschwitz is barbaric," Theodor Adorno wrote in 1949,[40] and much of painting now seems to share that sense of helplessness in the face of a terrible history. As if in direct response to Adorno's famous dictum, Tuymans made a painting of the gas chamber at Auschwitz (*Gas Chamber*, 1986). Of this painting he has written, "The picture, its aesthetic character, is the disguise of something that is absolutely inaccessible if it is not disguised."[41] The distance that Tuymans maintains in his overtly political and historical paintings is further evidence that the direct address, the representation of some dramatic or heroic incident, is no longer effective. Simply representing a climactic moment seems inadequate, and the painter instead filters the historical event through layers of memory and other forms of representation.

Jacques-Louis David
The Oath of the Horatii, 1784

Gerhard Richter
Record Player [Plattenspieler]
from *October 18, 1977*, 1988

Luc Tuymans
Gas Chamber, 1986

following pages:
Luc Tuymans
Chalk, 2000

Luc Tuymans
The Mission, 2000

Tuymans has been among the most consistent in continuing to explore the possibilities of a contemporary history painting. His series Mwana Kitoko addresses Belgian colonialism in Africa and the resistance to it. *Chalk* and *The Mission* (both 2000), paintings from that series, are simultaneously reticent and explicit. The images they present are stubborn. "The narrative is cut out of the painting," Tuymans has said,[42] but it lingers as an inescapable context. The starting point for *Egypt* (2003) was a photograph of Colin Powell meeting with Hosni

40 Adorno, "Cultural Criticism and Society," in *Prisms*, trans. Samuel Weber and Shierry Weber (Cambridge: The MIT Press, 1982), 34.

41 Tuymans, "Disenchantment," in Ulrich Loock, et al., *Luc Tuymans* (London: Phaidon, 2003), 133.

42 Tuymans, in Craig Garrett and Michele Robecchi, "The Dark Places: Interview with Luc Tuymans," *Flash Art* (March–April 2004): 79.

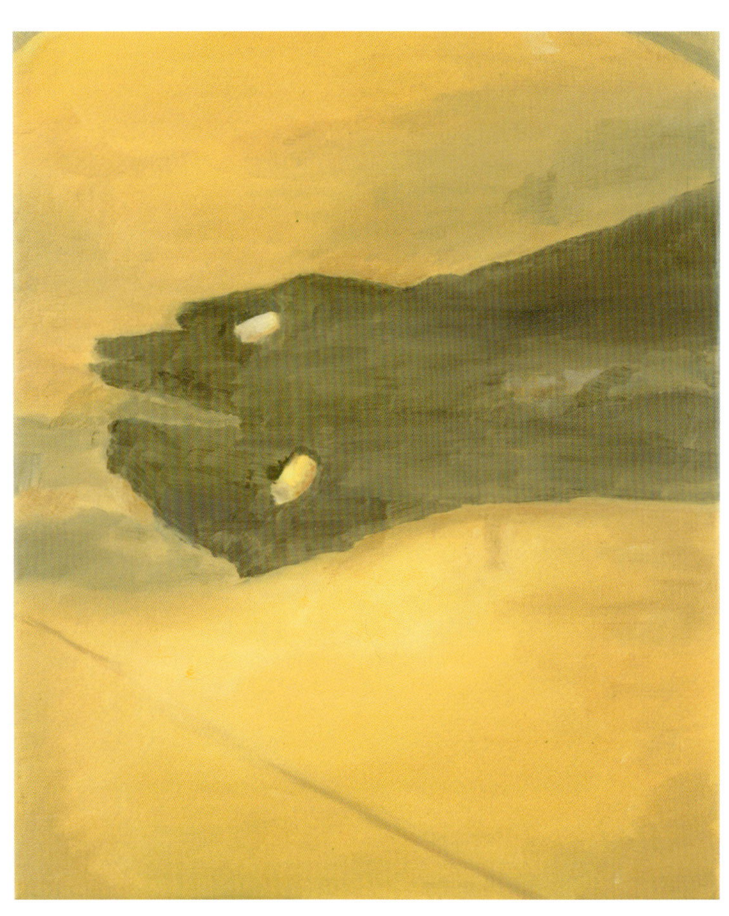

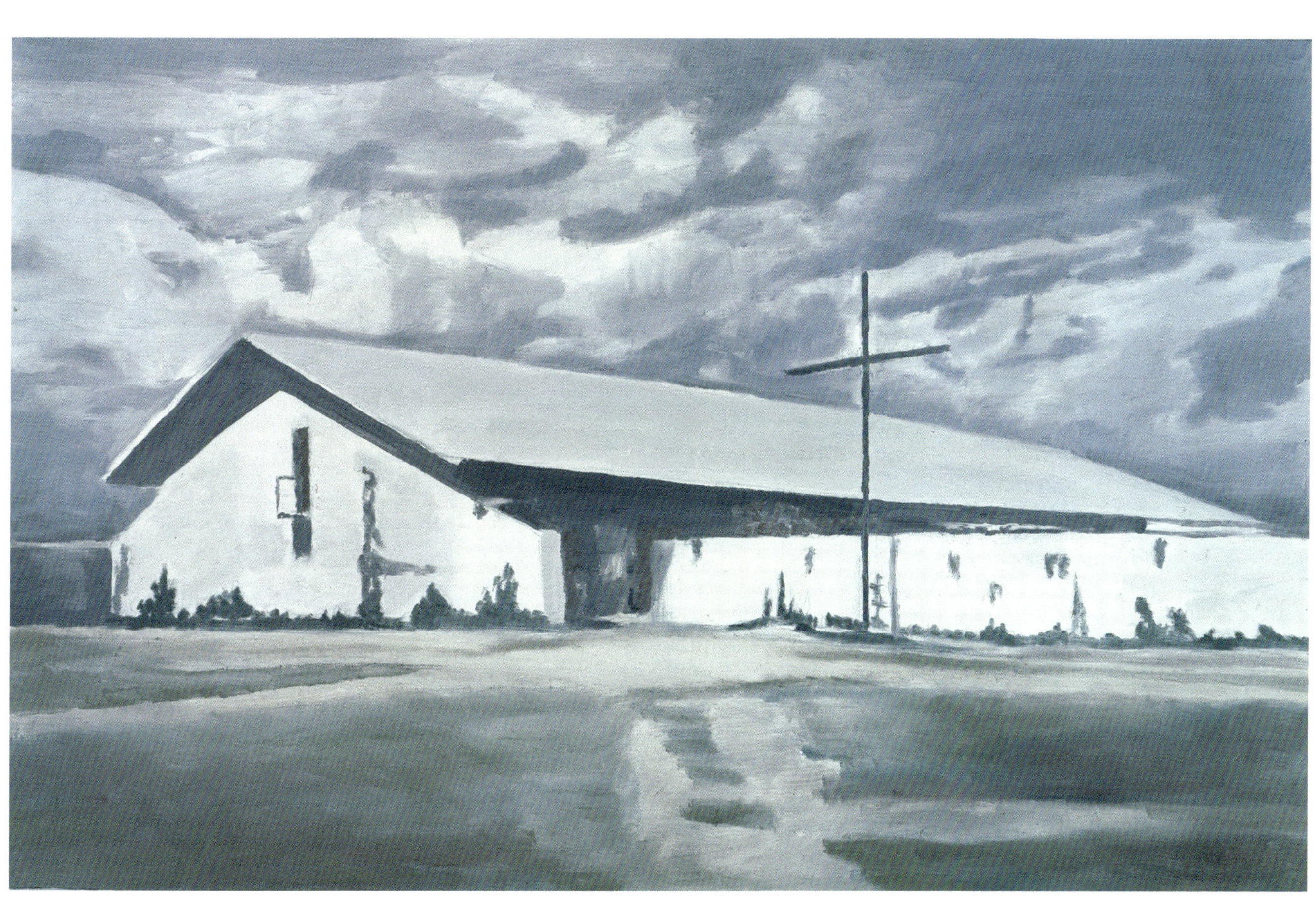

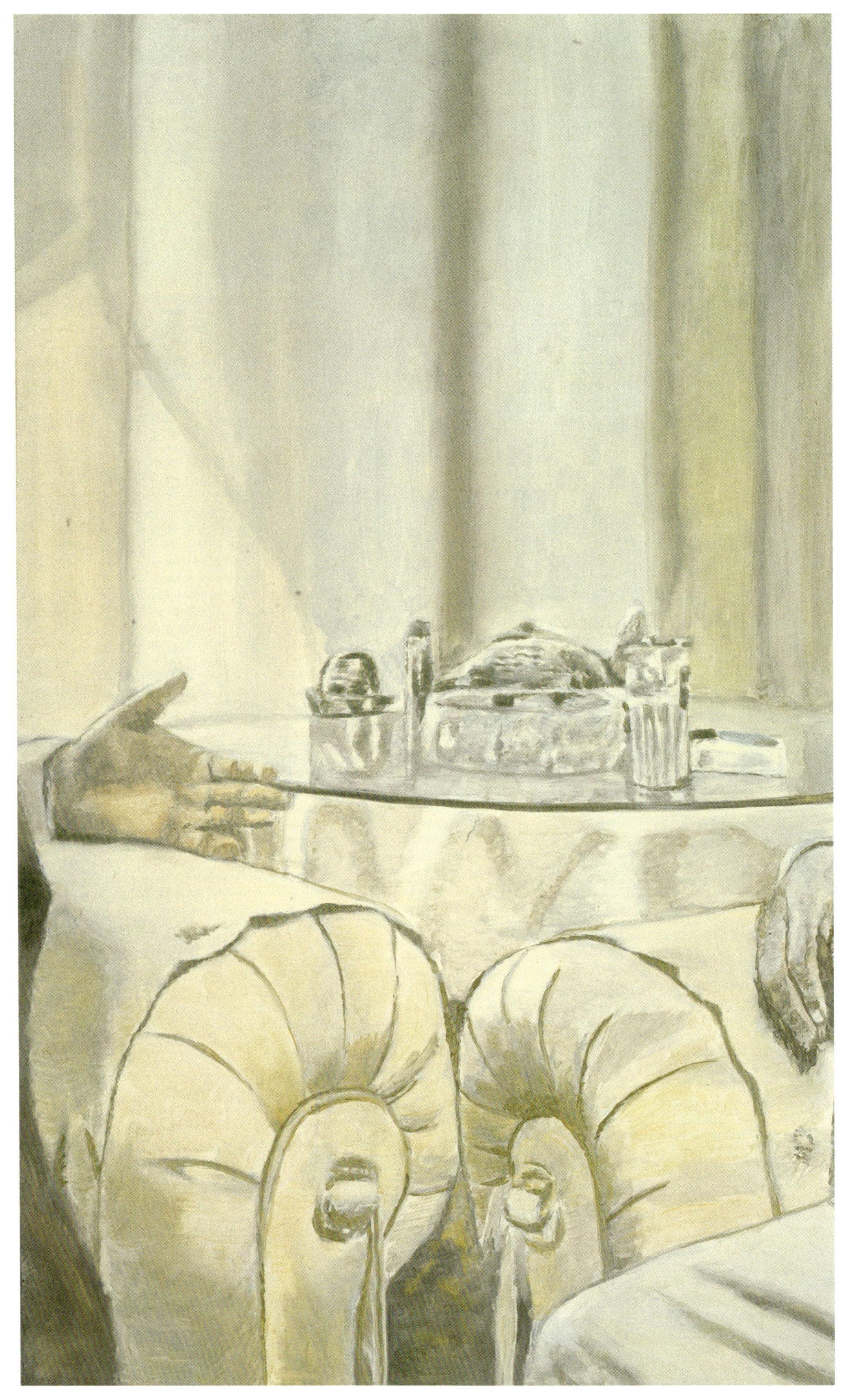

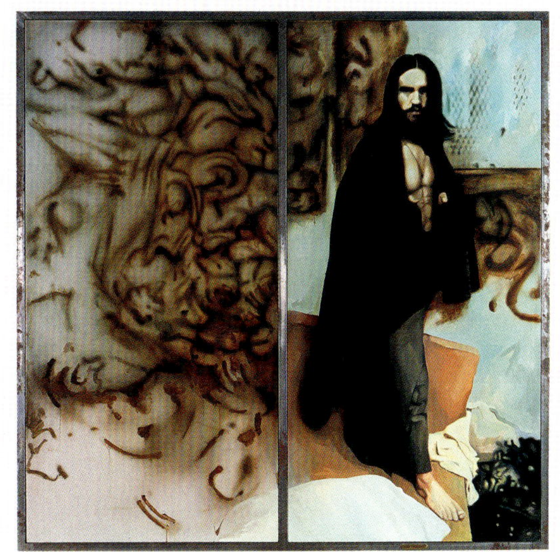

Mubarak in Egypt during the initial stages of the war in Iraq. The artist chose only that part of the image that shows the two men's hands and the space between them. The pale opulence of the surroundings suggests a kind of frozen, anaesthetized condition. The two isolated hands enact, in Tuymans's words, "the downfall of diplomacy through brutal power, symbolized by the one hand that speaks and dictates and by the other that is passive."[43]

Richard Hamilton's *Countdown* (1989) shows the charged image of a "Loyalist" marching in a parade in Northern Ireland. Such parades are historically overdetermined, commemorating as they do the seventeenth-century victory of William of Orange over Catholicism and at the same time the continuing desire of extremist Protestants to assert dominance over the Catholic minority. The subject of the painting is himself a form of historical palimpsest, with his archaic costume comprising elements both of seventeenth-century regalia (the ornamental sash and cuffs) and 1920s costume (the bowler hat), all carried defiantly into the present. Hamilton's image echoes these layers of historical reference. The image is filtered through various layers of photographic and video scanning (it even includes a frame number), completed by a further intervention in the form of a swath of red enamel paint that overrides everything else in the picture. The paint's bright color only partly conceals its relationship to the smeared shit that surrounds the figure in Hamilton's related painting of an IRA prisoner (*The Citizen*, 1981–83) during the so-called "dirty" protests of the 1970s. In turn, of course, the shit inexorably evokes abstract mark-making.

Luc Tuymans
Egypt, 2003

Richard Hamilton
The Citizen, 1982–83

following pages:
Richard Hamilton
Countdown, 1989

Kerry James Marshall
Souvenir I, 1997

Even an artist as invested in the idea of history painting as Kerry James Marshall explained his practice in terms that are themselves already historicized and institutional:

43 Tuymans, "Display," *Flash Art* (March–April 2004): 40.

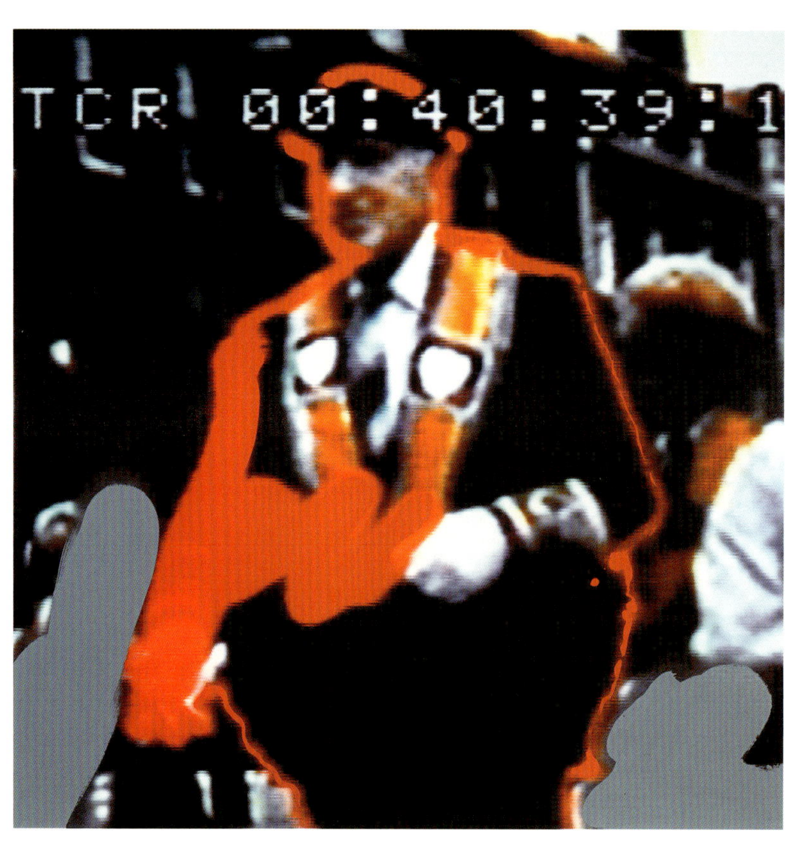
TCR 00:40:39:1

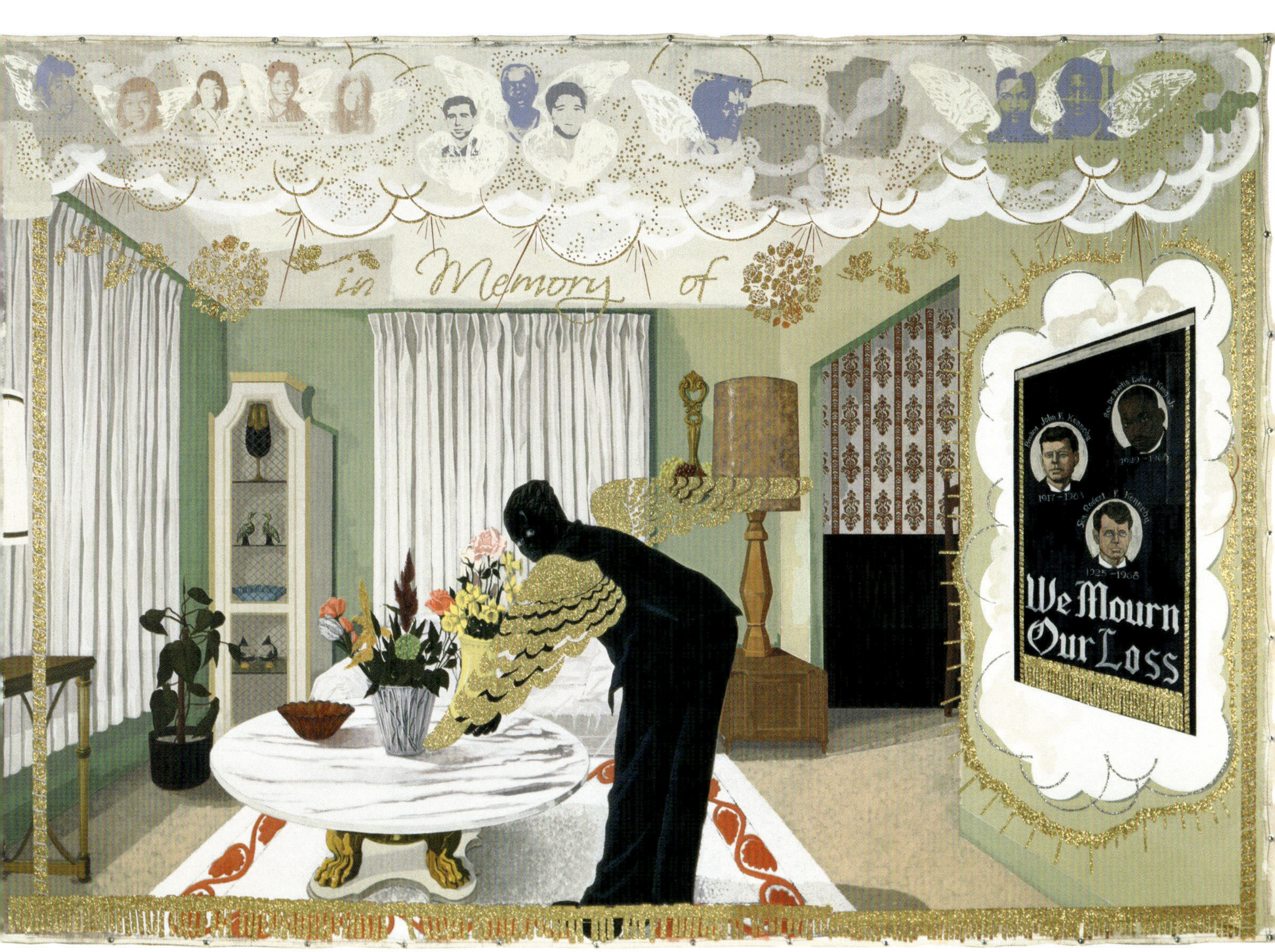
in Memory of
John F. Kennedy
1917–1963
Sen. Robert F. Kennedy
1925–1968
We Mourn
Our Loss

I look for ways to place works in the museum that foreground African-American subjects, which are otherwise largely missing. To do that, the works have to operate on the same scale and with the same aesthetic ambitions as the art we commonly see there. I made a conscious decision to position my work inside the genre of history painting because that tradition is the backbone of museology. If my work embodies the same principles as that work, handling imagery under the terms it sets, then it has a chance.[44]

Marshall recognized that the capacity of painting to act as an agent of change has increasingly been called into doubt when he said of his Souvenir series of paintings: "Instead of representing an event in history, they stand for a period of history."[45] In this context, despite the specificity of content in these works, the representational function is operating at a certain distance. The paintings are set in living rooms where actual historical events—the assassinations of John F. Kennedy and Martin Luther King, for example—are already represented as memorials. This arms-length approach—to make a representation of a representation—in itself suggests a melancholic awareness of lessened possibilities. "We mourn our loss," says a prominent inscription in *Souvenir I* (1997); while the mourning is explicitly for the assassinated, it can also be read as mourning for the very capacity of contemporary painting to address such issues.

As Buchloh has argued, "The history of history painting is itself a history of the withdrawal of a subject from painting's ability to represent, a withdrawal that ultimately generated the modernist notion of aesthetic autonomy."[46] The move towards such aesthetic autonomy does carry with it a sense of loss. For the historical avant-garde early in the twentieth century, the preservation of art's seriousness, paradoxically, had seemed to call for a retreat from socially determined issues into the realm of the self-contained.

44 Marshall, "Notes on Career and Work," in *Kerry James Marshall*, 123.

45 Ibid.

46 Buchloh, "A Note on Gerhard Richter's *October 18, 1977*," in *October*, no. 48 (spring 1989): 93.

THERE IS TO BE NO MORE REPRESENTATION

If photography stands at one pole in this argument because of its challenge to painting's primacy in representation, then abstraction is at the other, because it was abstraction that historically seemed to offer the greatest possible autonomy. The idea of pictorial autonomy had, of course, grown independently of abstraction. It was a crucial element in the reception of Cézanne's work. Kandinsky, for example, argued that "it is not a man, an apple, or a tree that are represented. All are solely used by Cézanne for the construction of an innermost artistically sound reality which we call a painting."[47] For Braque, "the goal is not to be concerned with the *reconstitution* of an anecdotal fact, but with the *constitution* of a pictorial fact."[48]

If actual subject matter was already reduced to nothing more than the anecdotal, however, then it was a relatively short step to its abandonment. For the pioneers of abstraction, the way forward for painting—the step necessary for the preservation of its autonomy—lay in the renunciation of representation altogether. For Mondrian, the represented object became only an obstacle to pure composition, which was now taken to be the real business of painting: "In painting you must first try to see *composition, color, and line* and not the representation *as representation*. Then you will finally come to feel the subject matter a hindrance."[49] Likewise, Rodchenko wrote of the paintings he made in 1921: "I reduced painting to its logical conclusion and exhibited three canvases: red, blue and yellow. I affirmed: It's all over. Basic colors. Every plane is a plane, and there is to be no more representation."[50]

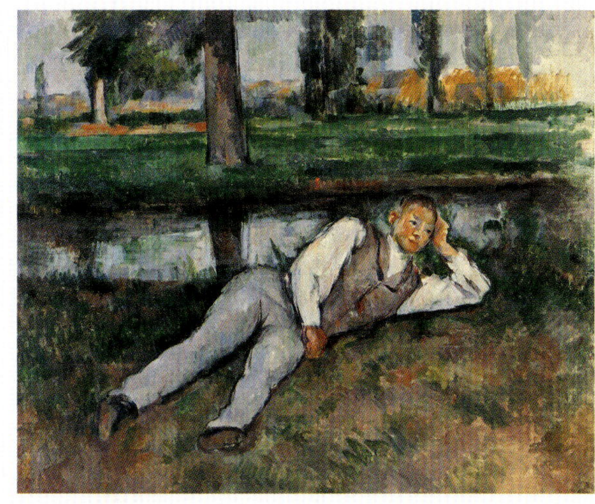

Paul Cézanne
Boy Resting, 1887

47 Kandinsky, *On the Spiritual in Art*, ed. and trans. Hilla Rebay (New York: Dover, 1977), 32.

48 Georges Braque, "Thoughts and Reflections on Art" (1917), in Herschel B. Chipp, ed., *Theories of Modern Art* (Berkeley: University of California Press, 1968), 260.

49 Mondrian, "Dialogue on the New Plastic" (1919), in Charles Harrison and Paul Wood, eds., *Art in Theory, 1900–1990* (Oxford: Blackwell, 1992), 283.

50 Rodchenko, from the manuscript "Working with Maiakovsky" (1939), quoted by Bois, "Painting: The Task of Mourning," 238.

Forty years later, Ad Reinhardt, who often spoke of his own work as constituting the "last" paintings, was conscious of this position as having become a tradition of its own. "I often feel I'm inventing a new language," he wrote, "the language of Manet, Monet, Mondrian, Malevich."[51] Despite the subtlety of Reinhardt's position, it is nonetheless true that the inexorability of painting's movement towards monochromatic pure abstraction was widely felt. For Clement Greenberg:

> *A modernist work of art must try, in principle, to avoid communication with any order of experience not inherent in the most literally and essentially construed nature of its medium. Among other things, this means renouncing illusion and explicit subject matter.... Modernist Painting meets our desire for the literal and positive by renouncing the illusion of the third dimension.*[52]

The "painterly" was a concept originally introduced by the art historian Heinrich Wölfflin in the context of Baroque art. For Wölfflin the painterly constituted an alternative system of representation to the linear, perspective-based system that had held sway since the Renaissance. It suggested the possibility of evoking depth in richer, more convincing ways. For the abstract painters of the New York School, perspective was out of the question, but a variety of painterly marks were very much part of their repertoires. In 1962, Greenberg identified—particularly in the work of de Kooning and Guston—a tendency that he called "homeless representation," by which he meant "a plastic and descriptive painterliness that is applied to abstract ends, but which continues to suggest representational ones."[53] Greenberg's identification of this "mannerist" trend of the 1950s proved to be prescient,

51 Quoted by Bois, "The Limit of Almost," in *Ad Reinhardt* (Los Angeles: The Museum of Contemporary Art; and New York: The Museum of Modern Art, 1991), 14.

52 Greenberg, "Sculpture in our Time" (1958, based on an earlier text, "The New Sculpture," of 1949), in *Modernism With a Vengeance, 1957–1969*, vol. 4 of *The Collected Essays and Criticism*, ed. John O'Brian (Chicago: The University of Chicago Press, 1993), 56.

53 Greenberg, "After Abstract Expressionism" (1962), in ibid., 124.

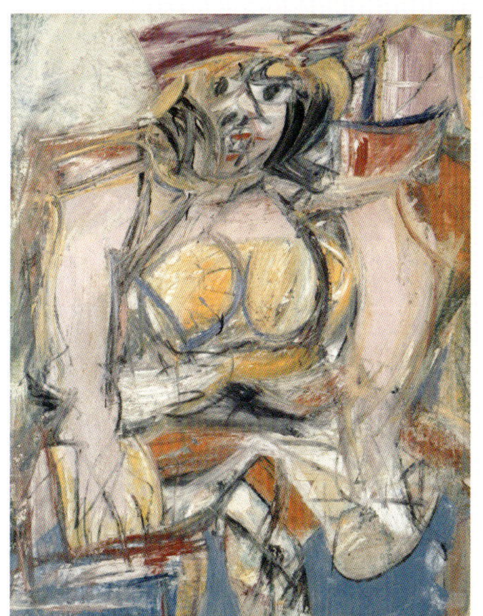

of course, especially as regards to Guston, at that time a purely abstract painter, while de Kooning's Woman paintings were already a notable anomaly in New York School painting of the fifties. As early as 1960, however, Guston had been wrestling with the implications of the Greenbergian rhetoric that painting had to be exclusively self-referential:

> *There is something ridiculous and miserly in the myth we inherit from abstract art—that painting is autonomous, pure and for itself, and therefore we habitually defined its ingredients and define its limits. But painting is "impure." It is the adjustment of impurities which forces painting's continuity. We are image-makers and image-ridden.*[54]

When Guston returned to the figurative, however, he did bring with him a dazzling painterly technique honed in the image-free crucible of Abstract Expressionism, and his "touch" is almost the same in both types of paintings.

Porter was among the most perceptive analysts of the issues raised by the renunciation of the relationship between painting and representation, and he himself remained persistently dissatisfied with both realism and abstraction. Taking an unorthodox position, Porter saw photography and abstraction as linked in their lack of relationship to a visual experience mediated through long and close observation of the physical world:

Ad Reinhardt
Abstract Painting, Blue, 1952

Willem de Kooning
Woman IV, 1952–53

> *The trouble with the realistic artist is that he is indirect, and between himself and his experience he puts concepts: a steely equality of detail, conceptualistic anatomy, or the metier of the old masters. The non-objective artist is closer to the photographer in his reliance on direct experience. But because he is not interested in nature he tends to lose contact with concrete variety. The trouble with this is that it leads to a loss of feeling for pluralism, as though all experiences were becoming one experience, the experience of everything.*[55]

54 Guston, quoted in Mayer, *Night Studio*, 141.

55 Porter, in "Eliot Porter," *The Nation*, 9 January 1960. Quoted in Rackstraw Downes, "Fairfield Porter: The Thought Behind the Painting," in Joan Ludman, *Fairfield Porter* (New York: Hudson Hills, 2001), 17.

Porter's prescient appeal for pluralism and his rejection of absolutism, however, reached very few in the 1960s. Reinhardt summed up the view of most artists of the period; for him, when "anything goes,' and 'it makes no difference whether art is abstract or representational,' the artists' world is a mannerist and primitivist art trade and suicide-vaudeville, venal, genial, contemptible, trifling."[56] Of course, the fact that Reinhardt felt the need to attack the idea that "it makes no difference whether art is abstract or representational" is evidence enough of the fact that the idea was at least in circulation.

In New York, it was abstract painting that had established the reputation of the city as the new worldwide capital of art, so it is not surprising that any return to the representational was particularly fraught there. While there might be a few in New York who could argue that abstract and representational painting were equally valid, the idea that a single artist could practice both was all but inconceivable, as Guston himself clearly felt, and as reaction to his 1970 exhibition demonstrated. While representational painting had certainly never disappeared, and indeed had enjoyed a certain revival in the form of Pop, the distinction still mattered profoundly. Most Pop was relentlessly flat, linear, and graphic, as if to distance itself as far as possible from the painterliness of the New York School. In its earliest stages, in fact, it was seen almost less as painting than as a kind of nihilistic neo-Dadaism. This was especially so in the light of the pervasive rhetoric that privileged unmediated self-expression over any engagement with historical precedent. As Harold Rosenberg famously put it, "At a certain moment the canvas began to appear to one American artist after another as an arena in which to act.... What was to go on the canvas was not a picture but an event."[57] Such a position left little room for a relationship with the pictorial tradition.

Guston was one of very few American artists to make significant abstract and representational work, and he could not do both at the same time. He had to renounce one to get to the other. His paintings might have made more sense in a European context that was all but invisible in the United States. While abstract

56 Reinhardt, "Art-as-Art" (1962), in *Ad Reinhardt*, 122. 1962 was also the year in which the well-known abstract painter Al Leslie began to make figurative work, and he too expressed great anxiety about the change of direction. As he said, "these figurative ideas could not be ignored, even though following them could seem to imply that I would be turning my back on the twentieth century." Interview with Barbara Flynn in *Alfred Leslie: The Grisaille Paintings, 1962–1967* (New York: Barbara Flynn and Richard Bellamy, 1992), p. 55.

57 Rosenberg, "The American Action Painters" *Art News* 51, no. 5 (December 1952): 22–23, 48–50.

painting in postwar Europe occupied an important position as representative of an avant-garde tradition that had been savagely attacked and almost destroyed by the Nazis, it never quite achieved the virtually unchallenged primacy that it held in the United States through the mid-1960s.

Guston, who was born in 1913, had had to fight his way *to* abstraction after an apprenticeship in 1930s social realism, and then out of it again. For a younger generation of artists, the conflation of representation and abstraction was no longer heresy. Painting itself was threatened, and to paint at all was enough. For Neil Jenney, like Richter, "There is actually no distinction between abstraction and realism."[58] Even before Guston finally returned to representation, Jenney had begun making paintings that sacrificed the mimetic in favor of clear content expressed through exuberant and undisguised painterliness. In *Tools and Task* (1969), despite the shovels and sledgehammer that are the nominal subject of the painting, we know that the real tools in question are paint and brushes. The task is to make by hand a representation that offers the viewer a realism that cannot be better delivered by photography.

When Jenney began painting recognizable images, he felt no need to pursue a polished facture: "When you do realism you have to decide what degree of realism you are going to attempt and I decided that I did not want to be concerned about the technical factors."[59] "Bad" painting seemed like a viable way forward, as it still does for many, although, as Jenney put it later, in an elegant and resigned formulation: "Even if I produced the worst paintings possible, they would not be good enough."[60] He executed his later work in a highly polished technique. Jenney's paintings, although they encompass a number of different styles, are all produced in the context of an explicit rejection of photographic images. As Jenney put it: "I am not trying to duplicate something that I see in nature because you must always compromise—it is always going to be paint, you cannot out paint the paint. I was not trying to disguise the fact that these were paintings. I was not trying to mimic photographs."[61]

58 Jenney, in Richard Marshall, *New Image Painting* (New York: Whitney Museum of American Art, 1978), 38.

59 Ibid.

60 Ibid.

61 Ibid.

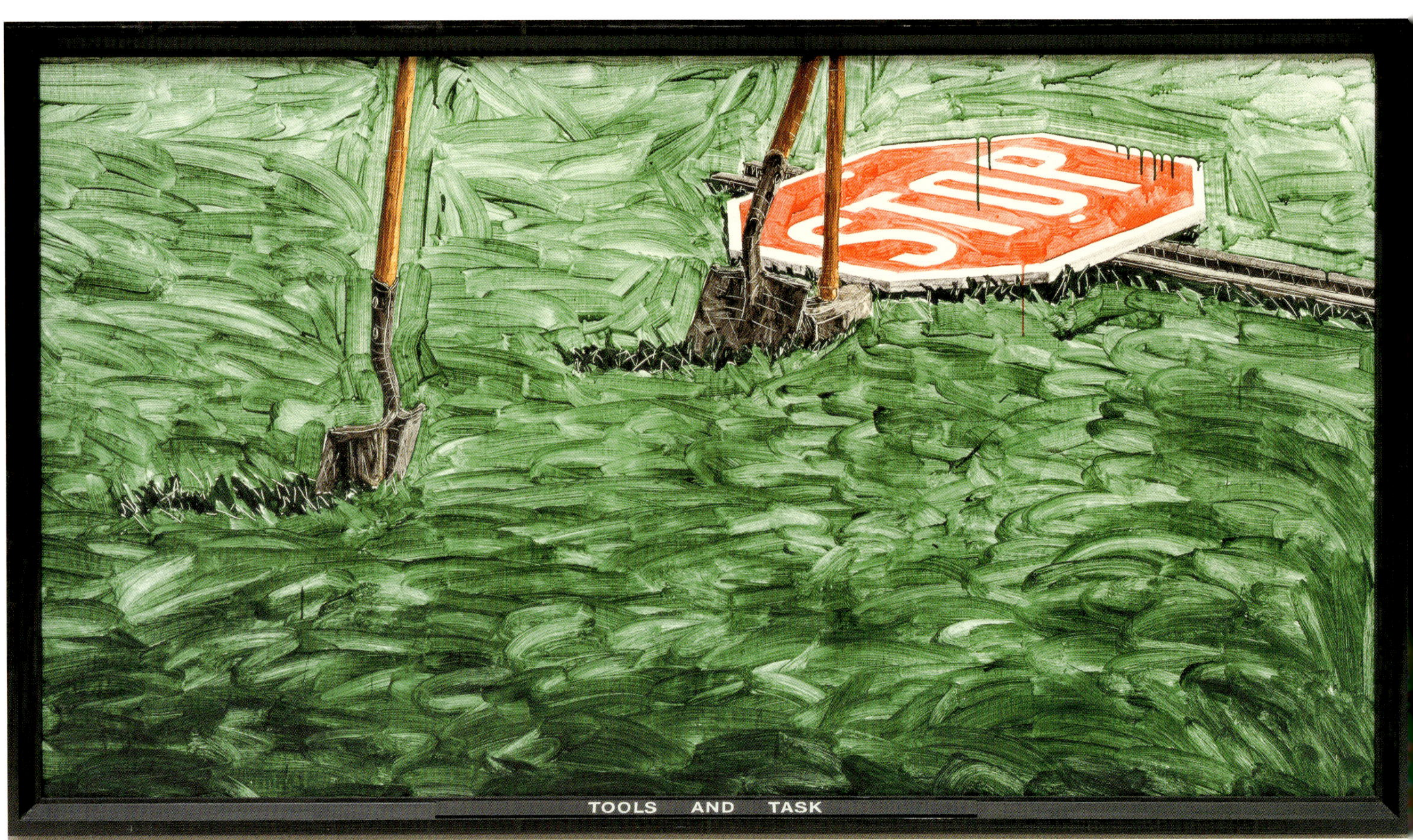
STOP
TOOLS AND TASK

This embrace of paint *as* paint is more common in the rhetoric of abstraction. Its appearance in the context of representation is a testament to a renewed crisis of confidence in painting in general that was steadily building during the 1960s. In 1964, Donald Judd wrote, "There is a vague pervasive assumption… that Abstract Expressionism is dead, that nothing new is to be expected from its original practitioners and that nothing will be developed from it, nothing that would be identifiable as coming from it and that would also be new. It sure looks dead."[62] Judd's own move into sculpture (or "specific objects," as he put it) was part of a widespread move away from painting by ambitious artists. Perhaps Reinhardt really *had* been making the last paintings. Many painters turned to versions of the serial that, consciously or not, mimicked industrial production. The abolition of painting as a craft that had appealed to earlier avant-gardists such as Malevich and Mondrian seemed to be on the point of realization. There was a sense, as Hal Foster put it, "that minimalism threatens modernist practice—more, that it consummates it, completes and breaks with it at once;"[63] in other words, that the crisis identified by Rodchenko in the 1920s was back, and more potentially lethal than ever: "there is to be no more representation." By the early 1970s, Porter, Guston, and Jenney all looked like eccentric figures who stood outside whatever remained of an avant-garde tradition, perhaps not even serious artists. Porter, indeed, was referred to dismissively as "amateurish" or a "Sunday painter."[64]

Neil Jenney
Tools and Task, 1969

62 Judd, *Arts Yearbook*, 1964.
63 Foster, "The Crux of Minimalism," in *Individuals* (Los Angeles: The Museum of Contemporary Art, 1986), 162.
64 See, for example, John Updike, "Violence at the Windows," in *Just Looking: Essays on Art* (Boston: Museum of Fine Arts, 2001), 114–25.

BACK TO LOOKING

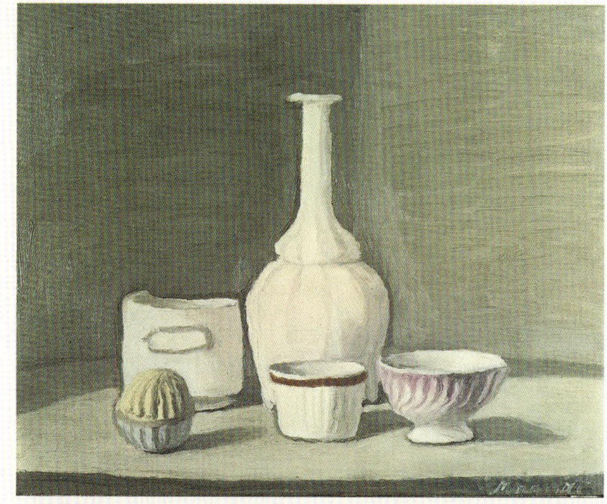

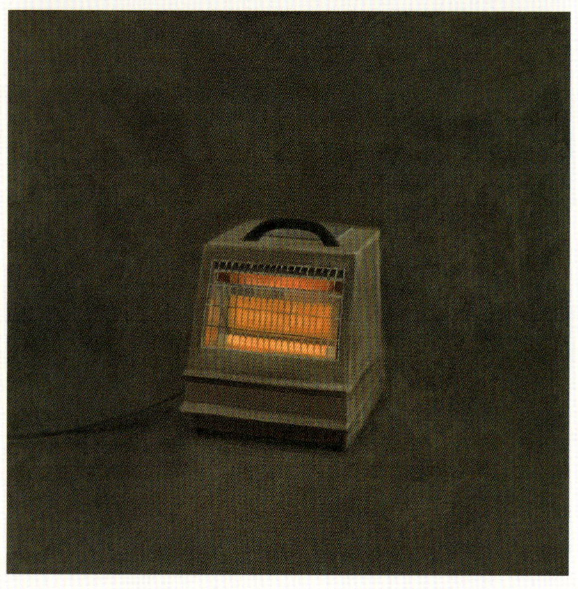

To focus, as Porter had recommended, on the long look at the visible world and the slow, painstaking process of making a version of it in paint was by the mid-1960s felt by many artists to be an outmoded practice of increasingly limited relevance. A teleological model of art, in which each movement, each artist, had to build on and supersede the achievements of the past, still held wide sway. For Vija Celmins, however, in 1964 still a student at UCLA, the more recent models also seemed to be somewhat played out, and she began to go "back to looking" under the influence of Giorgio Morandi's austere still lifes. She began in her own studio, focusing on the everyday objects that surrounded her—a lamp, an electric heater—and made slow, careful paintings of them. At first, she recalled, "I got no response at all. Sometimes people laughed."[65]

But in the long term there really had been little question that painting would return to representation—the whole history of the medium was bound up with it. The new question, however, was how painting would deal with the usurpation by photography of its *primary* role in representation. The return to representation was all the more problematic because of the long period during which non-representational work had been dominant. Abstraction had offered an alternative to the inexorable logic of language, which increasingly seemed synonymous with representation. Even today, to call a work of visual art "literary" is usually meant as a negative assessment. It is a somewhat backhanded way of acknowledging an important truth: that painting embodies an inherent resistance to linguistic models. The negative connotation of the term is there because we are reluctant to admit more directly how much of what we write about —and think about—painting is in fact thoroughly informed by language.

Giorgio Morandi
Still Life, 1946

Vija Celmins
Heater, 1964

Vija Celmins
Lamp #1, 1964

65 Celmins, telephone conversation with the author, 30 March 2004.

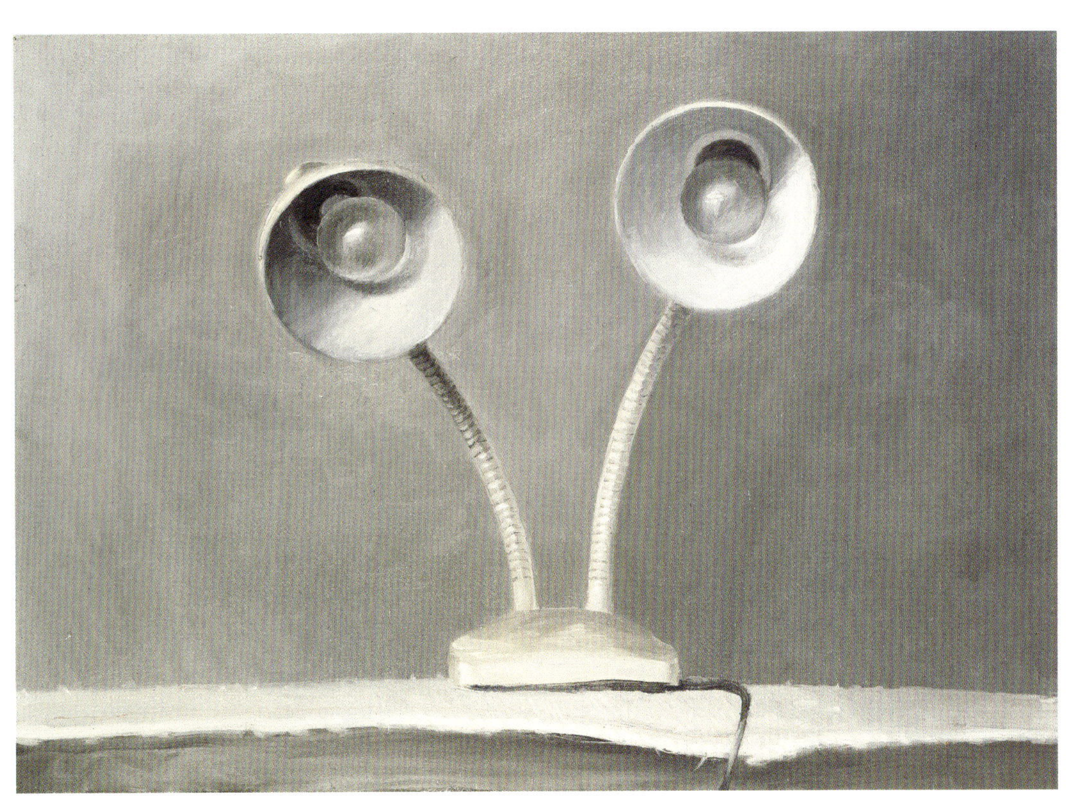

Paintings such as Celmins's, so evidently slow in their relationship to the image, call upon the viewer also to make a patient perceptual movement back and forth within the represented space. Even a pistol firing is painted as something that can be patiently observed. In a painting it can. There is a slowing down of the entire process of looking. Today we are increasingly accustomed to receiving, registering, and discarding images at very high speed. We are bombarded with images at a rate unprecedented in history and have become skilled at processing them. Part of painting's residual autonomy now rests in its insistence on a slower response, no matter how instantaneous the initial impression might be. As Guston said, "In the old painting I love, early Renaissance painting, the 'information' is fast, no? But the 'painting' is slow, dwelt upon."[66] The extended period over which most paintings are executed contributes to this implicit demand for patience. The unique, artisanal condition of painting in one sense limits it by making it easily convertible into a rare and expensive commodity, yet at the same time builds into it a certain resistance to the easy consumption of infinitely reproducible digitized images. The difference can be particularly dramatic in encounters with paintings that have become well known *through* photographs. Barnett Newman's paintings, for example, seem very graphic in reproduction, but when experienced in person reveal a quite different feeling. They are very evidently handmade objects. The surfaces are decidedly painterly, and they gradually reveal considerable depth.

Vija Celmins
Hand Holding a Firing Gun, 1964

Damisch has asked an important question: "Could there be a form of analysis whose aim was not to capture painting in the net of discourse but rather to allow oneself to be educated by it, even at the risk of undermining the linguistic model?"[67] He proposed "an analysis aimed less at helping us to understand than at helping us to see, and which would strive for a renewed intimacy with the work that is painting's own province."[68] This is not a position that seeks to deny painting its right to intellectual activity. The idea that painters are akin to *idiots savants* is a surprisingly persistent, but nonetheless false, model. Instead, Damisch posited a broader definition of the activity of painting, one that recognized it as an activity of the mind as well as the hand, but nevertheless strove to keep direct visual experience as present, and as valid, as the logic of language.

66 Guston quoted by Mayer, *Night Studio*, 152.

67 Damisch, *The Origin of Perspective*, trans. John Goodman (Cambridge: The MIT Press, 1995), 262.

68 Ibid., 263.

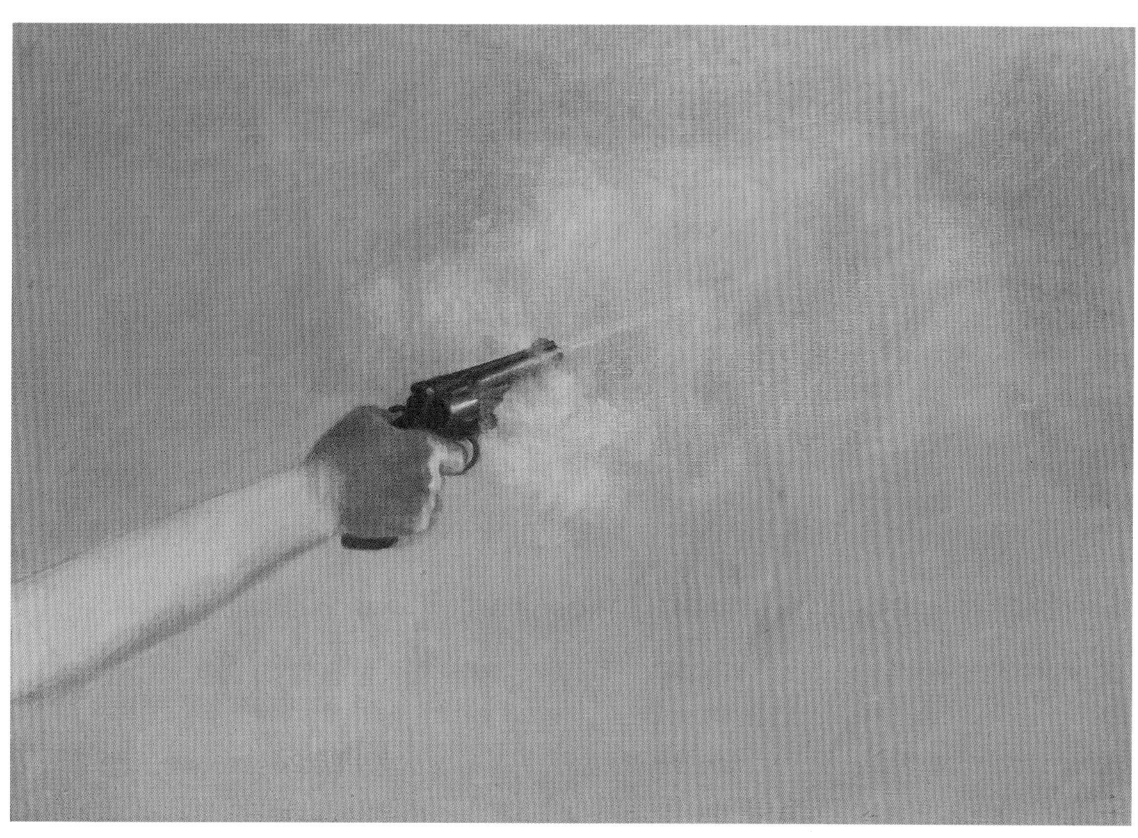

In National City, California, in 1969, John Baldessari was trying to think through the implications of art as a mental activity more than a physical one. "It seemed important," he said,

> *that I test this other premise—whether a person actually has to do his or her own work or can it just be a thought process? This came out of reexamining what art was supposed to be. And one of the fundamental assumptions, I suppose—and it still lingers—is that there should be the artist's touch in there in some way, otherwise it's not art.... So all that stuff is going through my mind at the time and I said again, "What's so bad if I didn't do it?"*[69]

Marcel Duchamp
Tu m', 1918

John Baldessari
A Painting by Hildegard Reiner, 1969

following pages:
John Baldessari
A Painting by Pat Perdue, 1969

John Baldessari
A Painting by William Bowne, 1969

One of the results of this analytical process was the series Commissioned Paintings, in which Baldessari essentially subcontracted the actual painting to other people: amateur painters whose work he had seen and liked at county fairs. He would supply them with a dozen or so slides (all of a hand pointing at an object) and ask them to choose one and make a painting of the image, reproducing it as faithfully as possible. The result was a series of fourteen paintings conceived by Baldessari but actually painted by someone else.

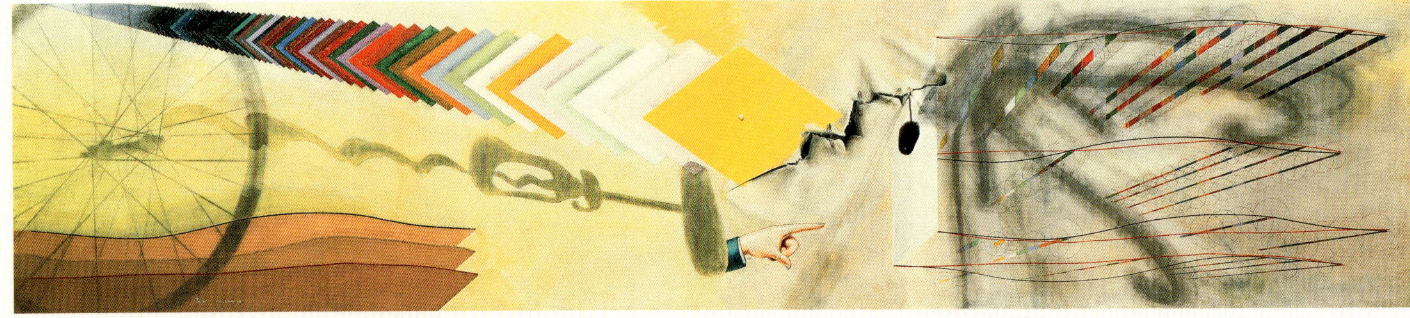

The image of the hand pointing is not arbitrary. By means of this motif Baldessari stressed that his real activity as an artist lies in the act of choosing, of making decisions. It is in this focus on close looking, on the act of looking, that this conceptual work finds a point of contact with Celmins's apparently quite different practice. In the case of the Commissioned Paintings, however, Baldessari subcontracted that activity, too. The hand was a friend's, and the choices were his, although Baldessari directed the project. The pointing hand makes a direct reference to the notoriously "anti-retinal" practice of Duchamp, one of whose last paintings, the derisive *Tu m'* (1918), includes a hand with a pointing finger, executed by a sign painter.

69 Baldessari, in an interview with Hugh Davies and Andrea Hales, in *John Baldessari: National City* (San Diego: Museum of Contemporary Art, 1996), 88–89.

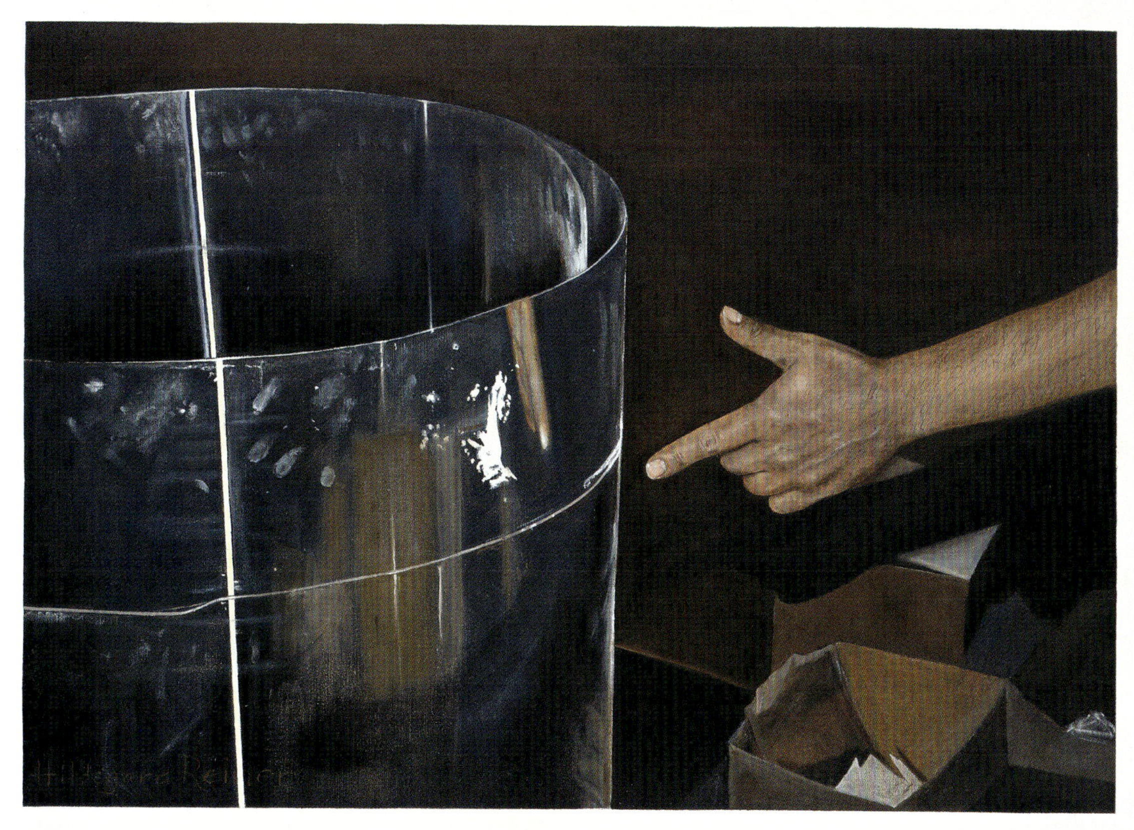

A PAINTING BY HILDEGARD REINER

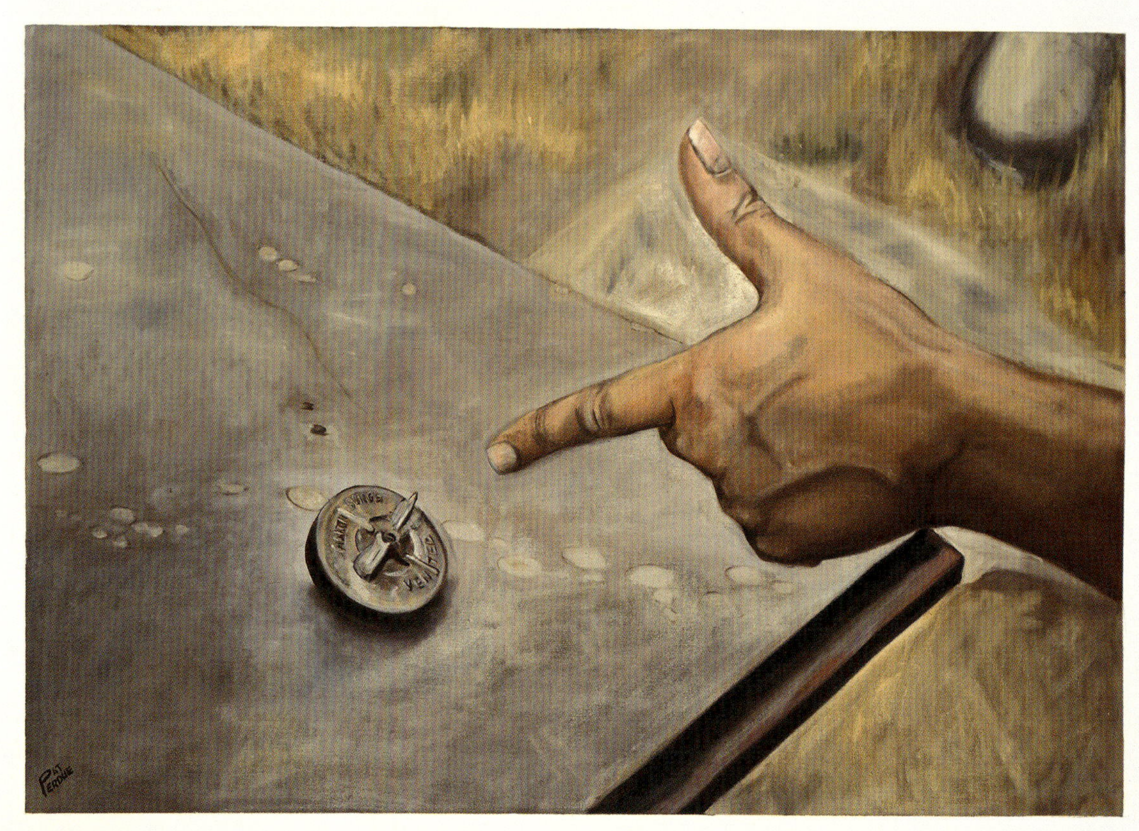

A PAINTING BY PAT PERDUE

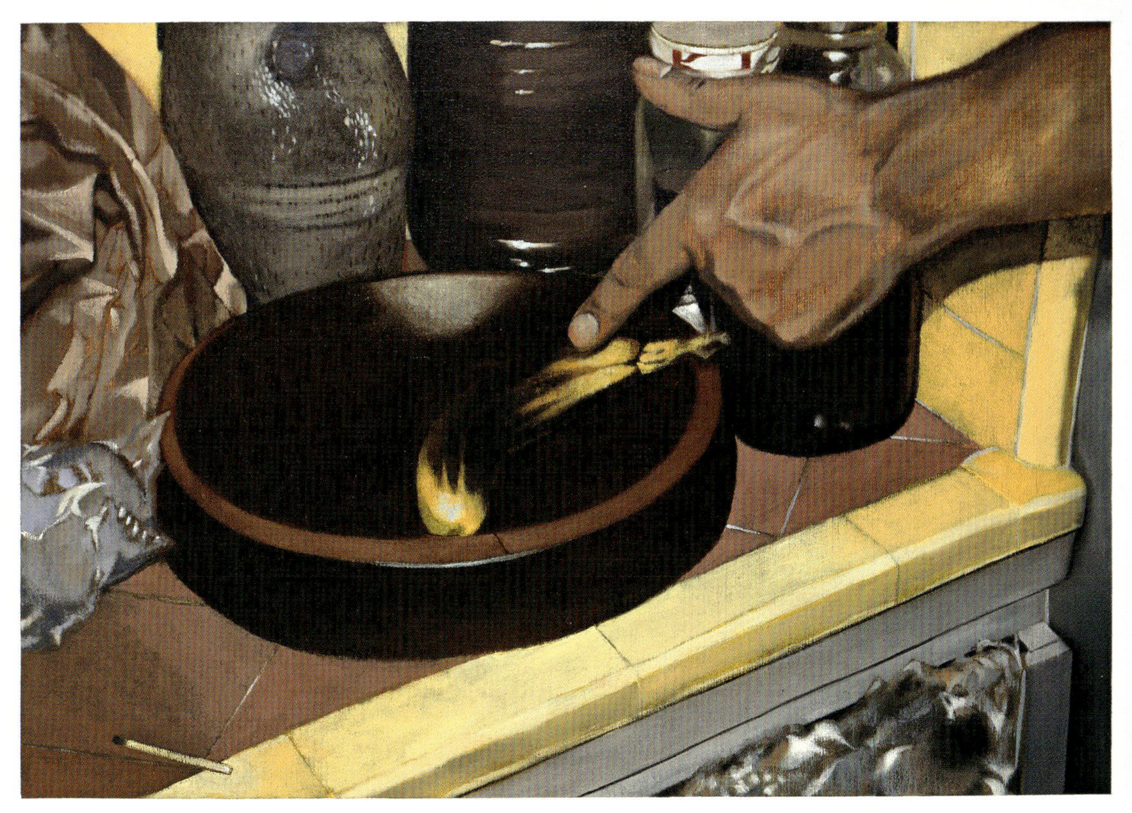

A PAINTING BY WILLIAM BOWNE

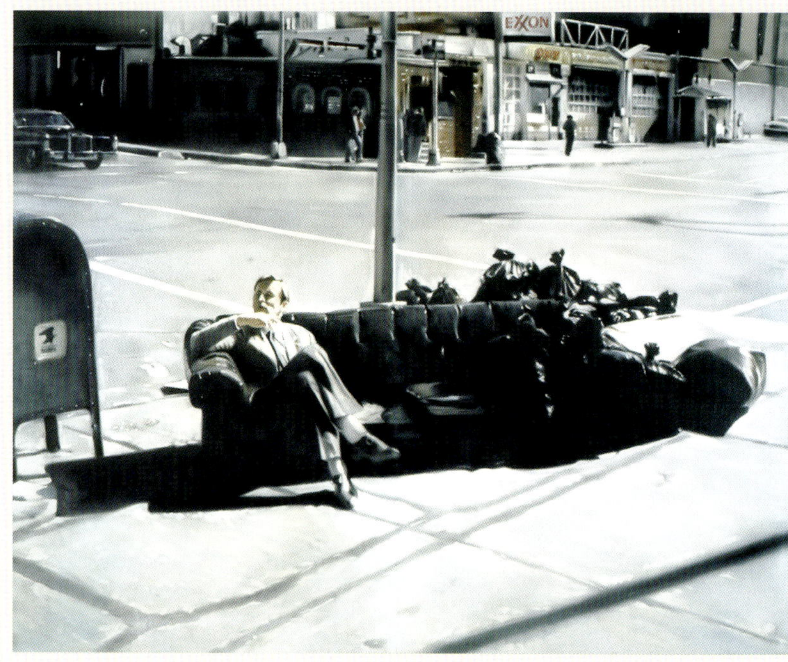

The use of such distancing tactics, maneuvers that hold the artist at arm's length from the work itself, reflect an alternative tradition to the recurrent appeals to faith in painting that I outlined earlier. What might be called the "insincere" tradition in art is relatively rare, but nevertheless strong, running as it does from Duchamp through Marcel Broodthaers ("I, too, wondered if I couldn't sell something and succeed in life.... The idea of inventing something insincere finally crossed my mind and I set to work at once."[70]) and on to Andy Warhol and Martin Kippenberger, who both at times had others execute their paintings. Nevertheless, such cool, ironic distance from the motif remains a distinctly minority tendency. More typical is Richter's characteristically ambiguous denial: "If I ever did admit to any irony, I did so for the sake of a quiet life. Because at some point, of course, I did care about motifs."[71] And by now, as Lawson has recognized:

> *One of the most troubling results of the co-option of modernism by mainstream bourgeois culture is that to a certain degree irony has also been subsumed.... From being a method that could shatter conventional ideas, it has become a convention for establishing complicity. From being a way to come to terms with lack of faith, it has become a screen for bad faith.*[72]

70 Broodthaers (1964), quoted in Michael Compton, "In Praise of the Subject," in *Marcel Broodthaers* (Minneapolis: Walker Art Center, 1989), 25.

71 Richter, interview with Sabine Schütz (1990), in *The Daily Practice of Painting*, 211.

72 Lawson, "Last Exit: Painting," 164.

HAPPY TO BE ALIVE

Reinhardt had been clear: "If I were to say that I am making the last paintings, I don't mean that painting is dying. You go back to the beginning all the time anyway."[73] By the late 1970s, a new generation was ready to start over. This time, however, the challenge to painting would be less direct, but possibly even more destabilizing. Douglas Crimp's landmark exhibition of 1977, "Pictures," included the work of artists who painted and artists who did not, without assuming any particular hierarchical relationship between different media. Crimp simply postulated a "renewed impulse to make pictures of recognizable things." In this context, painting was simply one medium among others, a blow to its primacy as damaging as the direct attacks of earlier, more absolutist critics. For Crimp, there were simply pictures, and he framed his discussion in the broadest terms:

> *To an ever greater extent our experience is governed by pictures, pictures in newspapers and magazines, on television and in the cinema. Next to these pictures firsthand experience begins to retreat, to seem more and more trivial. While it once seemed that pictures had the function of interpreting reality, it now seems that they have usurped it. It therefore becomes imperative to understand the picture itself, not in order to uncover a lost reality, but to determine how a picture becomes a signifying structure of its own accord.*[74]

Martin Kippenberger
Untitled, 1981

This way of thinking about representation simultaneously downgraded painting to the status not just of a photograph, but potentially to that of a snapshot or a newspaper clipping. Yet at the same time it raised the possibility of an enormous new field of activity for painters who shared the desire to engage again with recognizable images.

First, of course, it was necessary to reject the lingering traces of Greenbergian abstraction. Barbara Rose's would-be prophetic exhibition of 1979, "American Painting: The Eighties," was briskly dismissed by Lawson as "a funereal procession of tired clichés paraded as if still fresh; a corpse made up to look forever young."[75] Lawson's ready embrace of the vocabulary of death is echoed in the titles of the

73 Reinhardt, in Jeanne Siegel, *Artwords: Discourses on the 60's and 70's* (Ann Arbor: U.M.I. Press, 1985), 27.

74 Crimp, *Pictures* (New York: Artists Space, 1977), 3. The exhibition consisted of works by Troy Brauntuch, Jack Goldstein, Sherrie Levine, Robert Longo, and Philip Smith.

75 Lawson, "Last Exit: Painting," 154.

paintings that he himself began to make at this time: *Tragic Victim* (1980), *Don't Hit Her Again* (1981), and *Inches From Death* (1981). *Happy to Be Alive* (1982) is marginally more optimistic. While the titles, drawn like the images themselves from the *New York Post*, announce a new engagement with recognizable, indeed loaded, imagery, they are also barely concealed references to the parlous state of painting itself.

The frequent appearance of children in the work of many of the artists discussed here can be taken in part as a symbol of a lost or threatened innocence, and in that sense to refer as much to painting itself as to childhood. Richter covered the image of a child's face with paint. Baldessari carefully reproduced a child's coloring-book scribble. For the cover of his first exhibition catalogue, Eggerer chose a found photograph of two nervous children at the bottom of a deep stairwell. In the work of Lawson this vulnerability is explicit. The children in his paintings are defenseless, already damaged.

John Baldessari
A Picture to Treasure, 1966–67

Thomas Lawson
Happy to Be Alive, 1982

following pages:
Thomas Lawson
Don't Hit Her Again, 1981

Thomas Lawson
Inches From Death, 1981

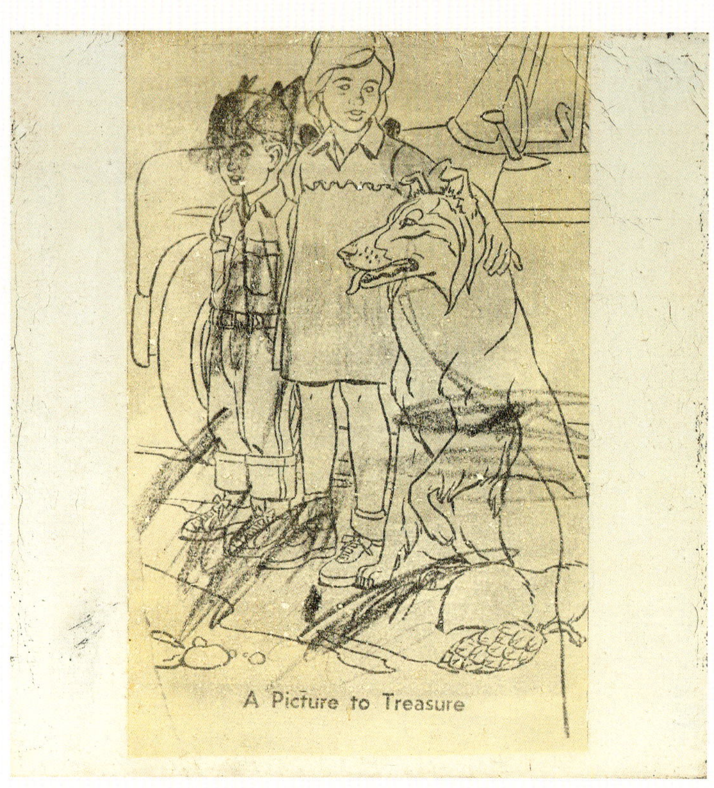

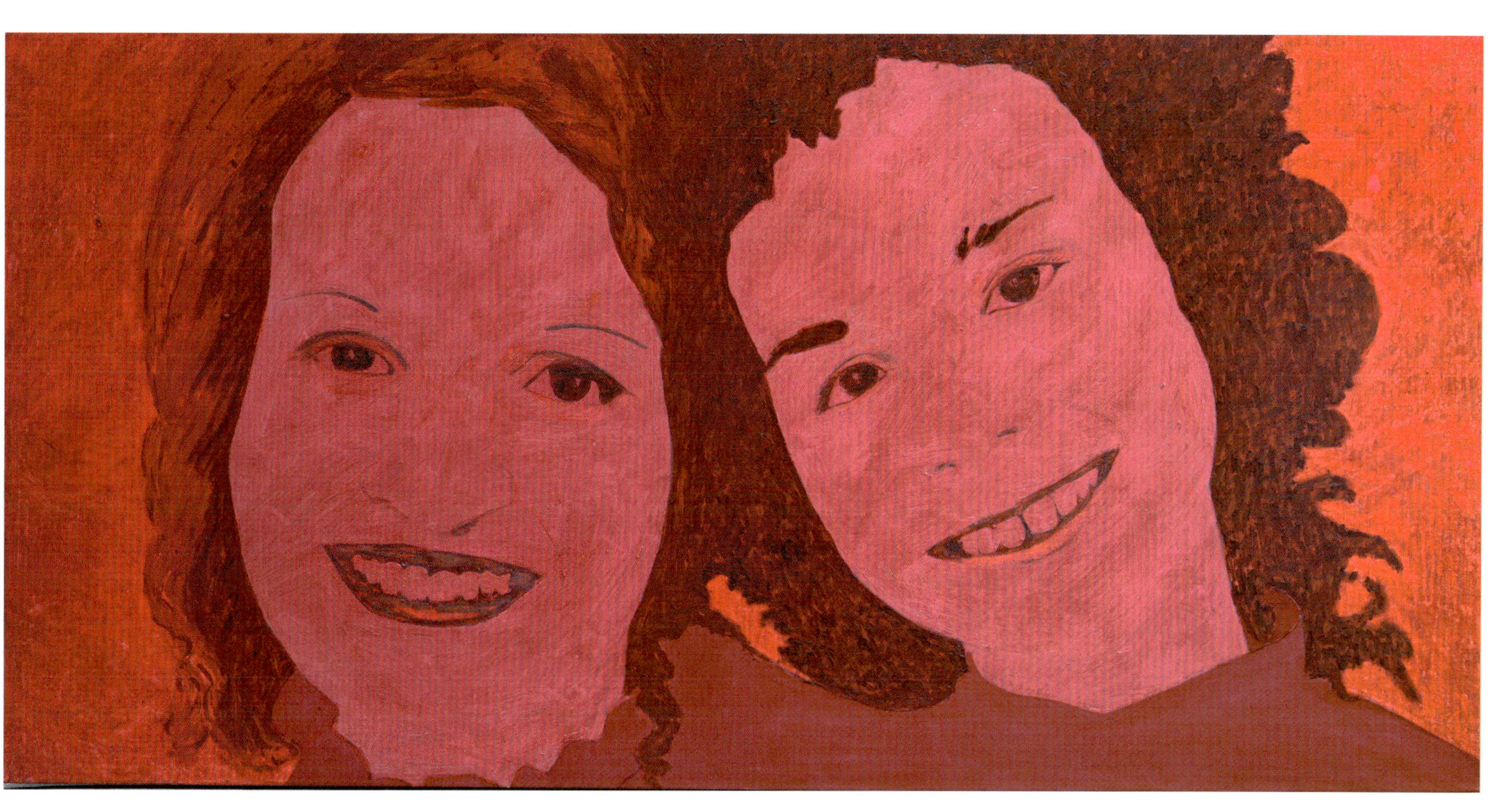

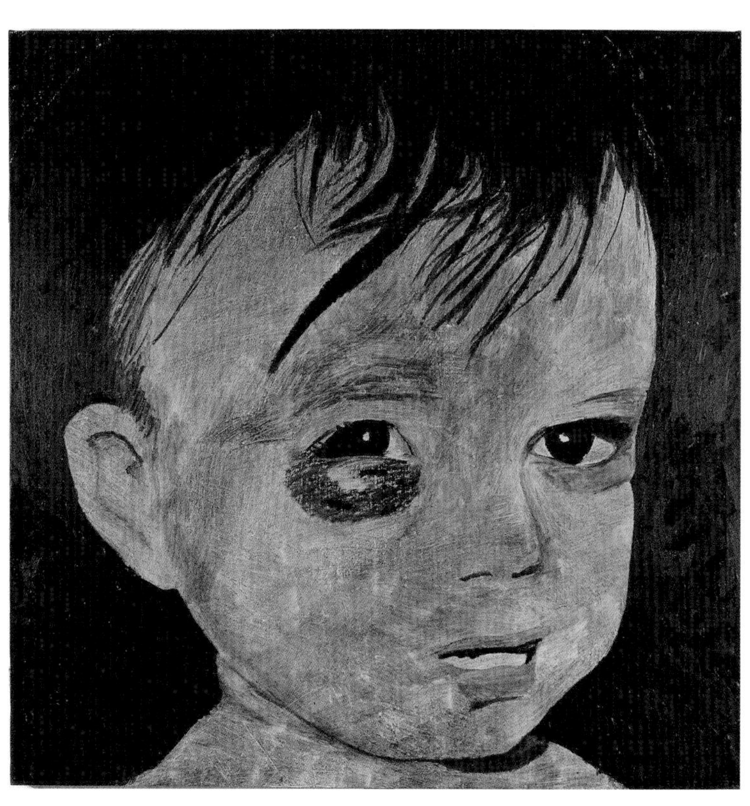

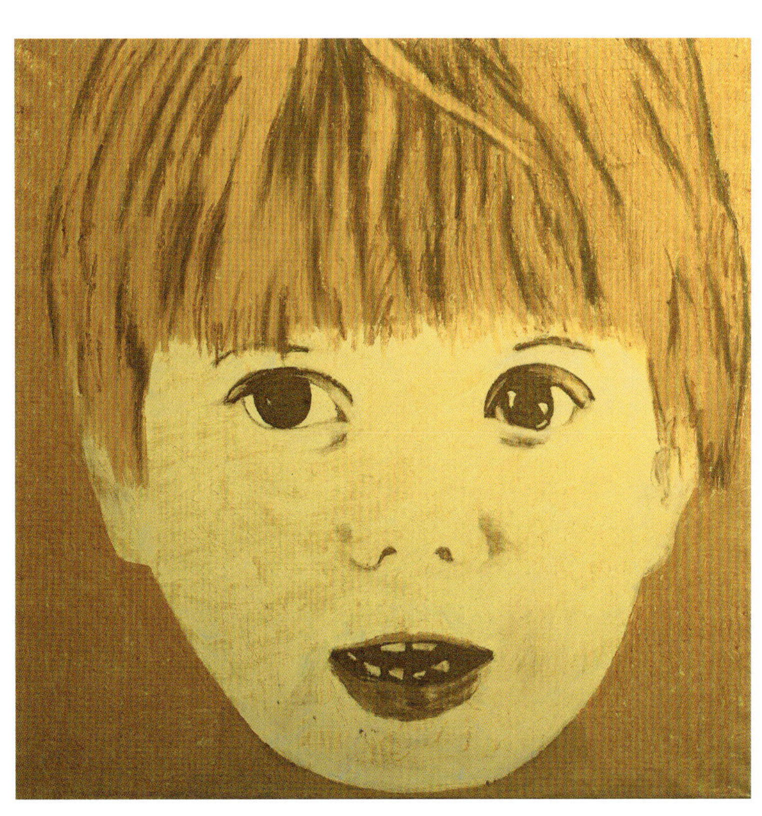

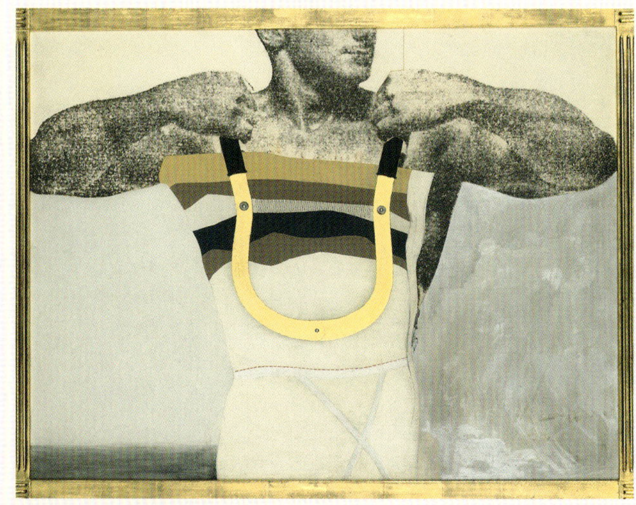

The baby in Hamilton's *Mother and Child* (1984–85) clings cheerfully to the mother but is surrounded by a whirling field of painterly instability. *Mother and Child* demonstrates a destabilizing fusion of elements. The source is an awkwardly composed snapshot that a stranger gave to Hamilton. The title, however, sets up a parallel connection with a long-established painting genre. In the painting itself, Hamilton has rendered the figures in a smooth, relatively neutral style, while the leafy background is given a more animated, painterly treatment. The consequent ambiguity between subject and background, and indeed between representation and abstraction, bears comparison with Porter's approach in *Six O'Clock*, in which two diminutive children pause in front of a landscape that seems to tower over them. The figures are represented by flat strokes of paint, just like the patches of light on the grass, or the roof of the house in the background. Unlike Porter, Hamilton preserves the distinction between figure and background, producing a nevertheless disorienting effect that is reinforced by the unsettling cropping of the original photograph. In both works the painted marks seem as fully present as the ostensible subjects.

Richard Hamilton
Towards a definitive statement on the coming trends in men's wear and accessories (c) Adonis in Y-fronts, 1962

Richard Hamilton
Mother and Child, 1984–85

Hamilton's paintings are only one part of an eclectic practice that has included an extended investigation of the relationship between art and popular culture. Hamilton, in fact, had prefigured Crimp's analysis of the new status of the image. By the late 1950s he had felt ready to move on from pure abstraction:

> *I began to move back to figuration. The return to nature came at second-hand through the use of magazines rather than as a response to real landscape or still-life objects or painting a person from life. Somehow it didn't seem necessary to hold on to that older tradition of direct contact with the world. Magazines, or any visual intermediary, could as well provide a stimulus.... Cinema, television, magazines, newspapers immersed the artists in a total environment and this new visual ambience was photographic.*[76]

76 Hamilton, "Notes on Photographs," in *Collected Words* (London: Thames and Hudson, 1983), 64.

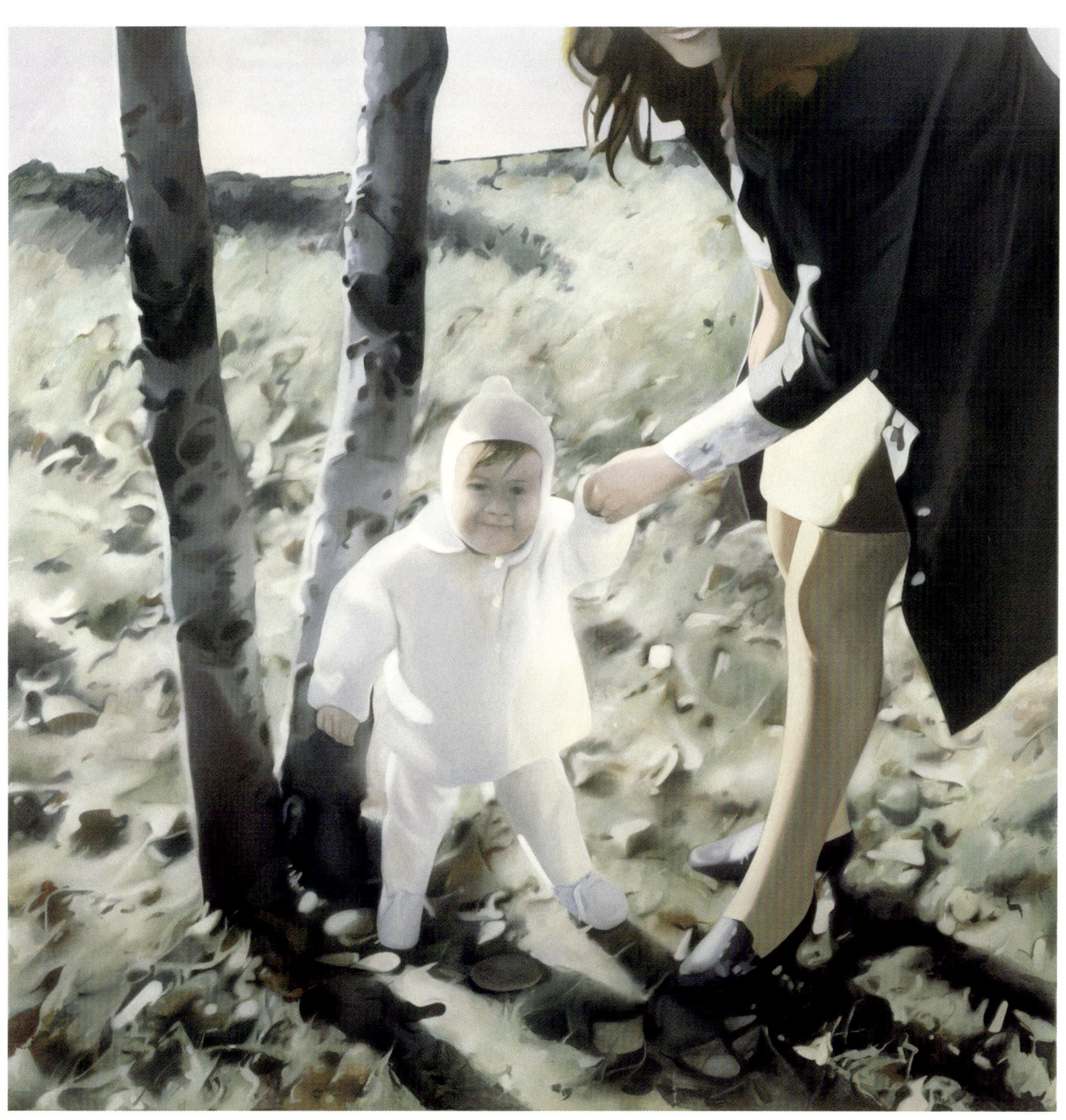

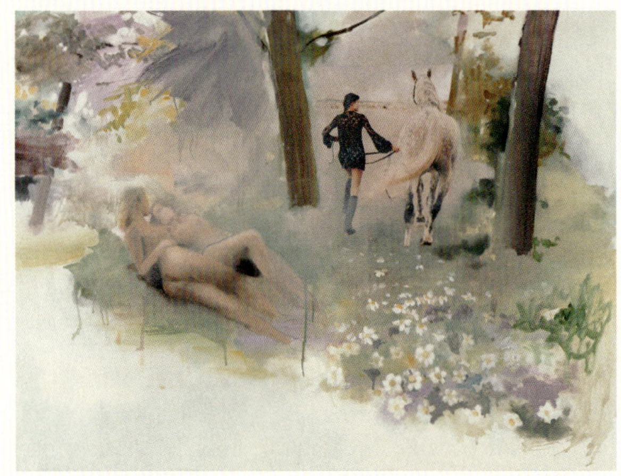

Despite his own skill as a painter, Hamilton could also argue that a painting was simply "documentary evidence that an artist has proposed a work of art."[77] His *Soft Pink Landscape* (1971–72) is a lush study of two young women in a forest landscape. Elements of photographic realism coexist with atmospheric evocations of light through the trees that in turn give way to passages of virtually abstract, dripping painterliness. While depth is suggested by the recession of the figures and the trees, the space overall remains on another level impenetrable, or shifting, or both at once. Puncturing the apparent romanticism, however, the source of the imagery in an advertisement is revealed by the presence in the foreground of a roll of toilet paper.[78]

Jochen Klein's seductive landscapes are also populated by figures of desire drawn from the worlds of advertising and mass culture, yet at the same time they too refer to abstract painting, in this case a soft, lyrical abstraction. The overall effect is a seamlessly integrated yet disturbingly fluid composition. For Klein, one starting point was the popular soft-core photography of David Hamilton; even more important, however, was the work of Richard Hamilton, whose relationship to both popular culture and painting prefigured Klein's interests. His simultaneous attraction to, demonstration of, and repulsion towards academic facility fascinated Klein and other younger painters. Klein's collaged elements of kitsch posters coexist with his own skilled painterly extrapolations from them, producing a result that is both totally coherent and profoundly unstable, in both its confounding of conventional pictorial hierarchies and the formal elements of its composition. Klein sought to lure the viewer with sweetness, but once that is accomplished the paintings, like Hamilton's, reveal an unequivocally excremental side, devolving into stains and smears.

Jochen Klein
#38, 1996

Richard Hamilton
Soft Pink Landscape, 1971–72

following pages:
Jochen Klein
#53, 1997

Jochen Klein
#57, 1997

77 Hamilton, "Propositions" (1971), in *Collected Words*, 266.

78 The advertisements, it emerged later, were conceived by the artist Bridget Riley when she was working for the J. Walter Thompson agency. See Hamilton, "Romanticism" in *Collected Words*, 78.

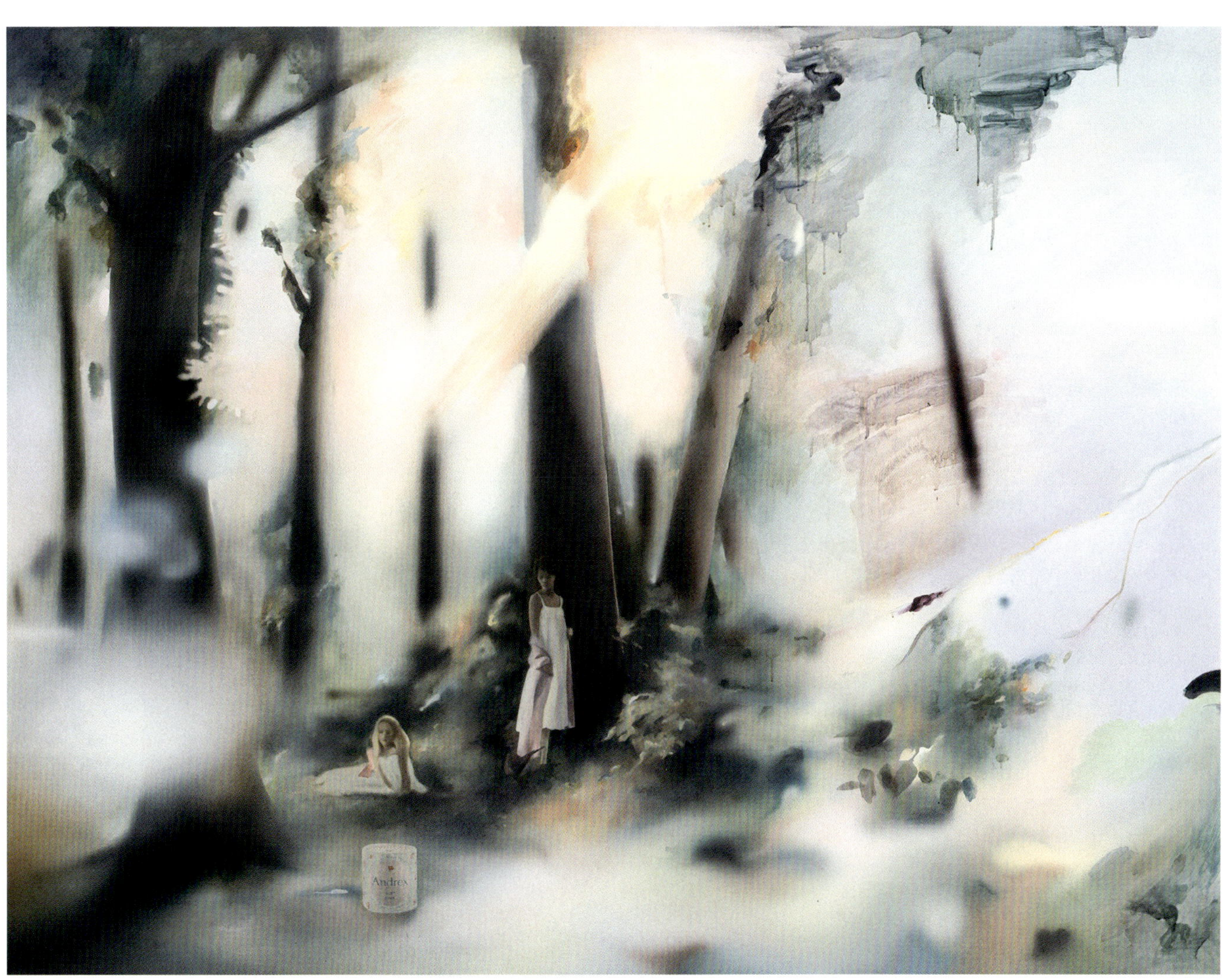
Andrex

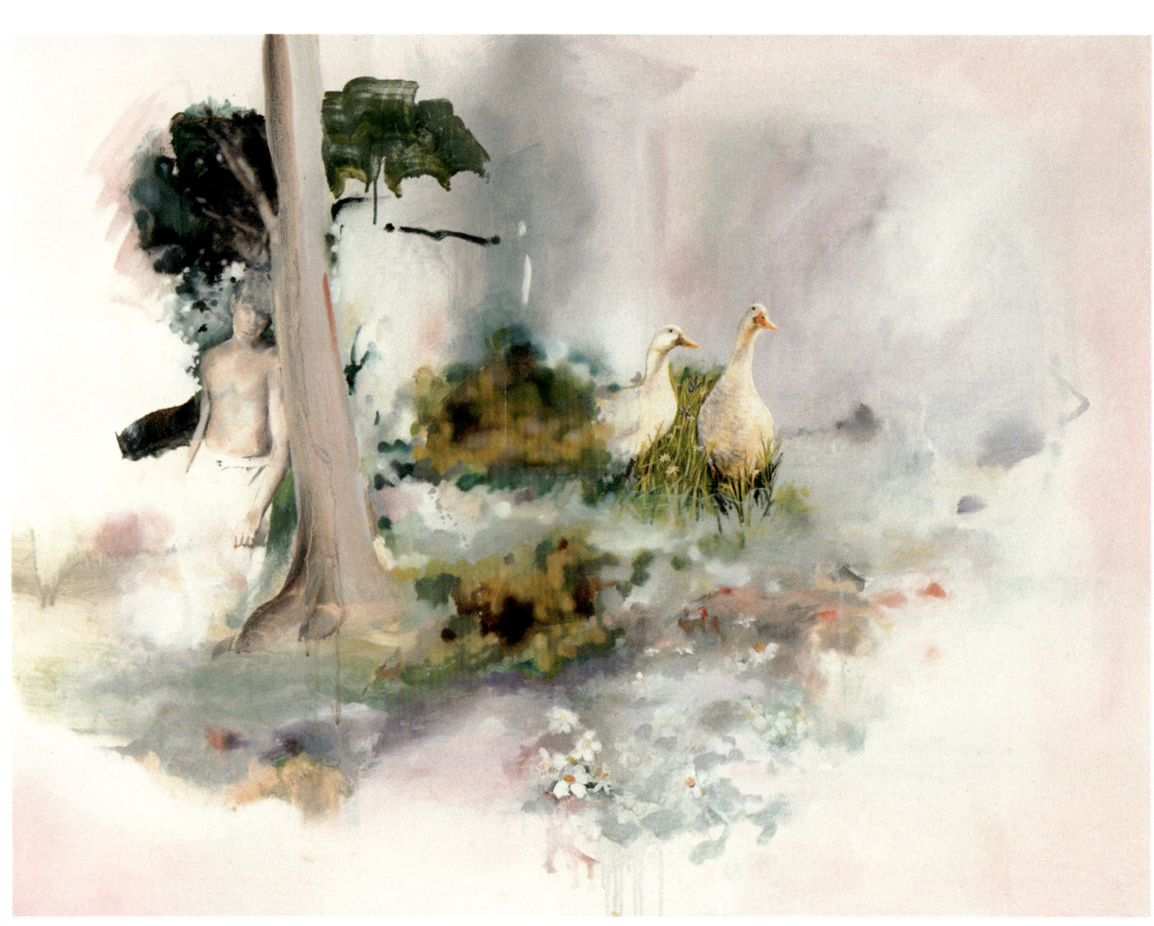

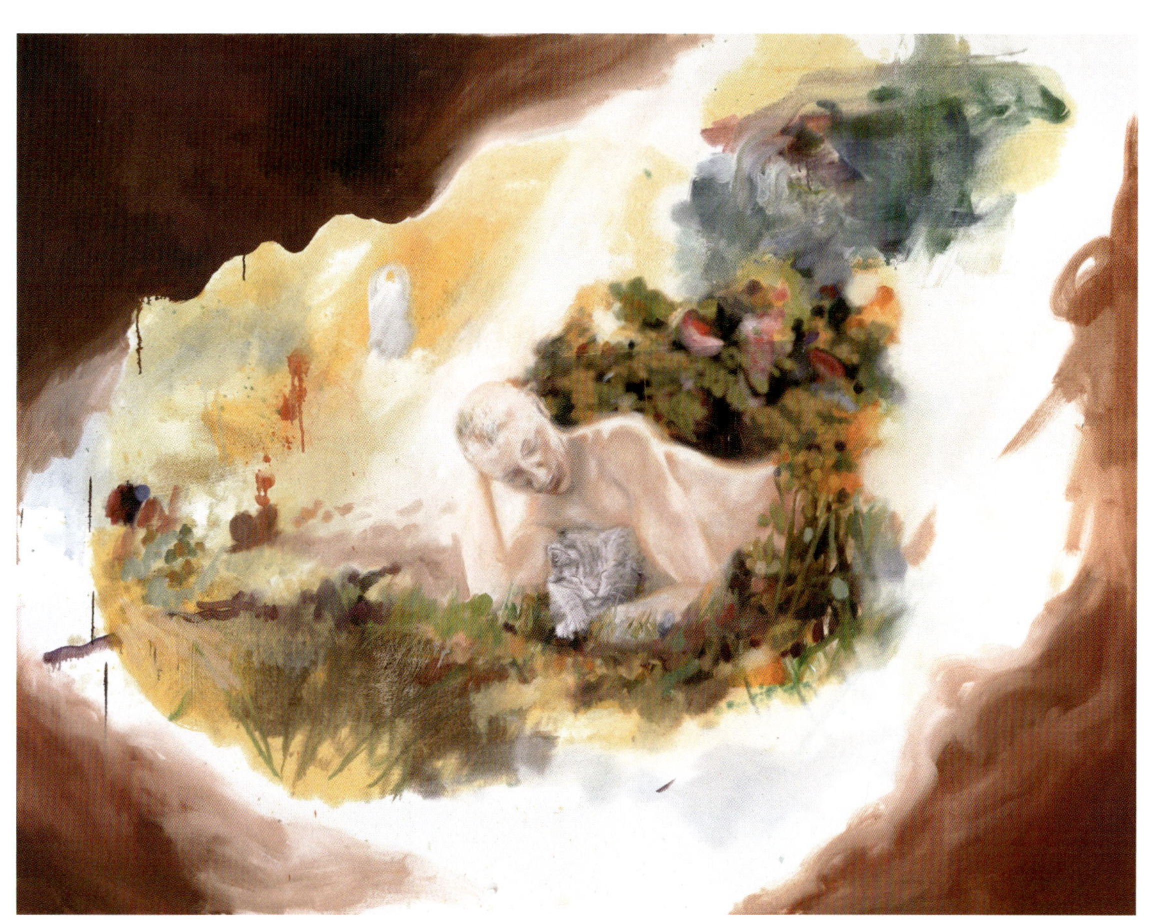

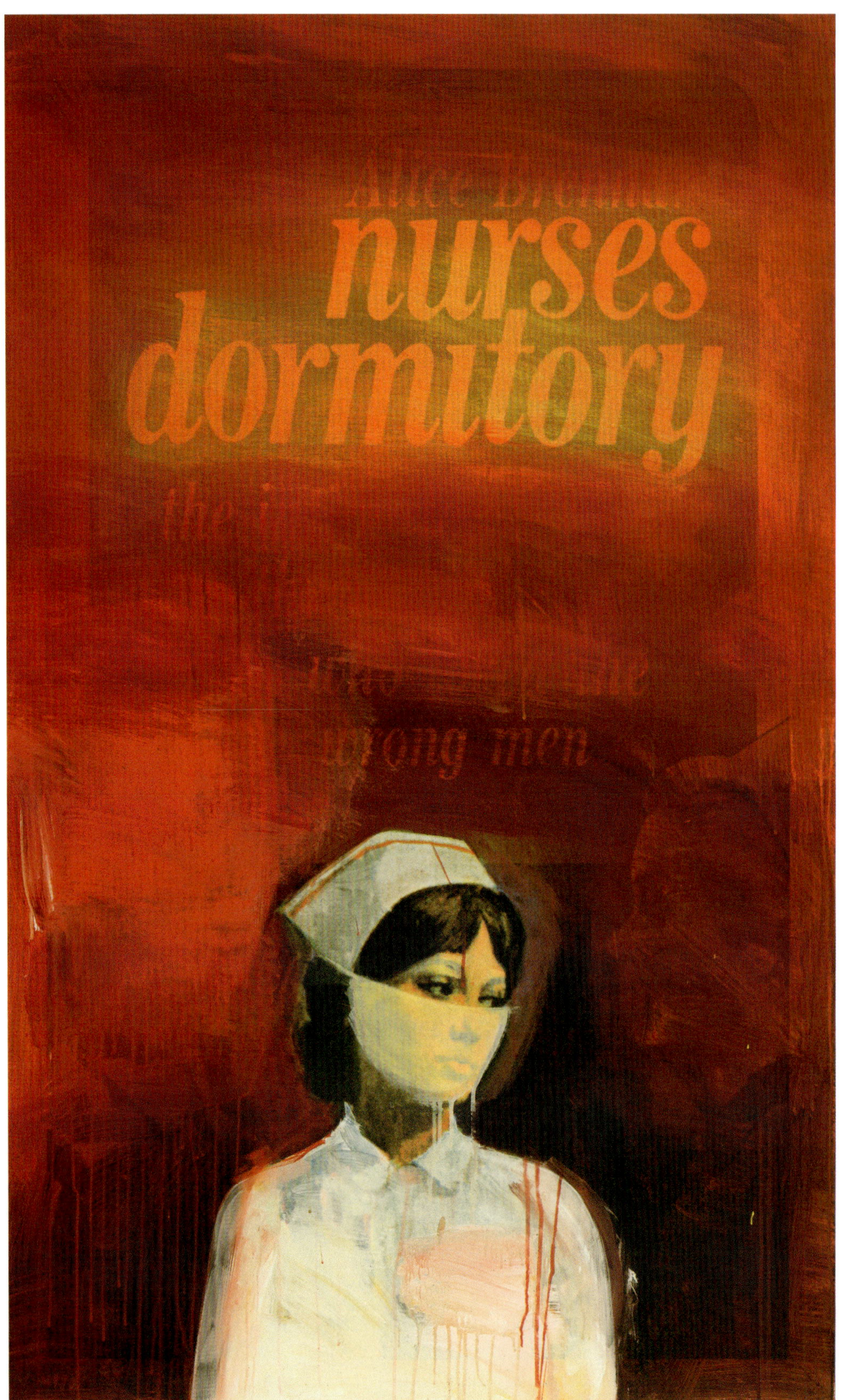
nurses
dormitory

PAINTED FICTION

Richard Prince, a pioneer of photographic appropriation and a key figure in the discourse of images since the 1970s, did not return to painting until the second half of the eighties. When he did, however, it was with a variety of styles, ranging from crisply typographical text paintings featuring ancient jokes to elaborately layered and overpainted canvases that mixed photo-silk-screening and painterly effects. His Nurse paintings continue to demonstrate the capacity of this approach to generate works that unpredictably veer between text and image, representation and abstraction, photo reproduction and painterly bravura. The Nurse paintings pursue the question of self-expression in the context of an overwhelming glut of pre-existing images. In them Prince continues to explore his ongoing interest in bad faith, as he presses pulp illustration into an uncomfortably close relationship to abstract expressionism. Prince's gestural swathes of paint confound the pictorial conventions of his source material, only to suggest another compositional order; one that refers as much to the formalism of New York School abstraction and the crudeness of *art brut* as it does to images drawn from mass culture.

Richard Prince
Nurses' Dormitory, 2002

Despite apparently attempting to obliterate the pulpy book covers, however, they remain viscerally present beneath the paint, pushing their way through like the return of the repressed. As Prince wrote in his semi-fictional book of 1983, *Why I Go to the Movies Alone*: "Sometimes I feel when I'm sitting there that my own desires have nothing to do with what comes from me personally because what I'll eventually put out, will in a sense, have already been out."[79] Prince embraces what Porter had identified as a crucial problem, that "all experiences were becoming one experience, the experience of everything." If the drips and gestures of painterly abstraction remain the signifiers of artistic authenticity, as they do, their juxtaposition with the siren-like but somehow sinister nurses of popular fiction creates a distinct sense of unease. In *Nurses' Dormitory* (2002), a trickle of red paint reads also as

79 Prince, *Why I Go to the Movies Alone* (New York: Tanam Press, 1983), 57.

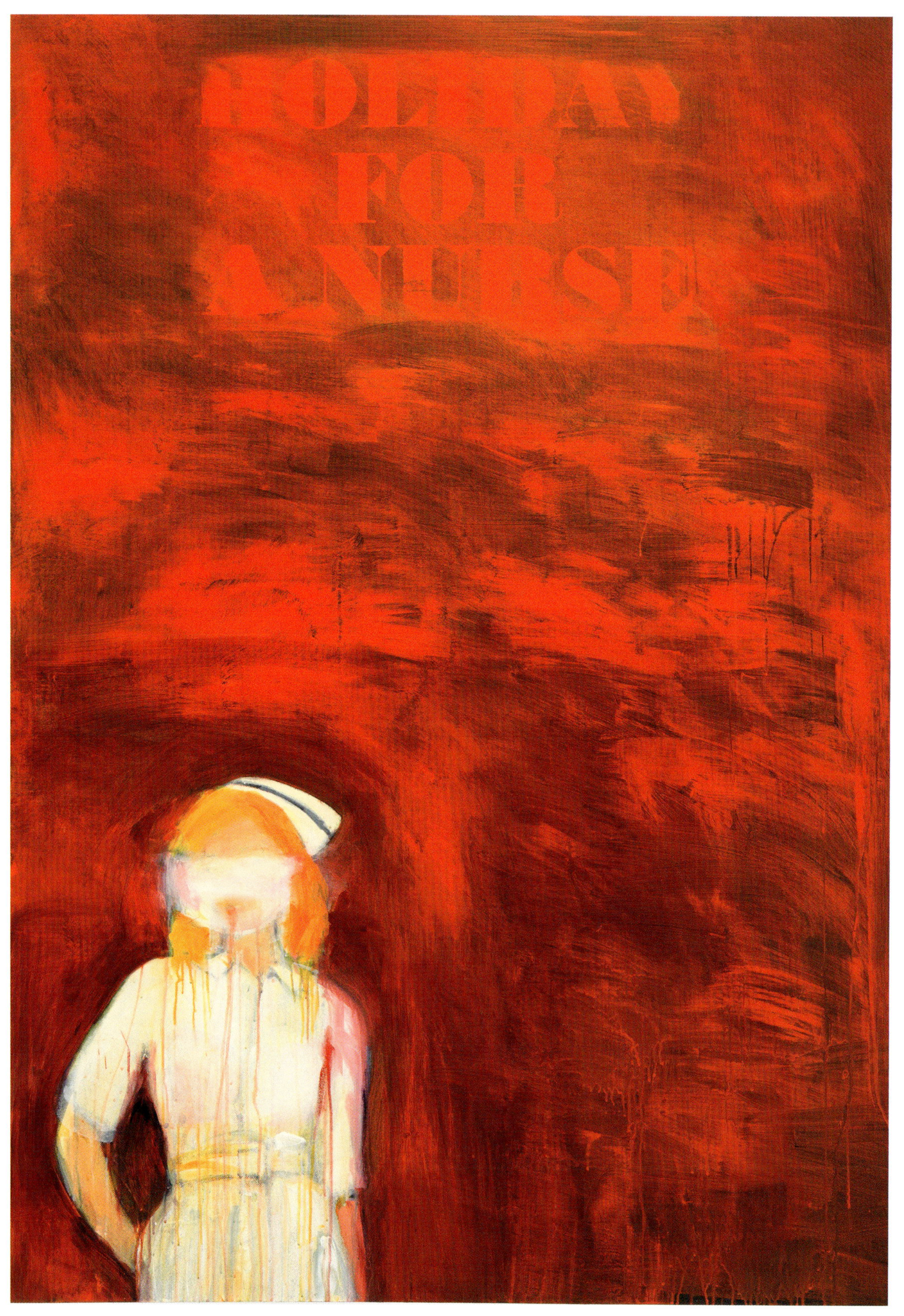
HOLIDAY
FOR
A NURSE

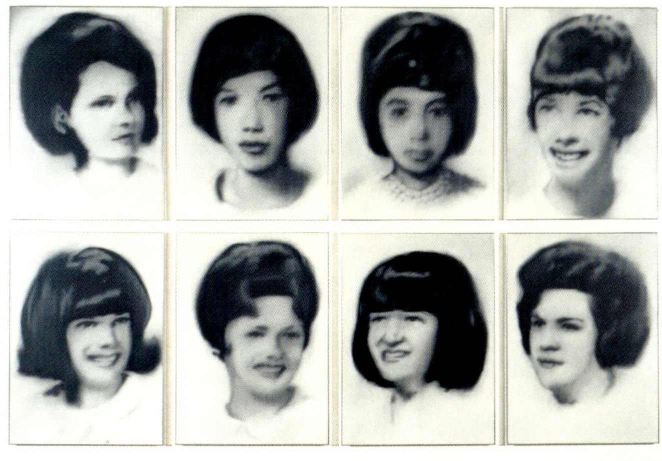

a trail of blood from the nurse's scalp. Recalling both Richter's *Eight Student Nurses* (1966) (all victims of the mass murderer Richard Speck) and Lawson's death-obsessed tabloid paintings, these works also raise the suggestion that painting itself is still perhaps not so far from the emergency room.

Prince's Nurse paintings can be seen as part of a deliberately vulgar strain in postwar painting that runs from Jean Dubuffet through Jean-Michel Basquiat to Lucy McKenzie. All of these artists have reacted to the elevated status of the classical tradition by attacking it directly. They resist more generally the implied power of painting—and their own facility in it—by launching assaults on the surfaces of their own work. This impulse challenges the conventional authority of painting by tapping into a rawer tradition of unschooled representational power. As McKenzie described her recent paintings: "A woman in a boiler suit is up a ladder painting a huge brain on the wall and you can see that the wall is all cracked and the whole scene is a painted fiction—it's obviously a painting as well. It was a little bit about creative masturbation, or a woman being violated by her own brain and creativity."[80] McKenzie makes the brain, represented either realistically or by a painted word, her target. But the danger even in such direct attacks is that they may in the end function more as homeopathic infusions of authenticity than as genuinely damaging assaults. Painting has long demonstrated its ability to absorb transgression, something McKenzie's frequent departures from painting in favor of music, writing, and various collaborative and socially-oriented activities may acknowledge. A key element throughout is a suspicion of "professionalism."

Richard Prince
Holiday for a Nurse, 2003

Gerhard Richter
Eight Student Nurses, 1966

following pages:
Lucy McKenzie
Untitled, 2002

Lucy McKenzie
Untitled, 2002

80 McKenzie, in John Slyce, "London: Last Exit Painting," *Flash Art* (October 2002): 69.

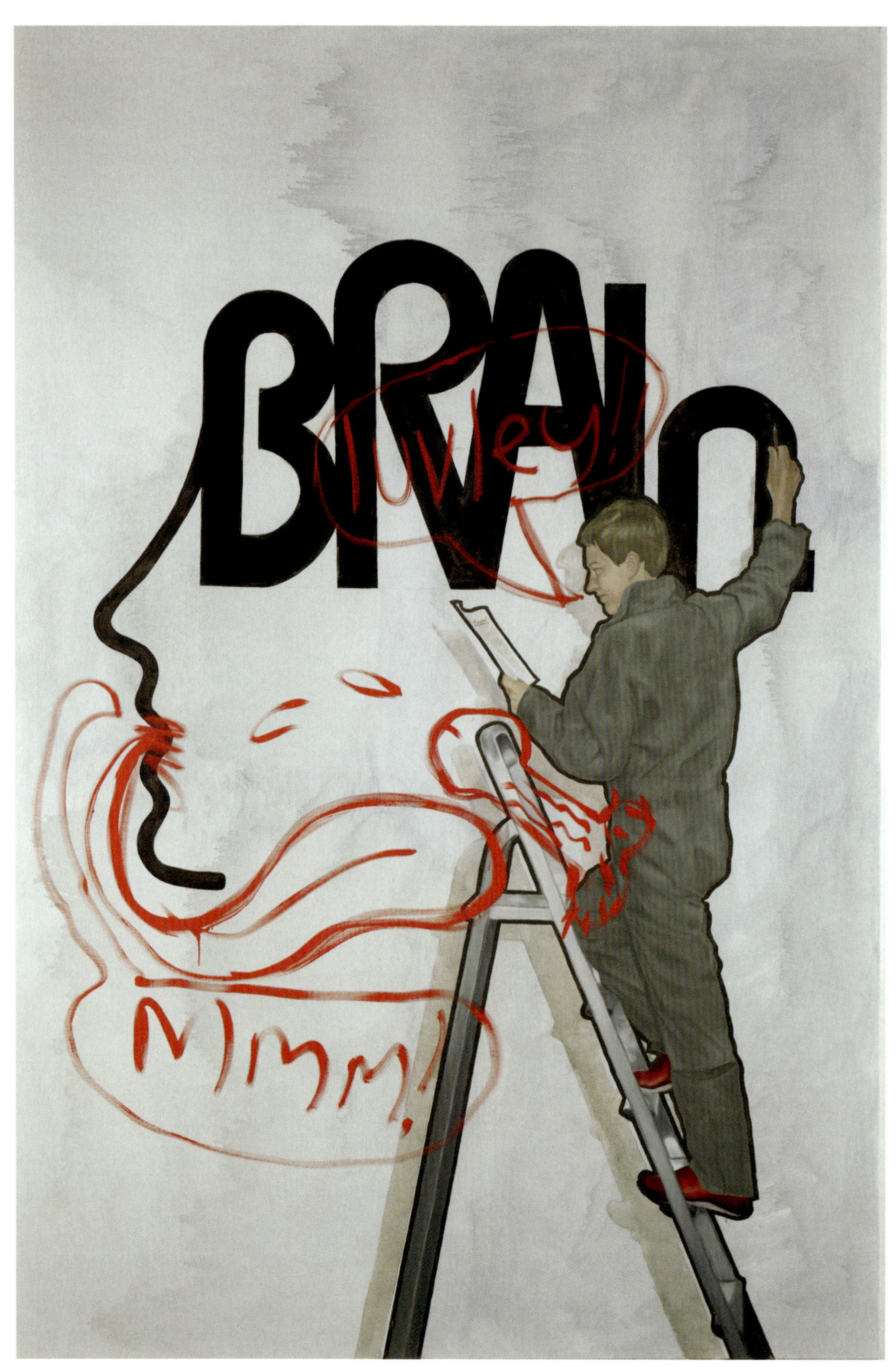
luvley!
MMM!

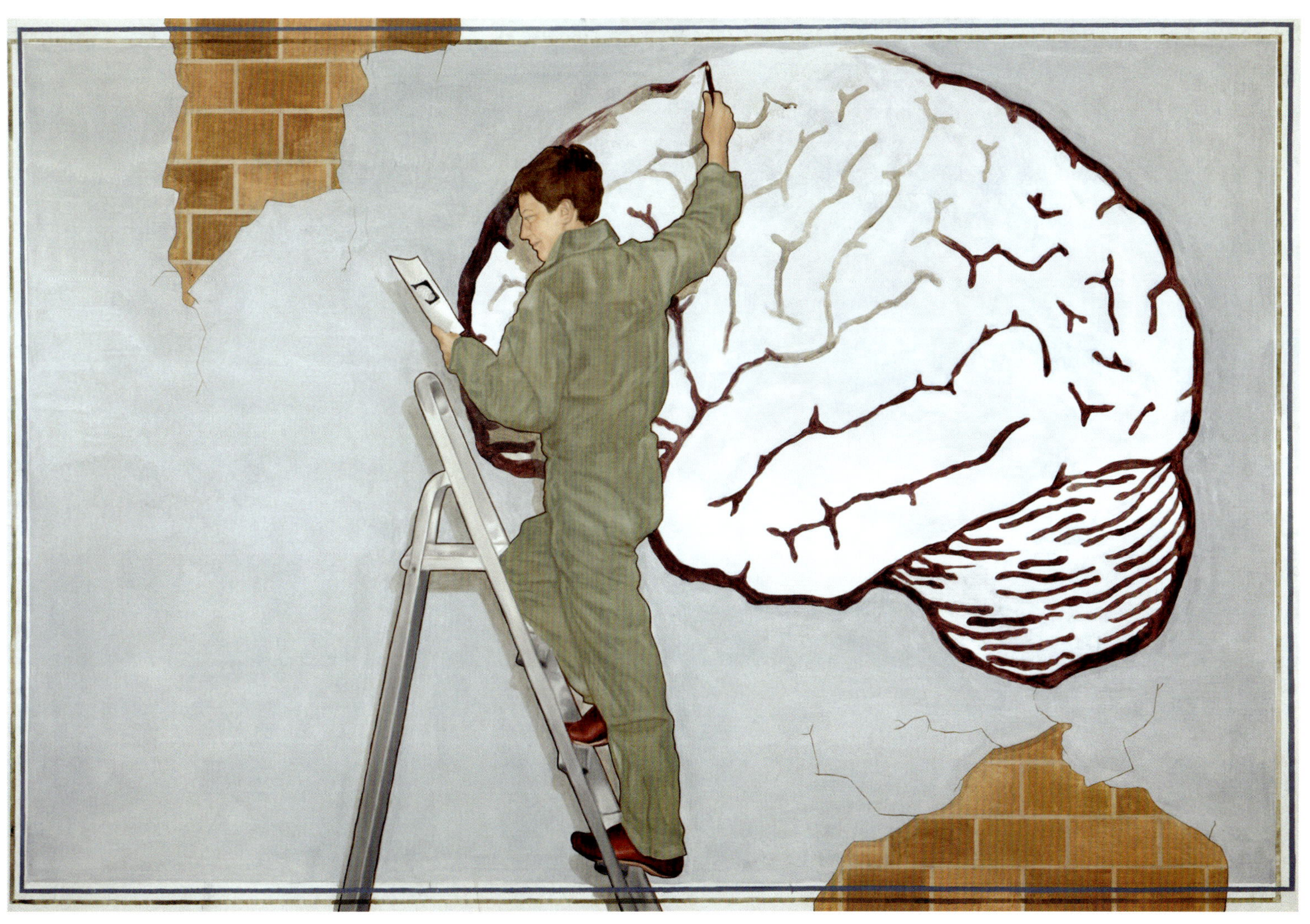

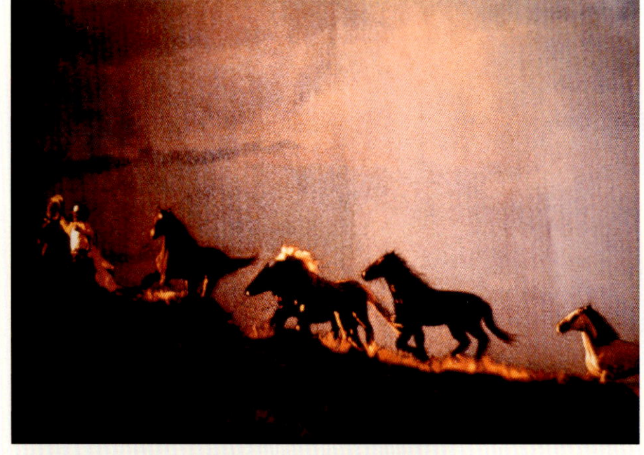

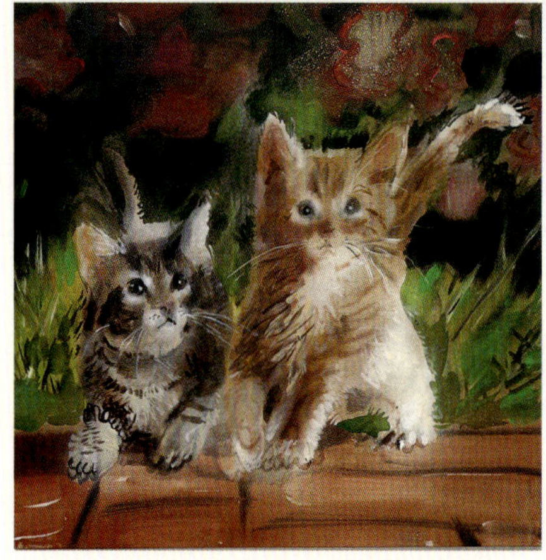

Richard Prince
Untitled (Cowboy), 1992

Mari Eastman
July, 2003

Mari Eastman
Marlboro Man, 2003

following pages:
Mari Eastman
Porcelain Bowl with Dragon Design and Red Glaze, 2004

Mari Eastman
U.S. Soldiers Dismantling the Bust of Saddam Hussein, 2003

Kerry James Marshall
Destiny Is a Rose, 1990

Laura Owens
Untitled, 2004

Mamma Andersson
We Do Boring Things Together, 2003

Other painters have sought out specific images and materials that lie beyond the bounds of acceptable taste. Eggerer, Prince, and Marshall have all worked with images taken from the covers of pulp novels. Klein, Marshall, and Mari Eastman have used glitter in their work. For Eastman, the glitter is part of a self-conscious but nevertheless sincere exploration of girlishness and adolescence that can embrace cute animals, bright colors, and romantic fantasy, although the nonchalance and spontaneity with which she appears to paint is in the end belied by the sophistication of the results. The same could be said of Laura Owens's prancing white horse, an apparently childish image rendered with all the skills of an experienced painter.

In Eastman's case, unlike Owens's, the source material is always photographic. A scene from the war in Iraq can thus become equivalent in one sense to an image pulled from an advertisement (her *Marlboro Man* (2003) refers both to Marlboro cigarette advertisements and to Prince's famous appropriations of them).

In Mamma Andersson's *We Do Boring Things Together* (2003) the faceless protagonists read and watch TV, but all around hover undefined presences, ghosts that surround them with an otherworldly nimbus of memory. As Andersson described her work: "For as long as I can remember, I have been captivated by the unconscious and obscure in the everyday."[81] Duwenhögger, Eastman, and Klein all come close in places, albeit in different ways, to this uncanny yet nostalgic sensibility, in their case drawing in part on the vocabulary of book illustration. They evoke in the process not just childhood memories, but also the kind of representation that takes an unselfconscious pleasure in narrative.

81 Andersson, in "The Nordic Pavilion at the Venice Biennial 2003," interviewed by Paula Toppila, 2003, www.frame-fund.fi/news/pavilion.

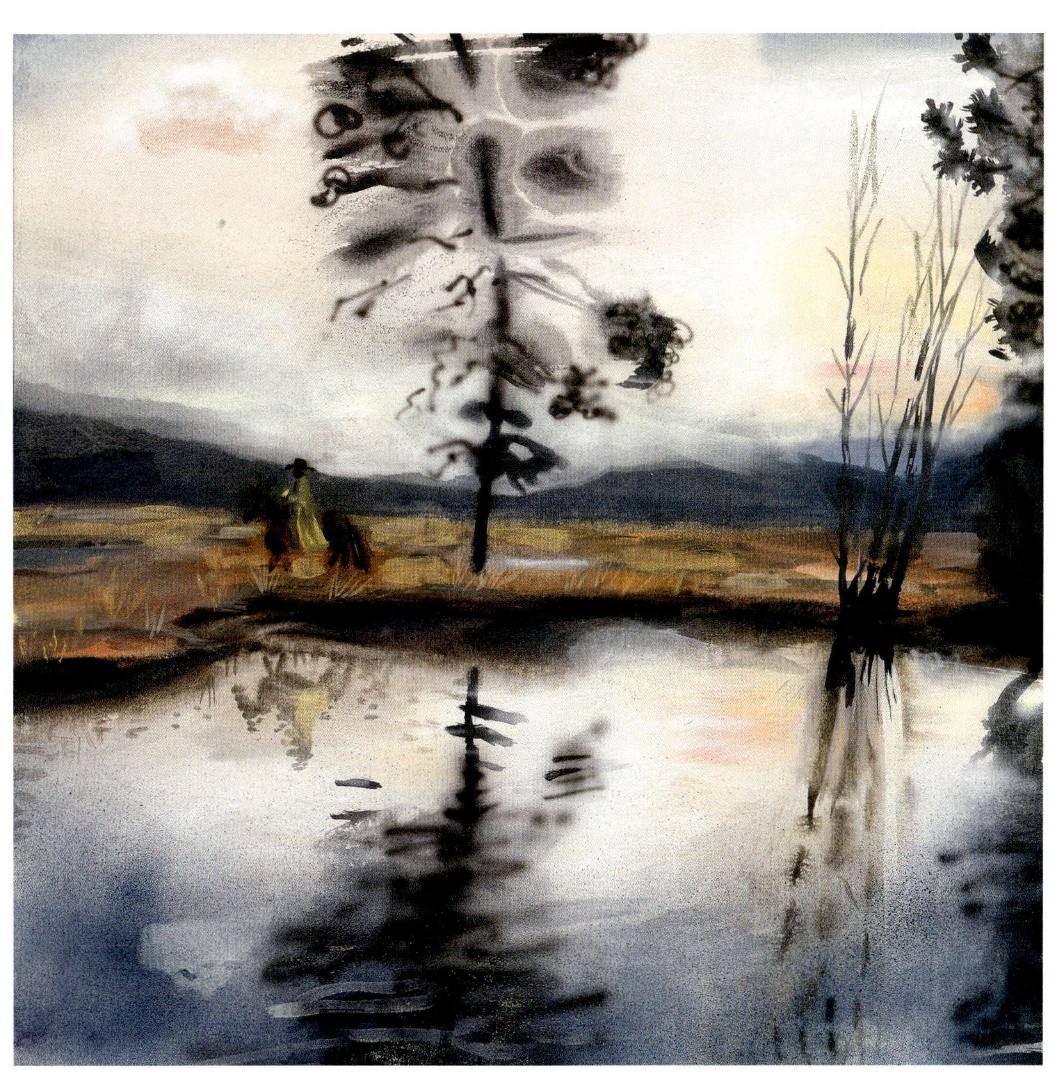

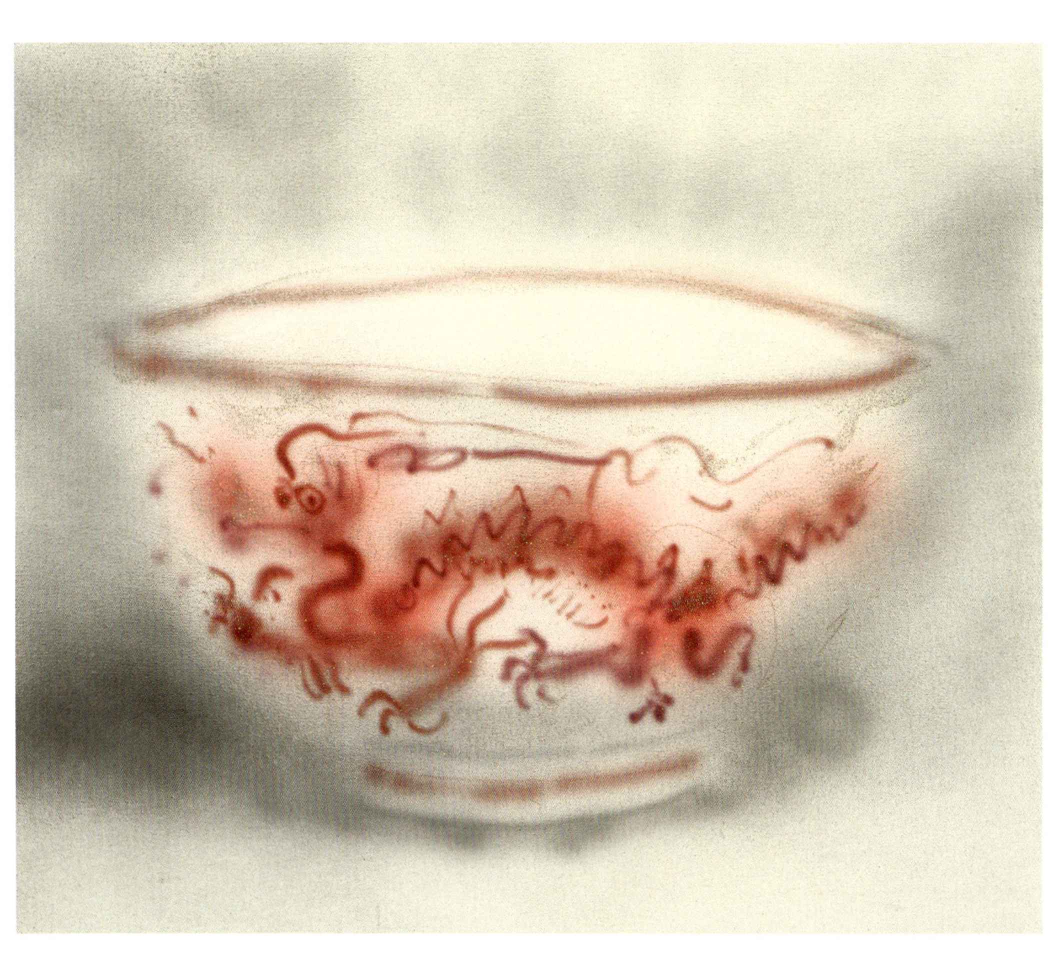

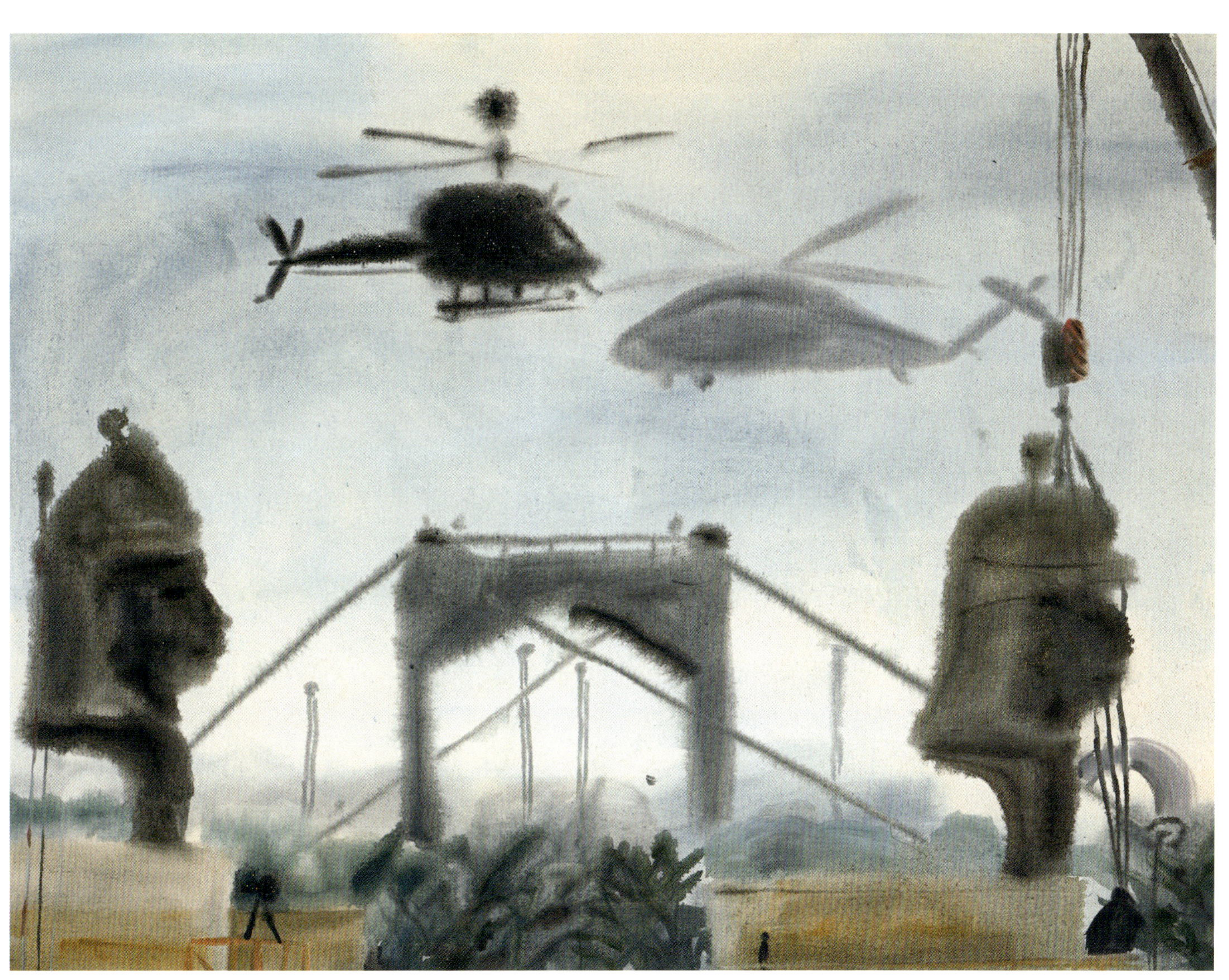

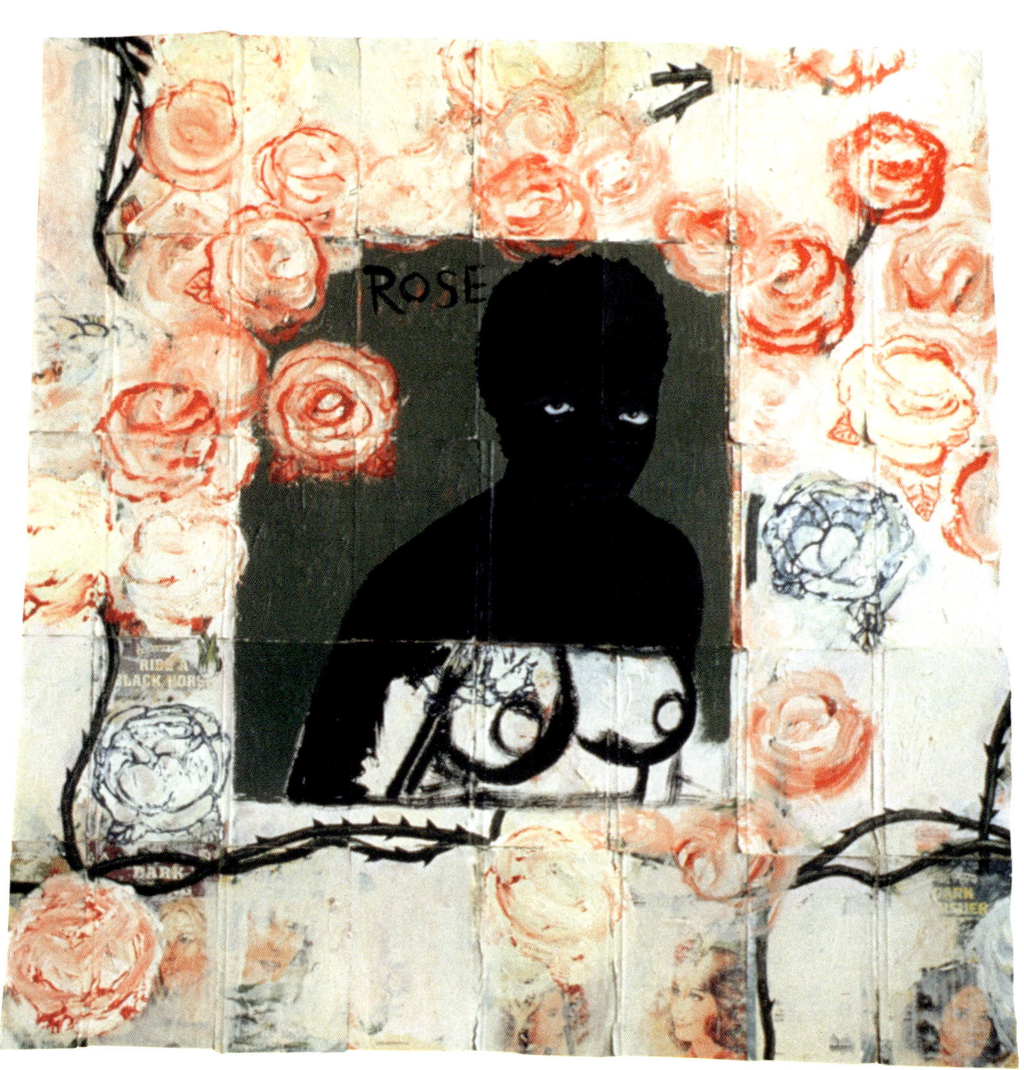
ROSE

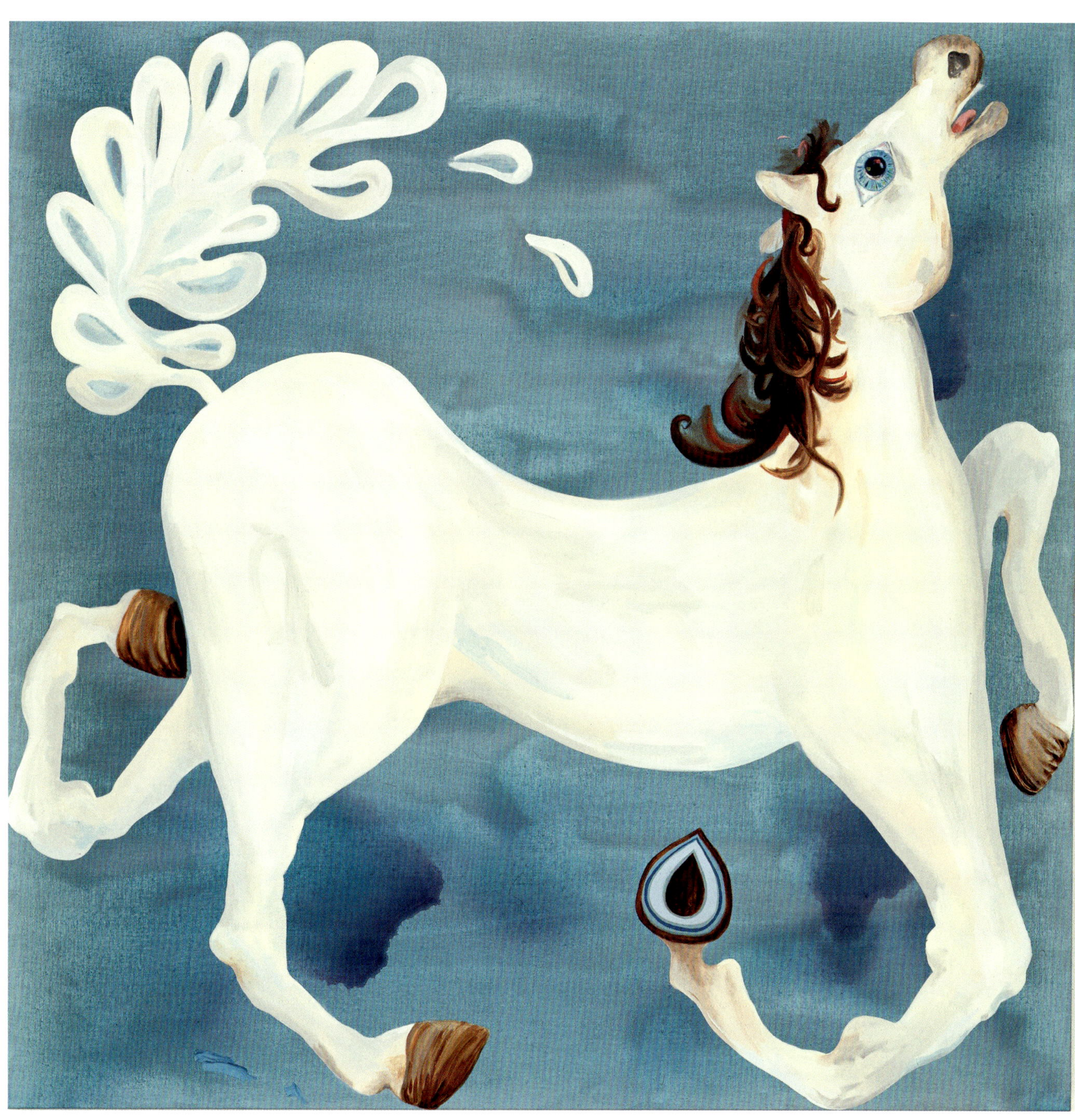

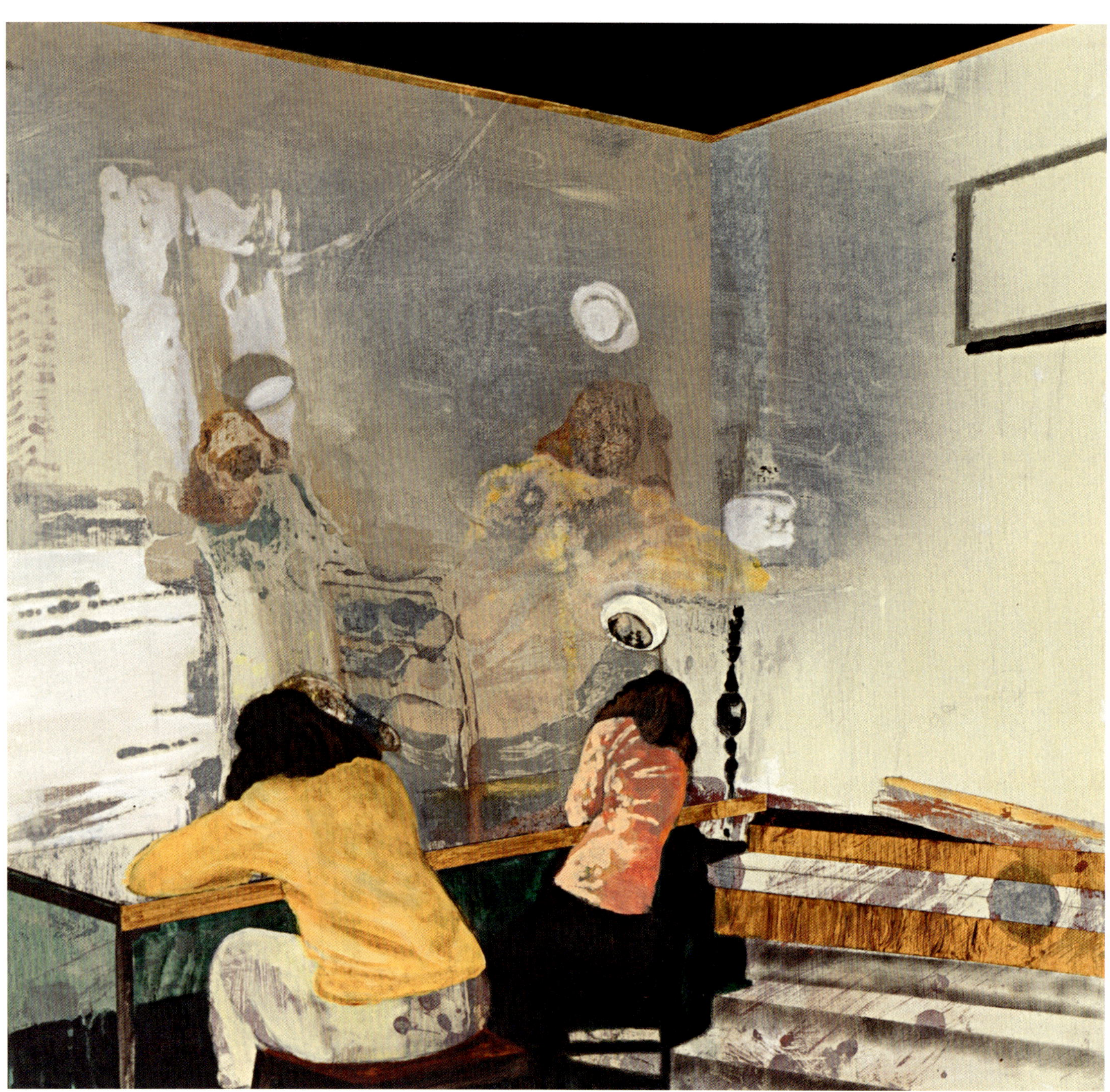

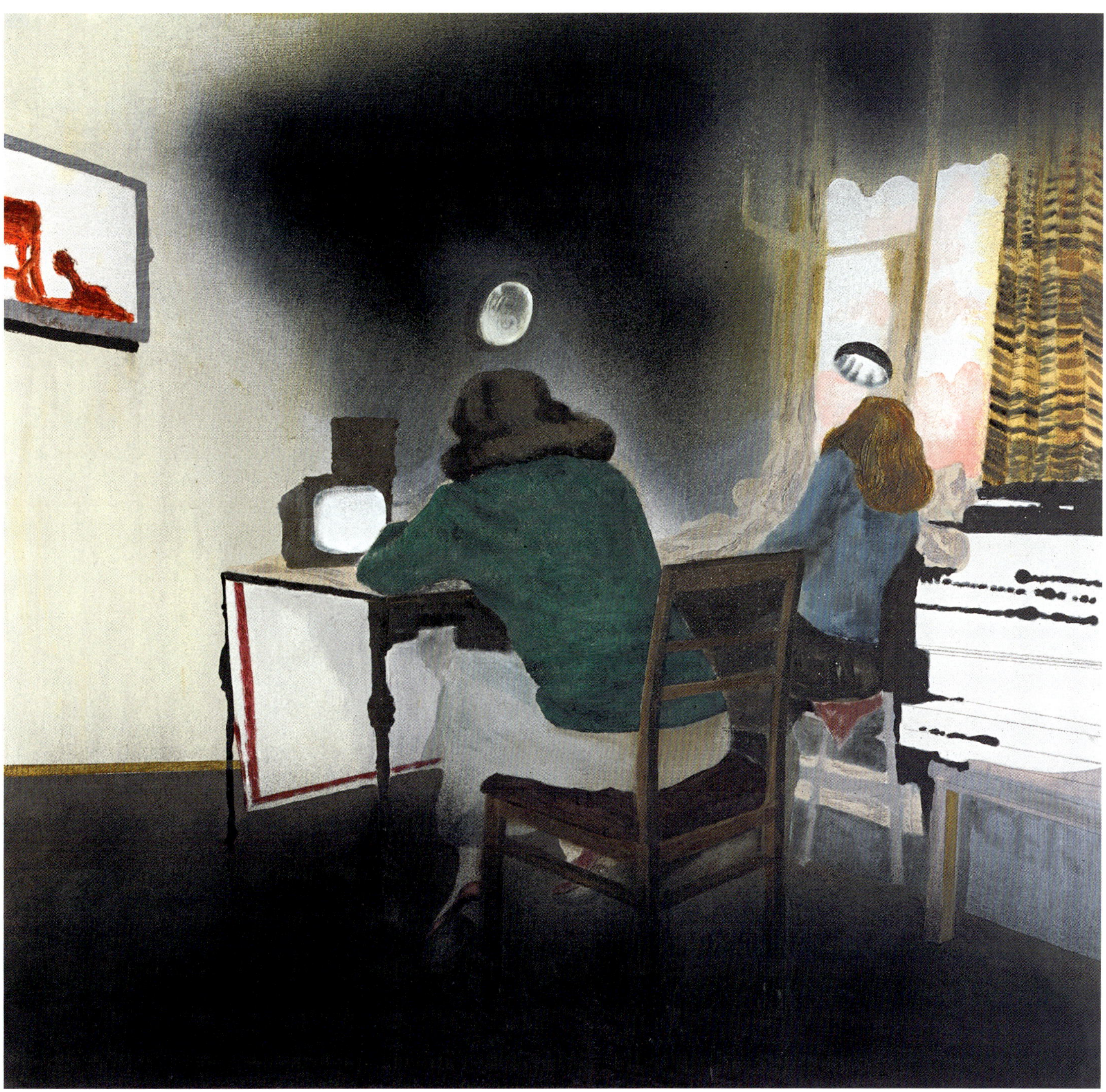

Mamma Andersson
Fatherland, 1997–2004

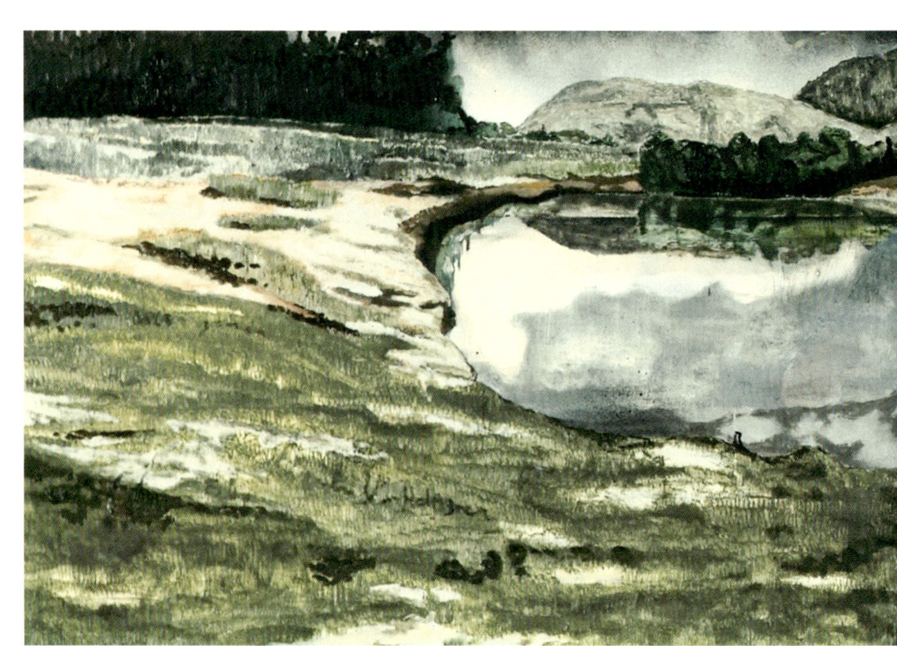

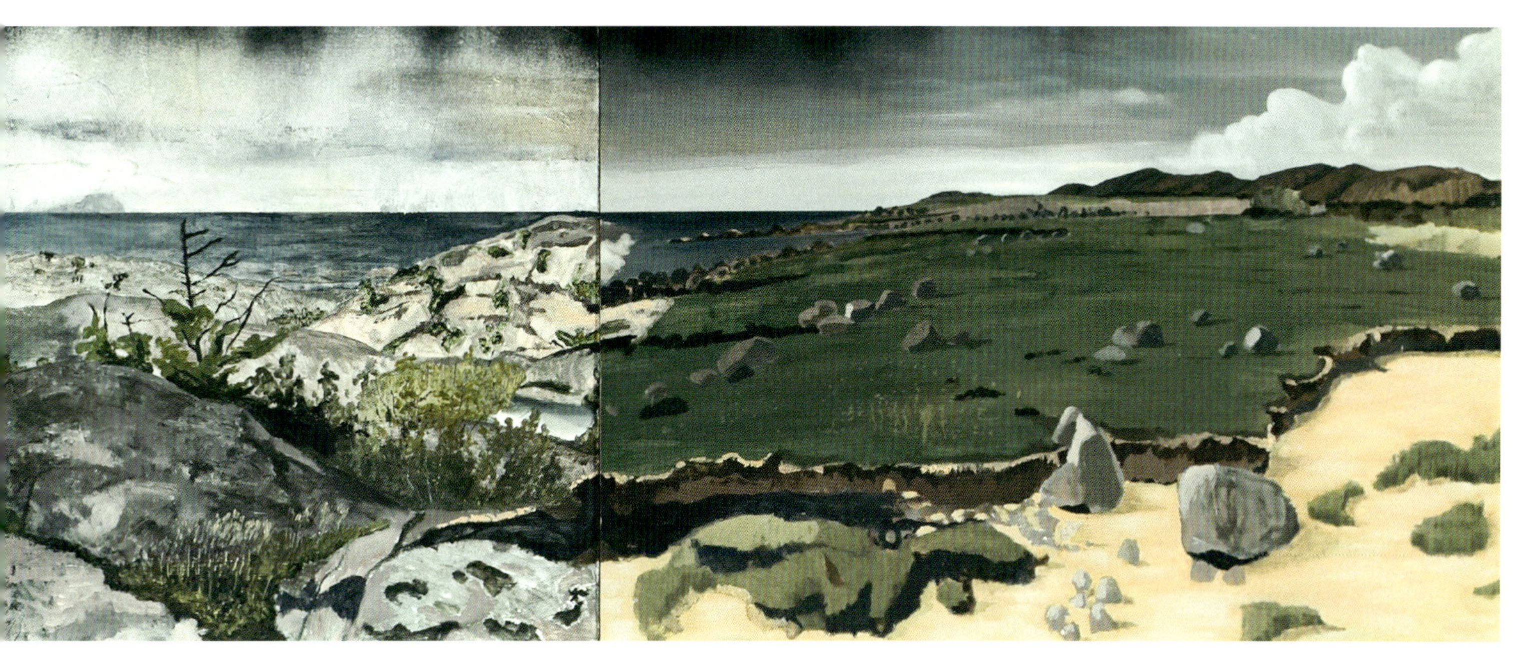

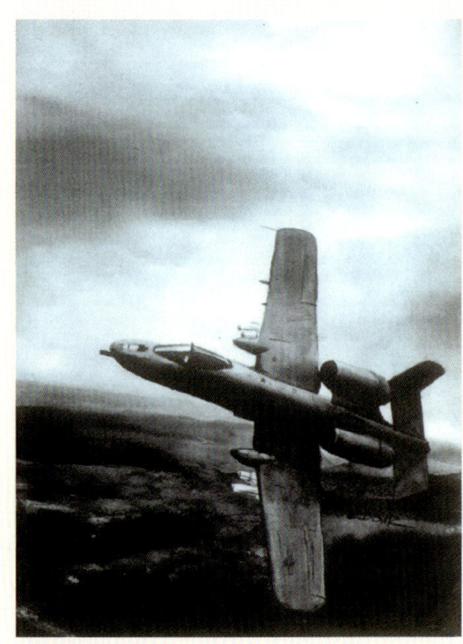

Edgar Bryan's self-portrait as a (young) painter, *The Ledge* (2004), seems almost to have come directly from a children's book. His concentration on his painting makes him almost one with the plant that he represents, even as it slowly envelops him. The overt romanticism of the image might be difficult without this appeal to a genre outside conventional art criticism. Illustration for children is one of those left-over areas of pictorial representation that have retained a certain independence of both art history and the dominance of photography. Although Bryan only recently began to look at children's book illustration specifically, he served as an illustrator in the United States Air Force for five years before studying at the Art Institute of Chicago and UCLA. As he recalled: "I painted murals of proud airmen and women, and I designed logos for the Air Force in Europe. I also did illustrations of the Berlin Wall coming down, since I arrived in Europe soon after it fell. I drew airplanes quite a bit too, especially the B-2 Stealth Bomber." Yet at the same time, he made another connection, to the clarity of the Neue Sachlichkeit artists of the 1920s, Karl Hubbuch and Rudolf Dischinger in particular. As Bryan explained,

> *It's interesting to me that "objectivity" and photo-realism are so different. These artists were taught academic drawing obsessively. I think their drawings look like children's book illustrations, I guess because they are trying to tell a story about life experiences, emotions and attitudes, etc. Simple drawings of faces and hands are the way to express these things. So this is a bridge from illustrations to the cold precision of the New Objectivity.*[82]

Edgar Bryan
illustration for *AirScoop News*
USAFE, 1992

Edgar Bryan
The Ledge, 2004

82 Bryan, e-mail to the author, 2 June 2004.

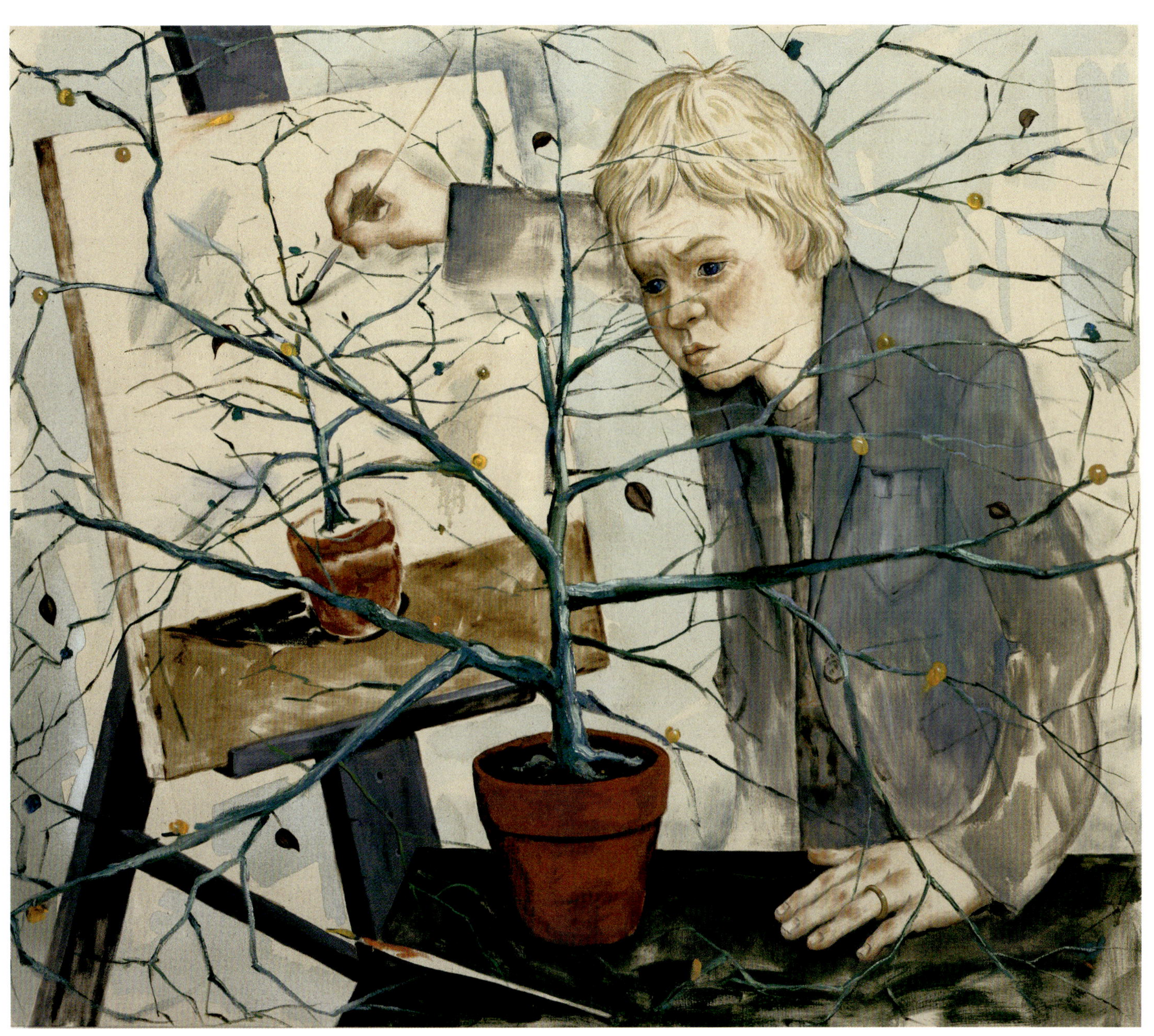

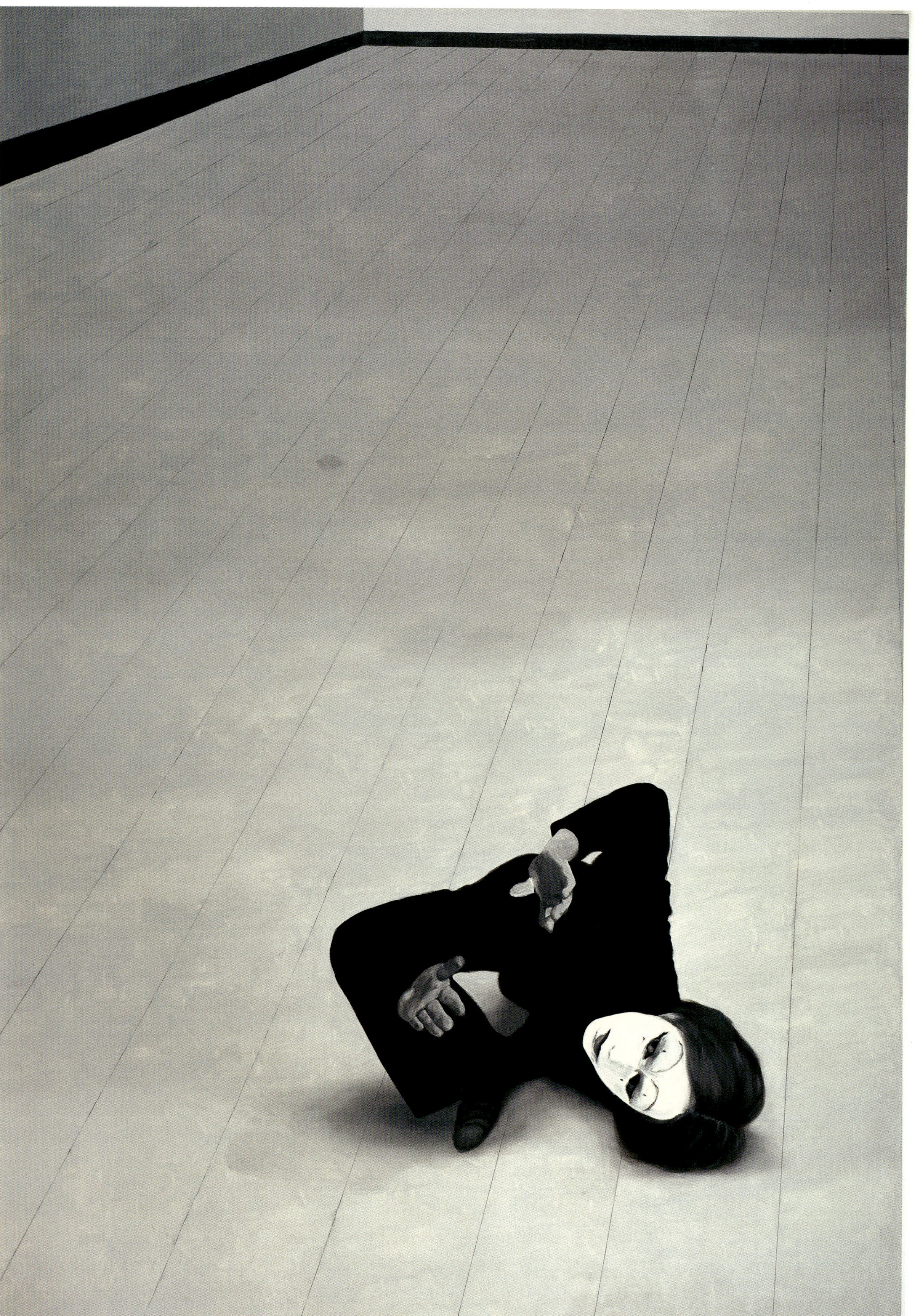

Edgar Bryan
Night in the Alte Pinakothek, 2002

In his huge painting of a posturing mime, Bryan found an image that tests the sensibilities of even the most blasé audiences. Its portentous title, *Night in the Alte Pinakothek* (2002), only ups the ante on what for many viewers seems a deliberate plunge into bad taste. "I did not fully appreciate the inexplicable level of disgust many people have for the mime," Bryan has acknowledged. For him, though, even this subject must be approached with sincerity. "Although it is rewarding to occasionally provoke disgust, it is more important that I take the subject seriously and approach the mimes from their own point of view."[83] This willed sincerity echoes the repeated struggles of contemporary painters to put aside their crises of faith in the very validity of their medium. The white painted face of the mime recalls Richter's painting out of the child's face, and the upraised hands seem to plead for mercy, as the space of the painting shoots back vertiginously. This is representation under pressure.

83 Bryan, e-mail to the author, 3 June 2004.

AN EPHEMERAL PLACE

Many contemporary painters favor compositions that are ambiguous, empty, or unstable. The figures in McKenzie's *They Are Lying on Their CVs* (2000) repeat and spiral out into a welter of nonobjectivity. The tree in the center of Eastman's *Marlboro Man* is in one sense a straightforward representation, yet it is also an exercise in virtually abstract paint handling, as is her *Evening Landscape* (2004). A space has opened up in which the transition between explicit representation and totally nonobjective painting is increasingly difficult to identify with any precision.

If the task of painting is the task of mourning, then we can perhaps see it not just in the quest for overlooked forms of representation, in the overt renunciation of representation, or in the deliberate blurring of the boundaries between representation and abstraction. It can also be found in the air of melancholy that suffuses many of the works included in this exhibition.

Mari Eastman
Evening Landscape, 2004

Lucy McKenzie
They Are Lying on Their CVs, 2000

following pages:
Kirsten Everberg
Lobby, 2003

Kirsten Everberg
Bar, 2003

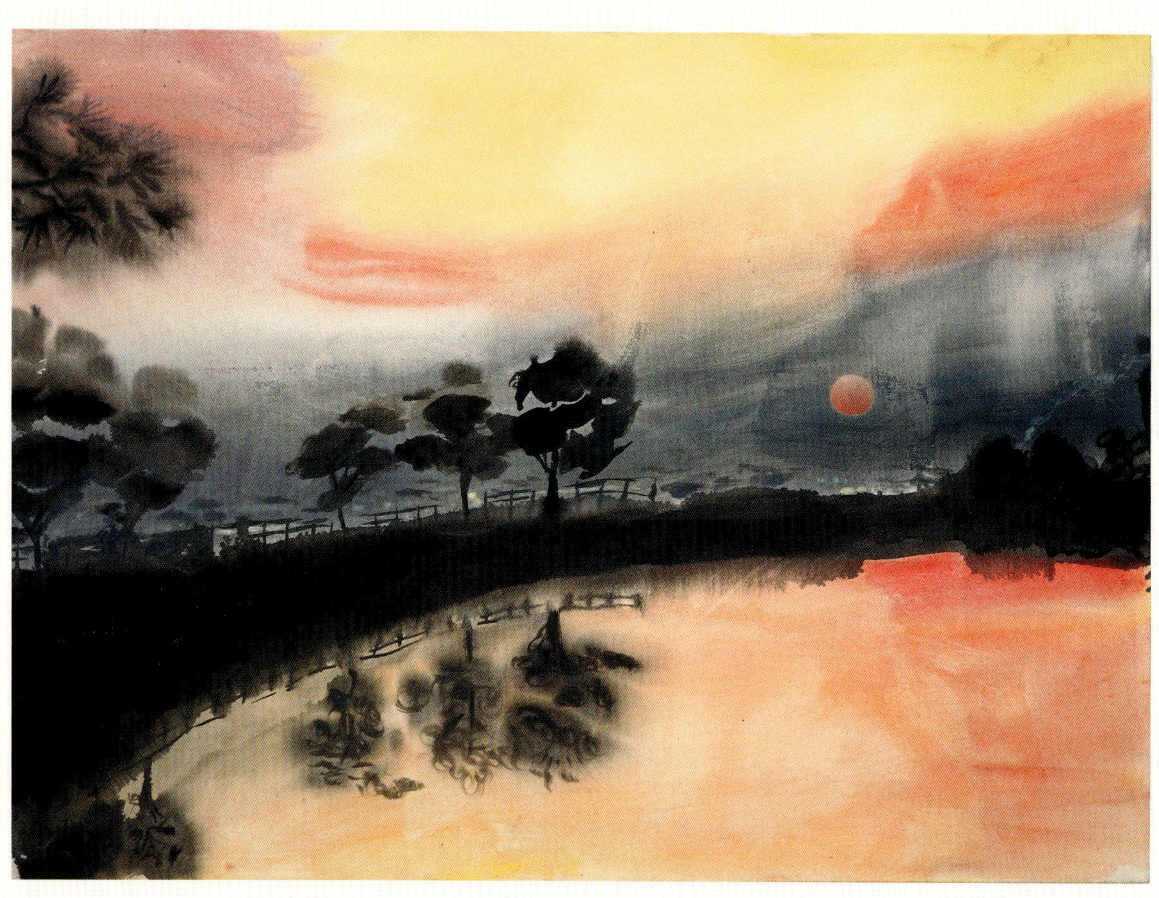

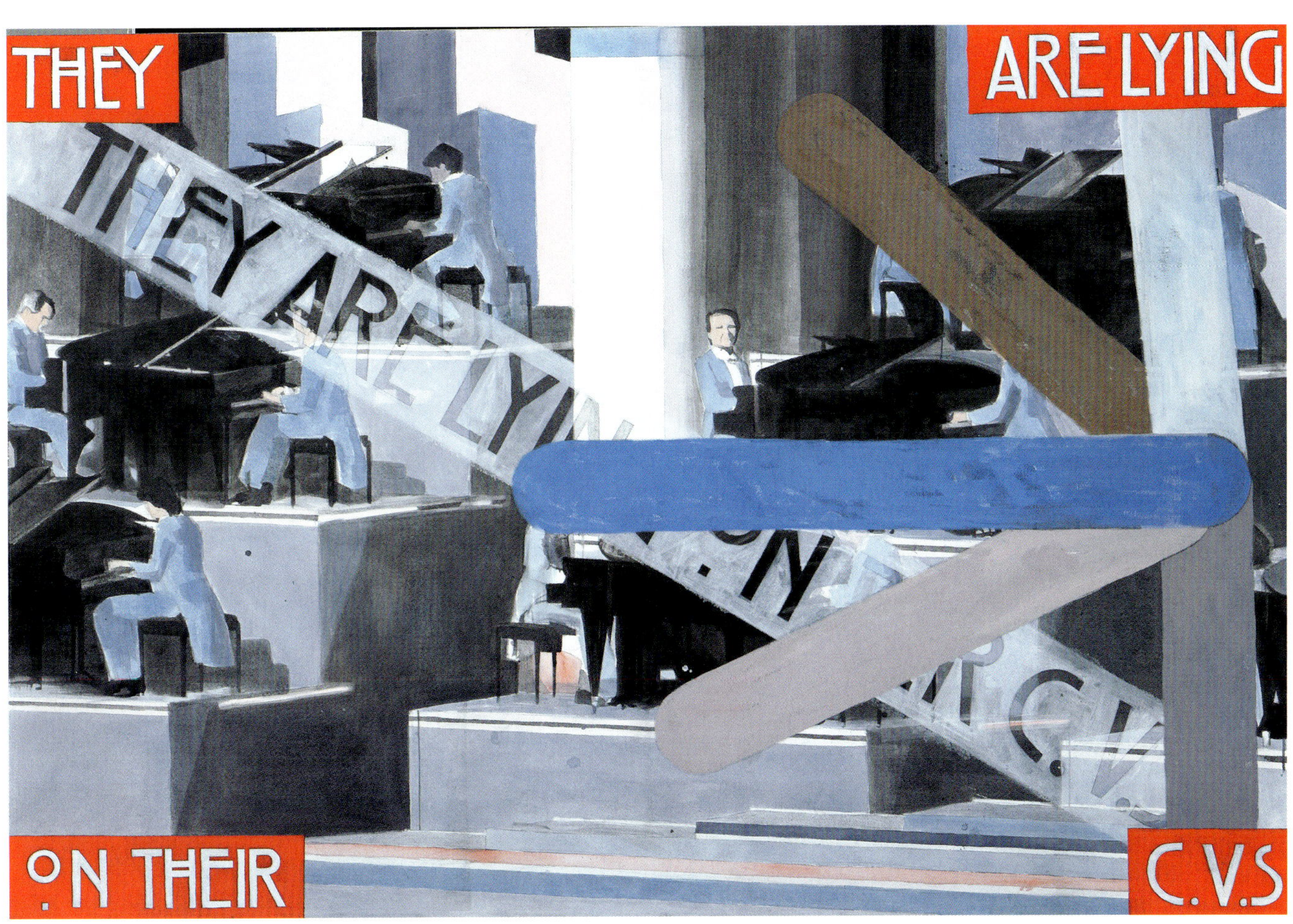
THEY
ARE LYING
ON THEIR
C.V.S
THEY ARE LYIN

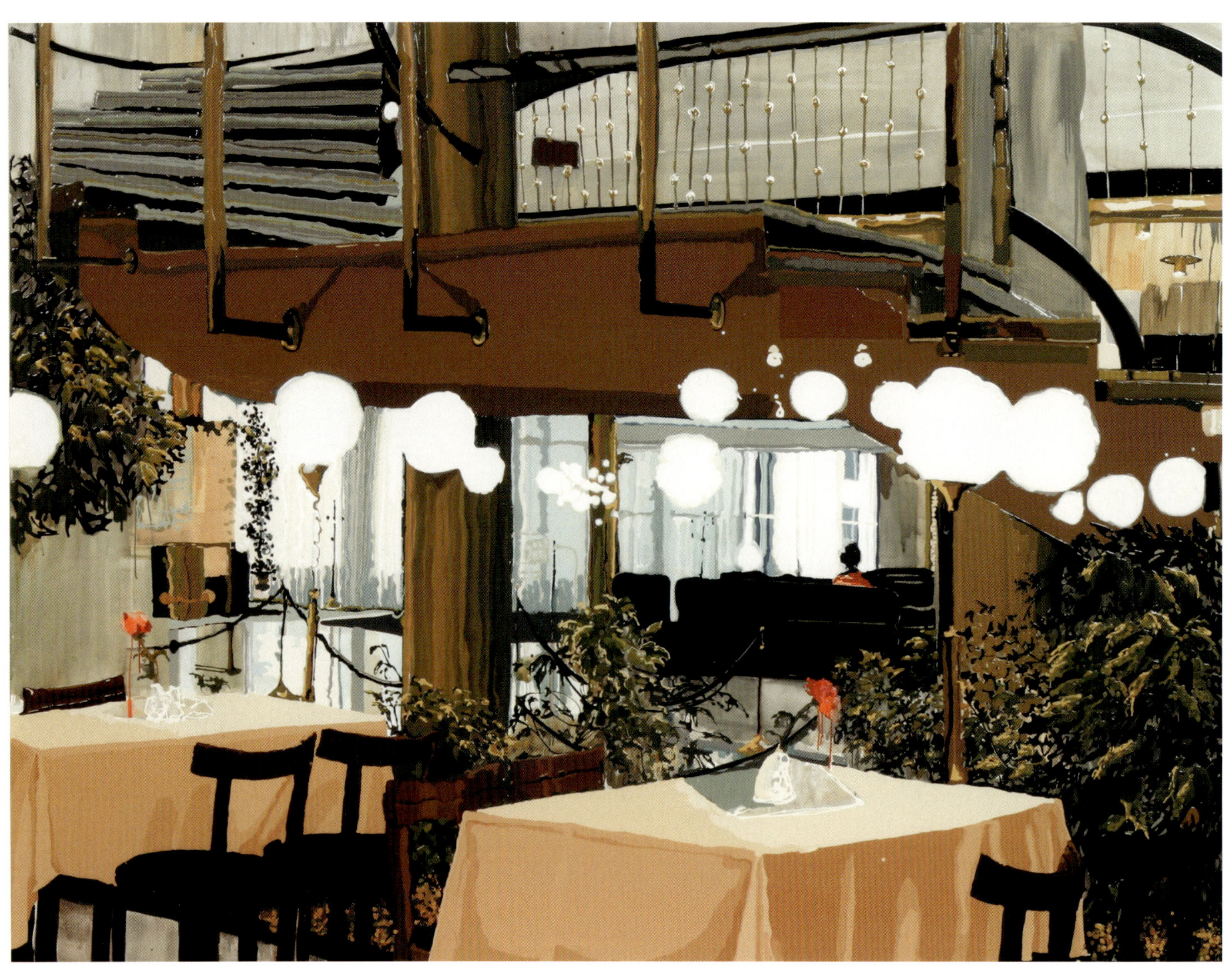

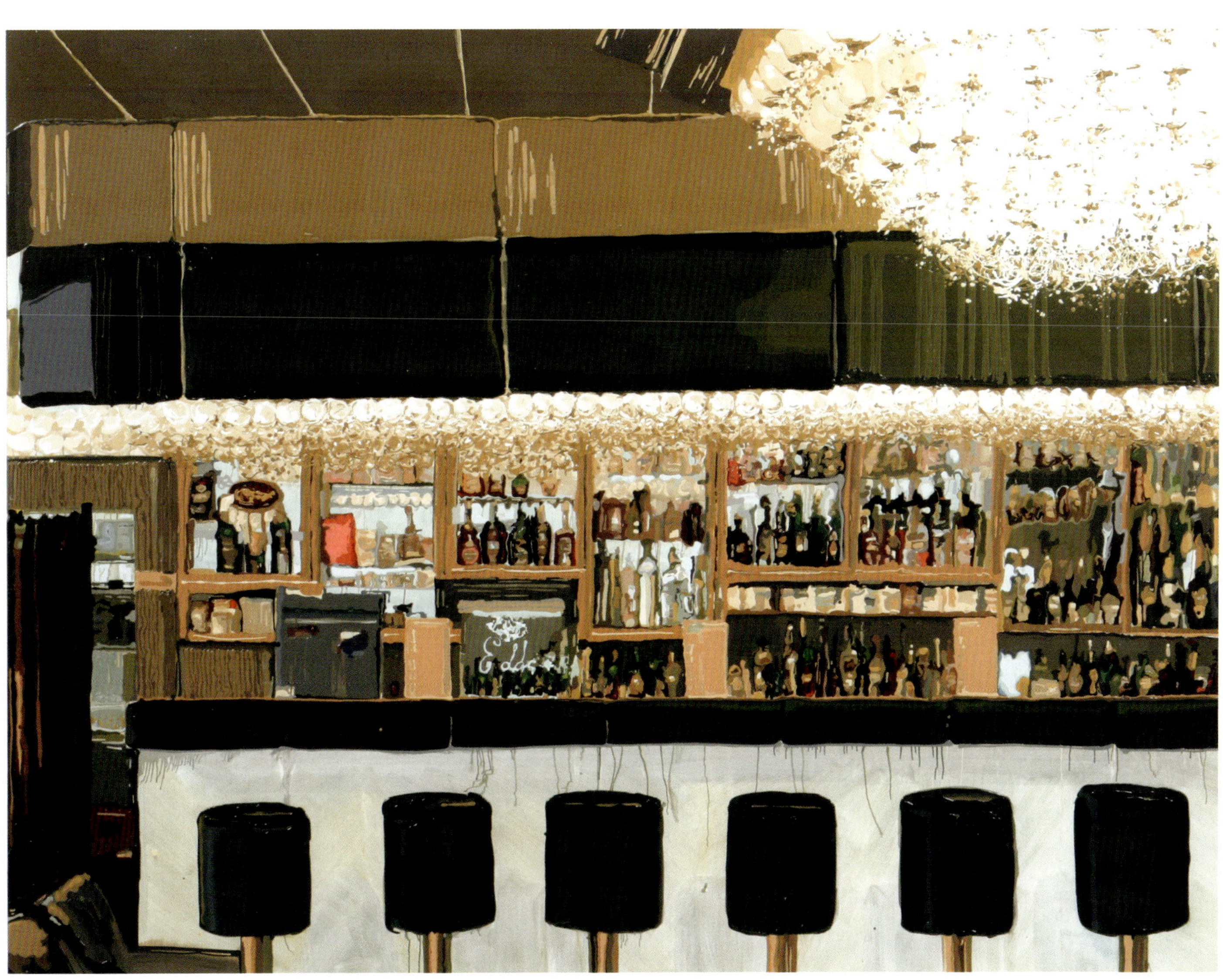

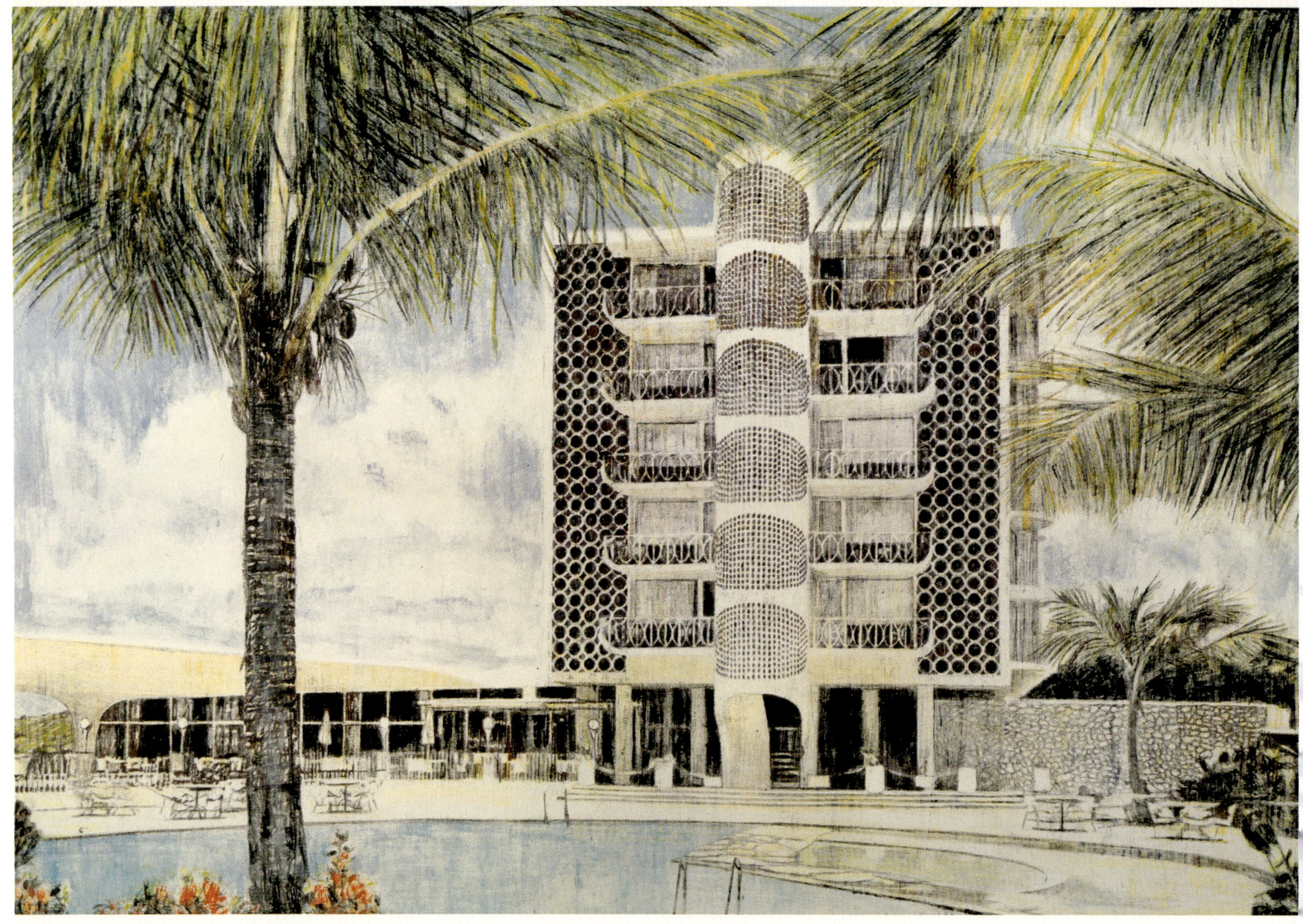

Kirsten Everberg's *Bar* and *Lobby* (both 2003) show the empty interior of a hotel in Brno, Czech Republic. Brno was a center of modernism before the Second World War and is the site of Mies van der Rohe's Tugendhat House (1928–30). The faded glamour of the rooms is redolent of a departed era, not so much that of the historic avant-garde as that of sixties Eastern European Communism. Everberg's thick enamel paint simultaneously seduces and repels the viewer as it seals the image of the place. The shiny paint echoes the glittering surfaces. It fixes and preserves them, as if in amber, yet at the same time its fluidity suggests that the whole scene could be at the point of melting away forever. The emphatic materiality of the paint threatens the very stability of the image it represents.

Enoc Perez has found his own kind of overlooked representation. His paintings of Puerto Rican hotels derive from the cheap postcards available in their lobbies, souvenirs of the luxury, modernism, and optimism that characterized the public rhetoric of leisure in the fifties and sixties, in Ponce as much as in Brno. Avoiding traditional painting techniques, Perez makes his paintings with oil stick pushed onto the canvas from the back, color by color, echoing the crude separations used in printing the original postcards. His paintings are thus both resolutely handmade and stubbornly mechanical, resistant to the temptations of the painter's fetishized "touch." If Everberg's shiny enamel paintings of hotel lobbies and bars seem to preserve something plangent from the past, Perez's dry, almost abraded surfaces reflect worn-out memories. Perez does not shy away from an overt nostalgia for the landscape of his childhood and adolescence. The sweetness of the memories, however, does not defuse the undercurrent of economic exploitation in the tropical tourist economy, an implication made explicit in the very name of one of the hotels: El Conquistador. Despite this, Perez identifies most of all with the fundamental optimism of these buildings' modernist aspirations, the idea, as he puts it, that their architecture represented a "better tomorrow."[84] In the very act of painting these images he asserts his own continuing faith in the medium as well as in the subject.

Enoc Perez
Ponce Inter-Continental Hotel, Ponce, Puerto Rico, 2003

following pages:
Enoc Perez
El Conquistador, Fajardo, Puerto Rico, 2003

Enoc Perez
Normandie, 2003

Silke Otto-Knapp
Grey Garden, 2000

Silke Otto-Knapp
Mandalay Bay (Night), 2003

Silke Otto-Knapp also paints the world of lush resorts—she particularly favors Las Vegas and the more lotus-land-like aspects of Los Angeles—though in her case they are largely imagined or derived from photographs. As Jennifer Higgie has written, "she is drawn to places and people so iconic and exhausted by their various representations in the popular imagination that, notwithstanding their vivid physicality, they almost cease to exist."[85] Otto-Knapp paints on canvas in watercolor, a technique almost as resistant to facility as Perez's scratchy oilstick. The results are landscapes that seem inherently fragile: fugitive environments that are always right on the edge of dissolution. As she has explained, "I use watercolor in such a way as to bring the transparent quality of the paint into conflict with the clarity of the photographic image. This painted space develops its own dynamic."[86]

84 Perez, e-mail to the author, 20 June 2004.

85 Jennifer Higgie, "Vanishing Act," *Frieze*, no.79 (November–December 2003): 82.

86 Otto-Knapp, in Anette Freudenberger, "Azalea Gardens," in *Silke Otto-Knapp: Orange View* (Düsseldorf: Kunstverein für die Rheinlande und Westfalen, 2003), 11.

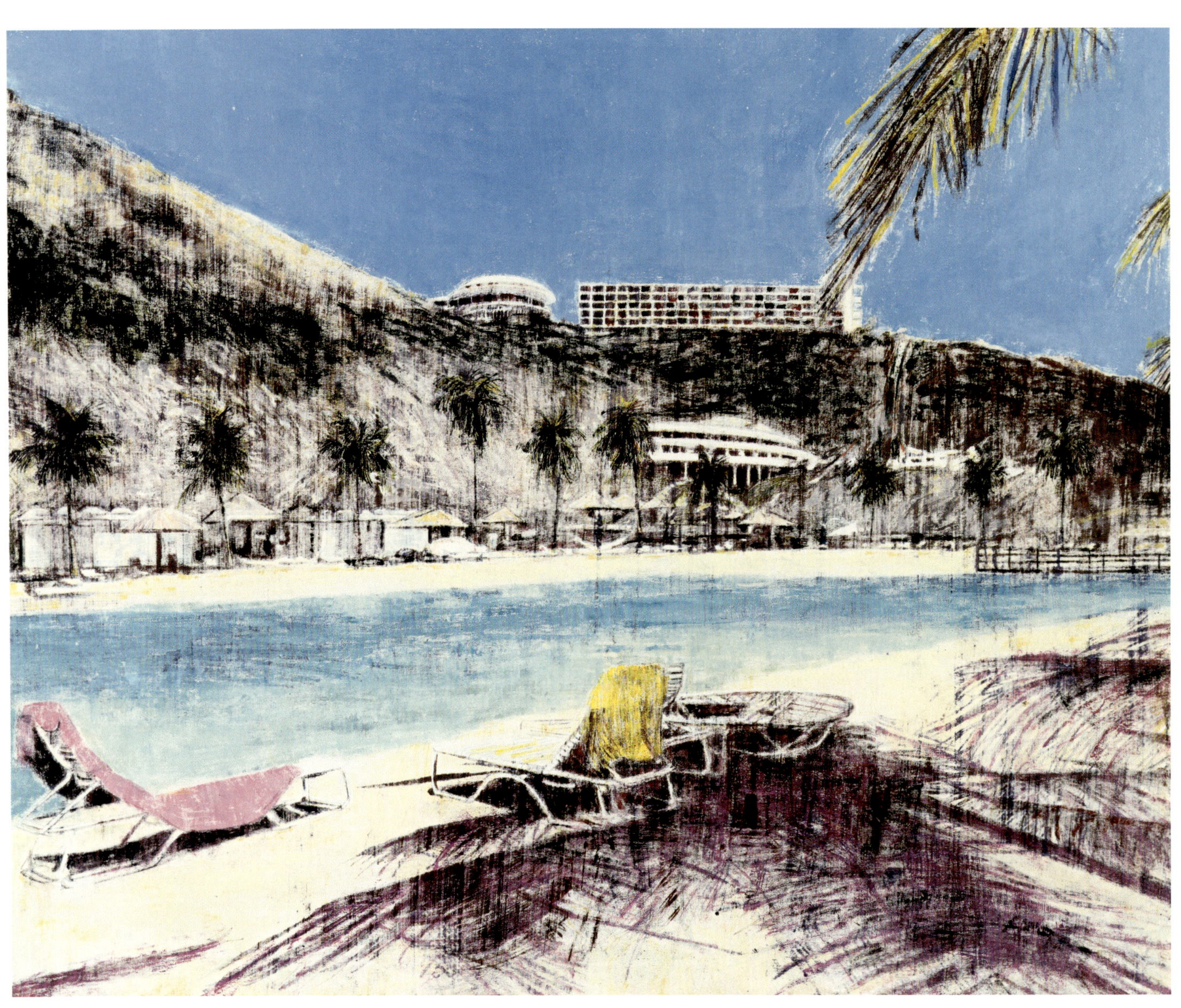

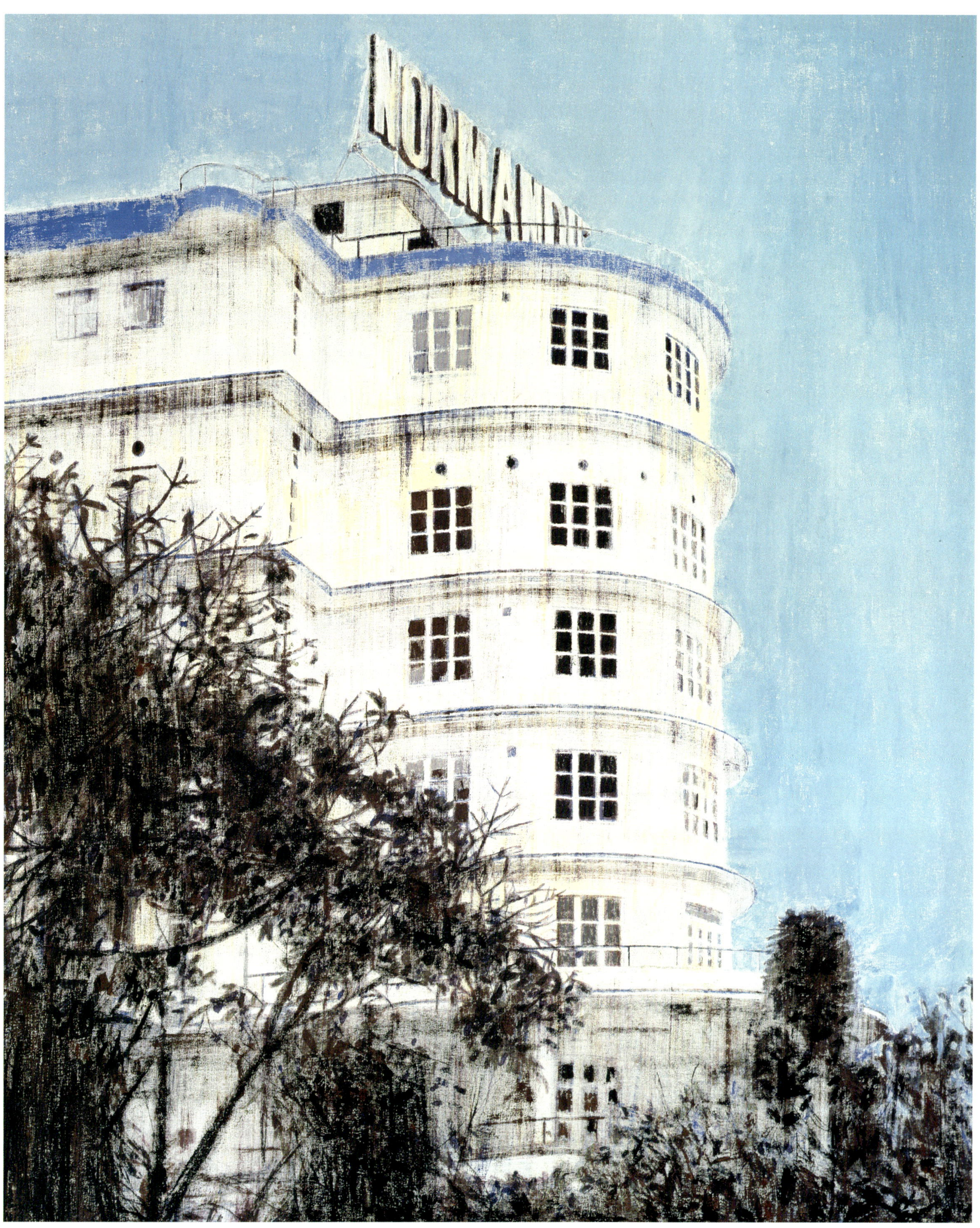
NORMANDIE

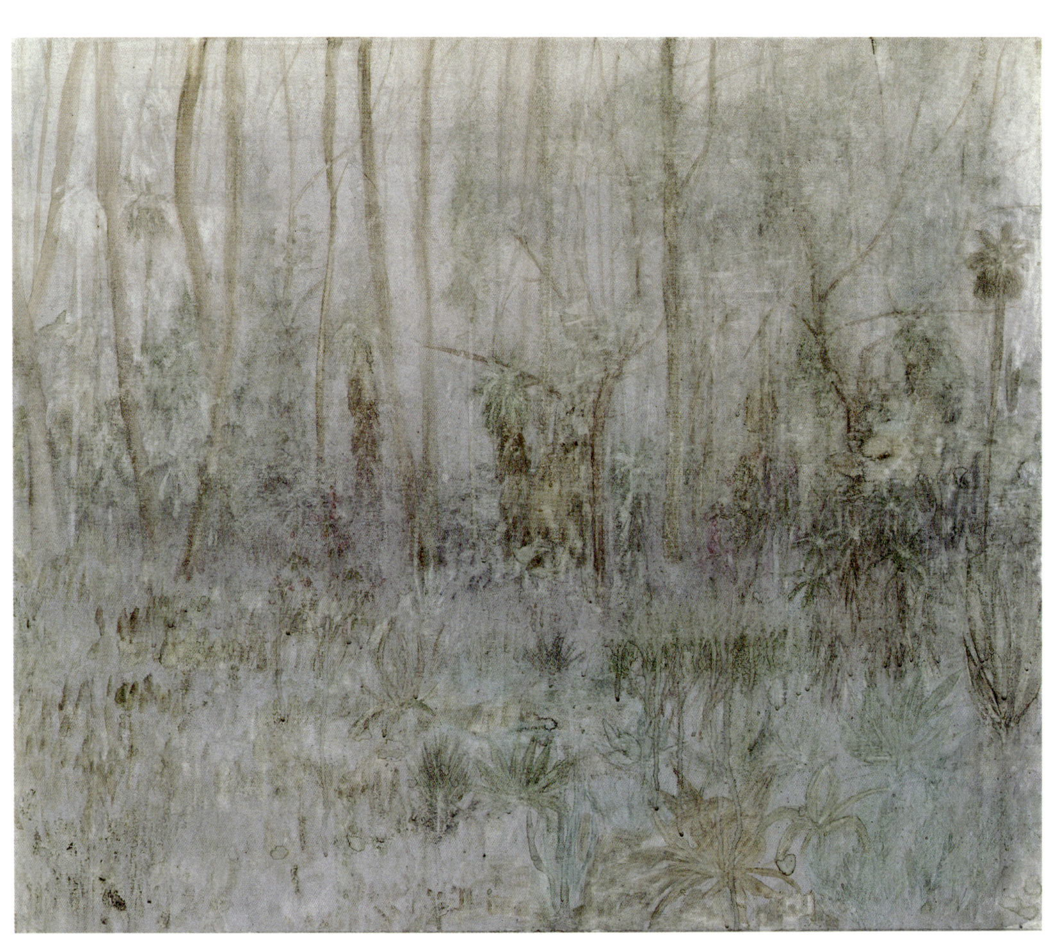

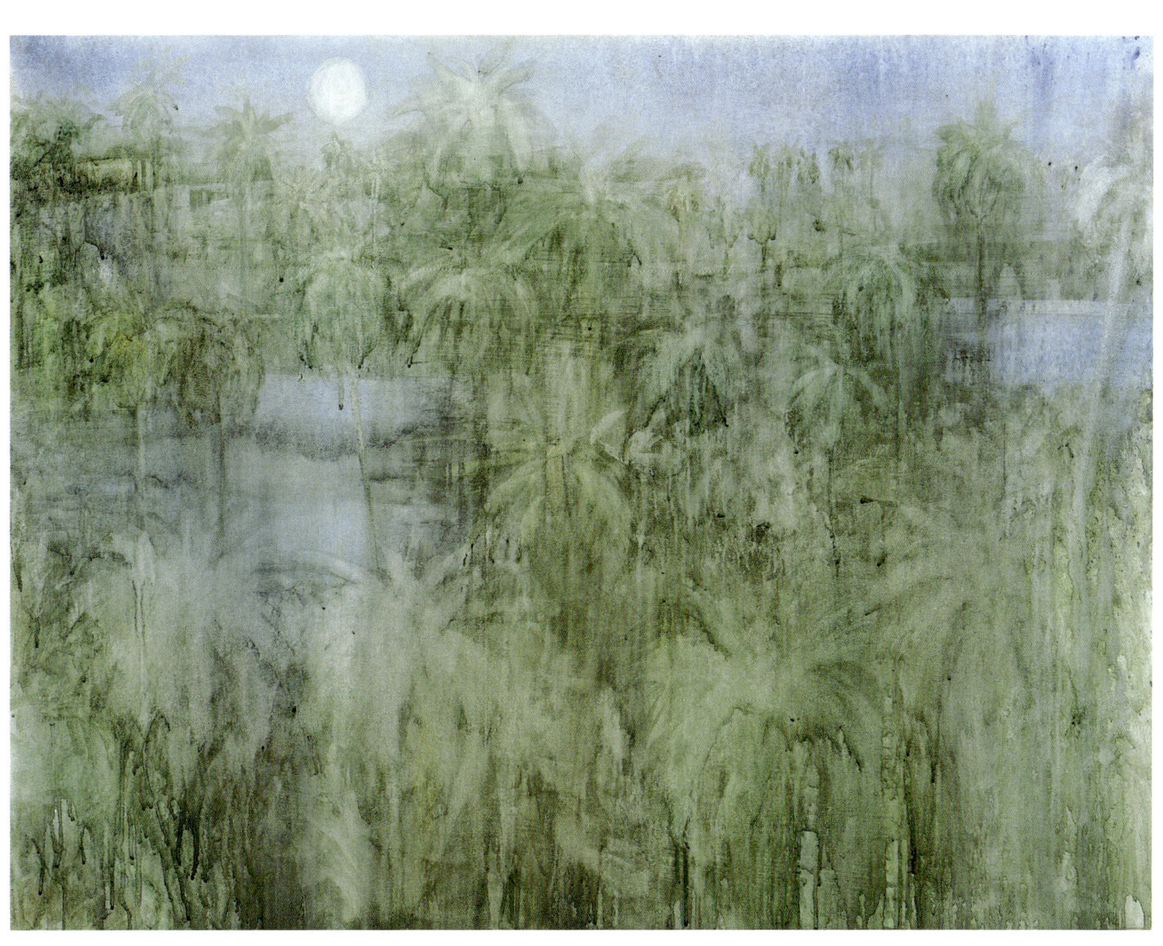

It is no accident that Everberg, Perez, and Otto-Knapp have all chosen to paint hotels. Hotels are inherently liminal spaces. One passes through them as a stranger. The same could be said about Doig's *City Entrance* (1998–99), in which train tracks cut anonymously through an urban setting that could be almost anywhere, or of Eggerer's generic *Atrium* (2003). Such motifs echo the transitional and ephemeral qualities that are also manifest in the paintings themselves.

Shakespeare's line in *The Tempest*, "All that is solid melts into air," became a touchstone for all of modernity via Marx and Engels's use of it in *The Communist Manifesto* (1848).[87] In the paintings of Eggerer, we can see this destabilization quite clearly, as both architecture and figures lose their bearings. Countless *pentimenti* reveal the ghostly evidence of figures that have all but disappeared, yet remain present nevertheless. The concrete and the ethereal are conflated in compositions that are simultaneously rigorous and indefinable. David Joselit has written that in Eggerer's paintings, "the placement of a figure within a ground is almost always traumatic. And this *formal* trauma—in which the ground rejects the figure as a body might reject a transplanted organ—allegorizes social alienation."[88] Joselit perceptively makes the connection between the instability of the composition and the instability of social relationships in a society riddled with false consciousness. Eggerer tears holes between the myth of community and its reality: fragmentation and anomie. His paintings are full of potential allegory: children under surveillance, people hemmed in by oppressive architecture. His tessellated compositions are constructed by means of glances between these characters, of gestures that point from the center to the margins. This tentative structure connects his painting to his earlier, more overtly political work, in which the public toilet could be read as "an ephemeral place which is only made up of gestures, glances, and craving."[89] Yet as Berger has written, "Without an acknowledged coexistence of the ephemeral and the timeless, there is nothing of consequence for pictorial art to do."[90]

Peter Doig
City Entrance, 1998–99

following pages:
Thomas Eggerer
Outdoors, 2003

Thomas Eggerer
Atrium, 2003

87 Paul Berman makes effective use of it to characterize the protean quality of modernity. See his *All That Is Solid Melts Into Air: The Experience of Modernity* (New York: Penguin, 1982).

88 Joselit, "Thomas Eggerer," *Artforum* (October 2001): 148.

89 Klein and Eggerer, "Leave a Message," in Hedwig Saxenuber and Astrid Wege, eds., *Oh, Boy, It's a Girl: Feminismen in der Kunst* (Munich: Kunstverein, 1994), 72–73.

90 Berger, "Painting and Time," 210.

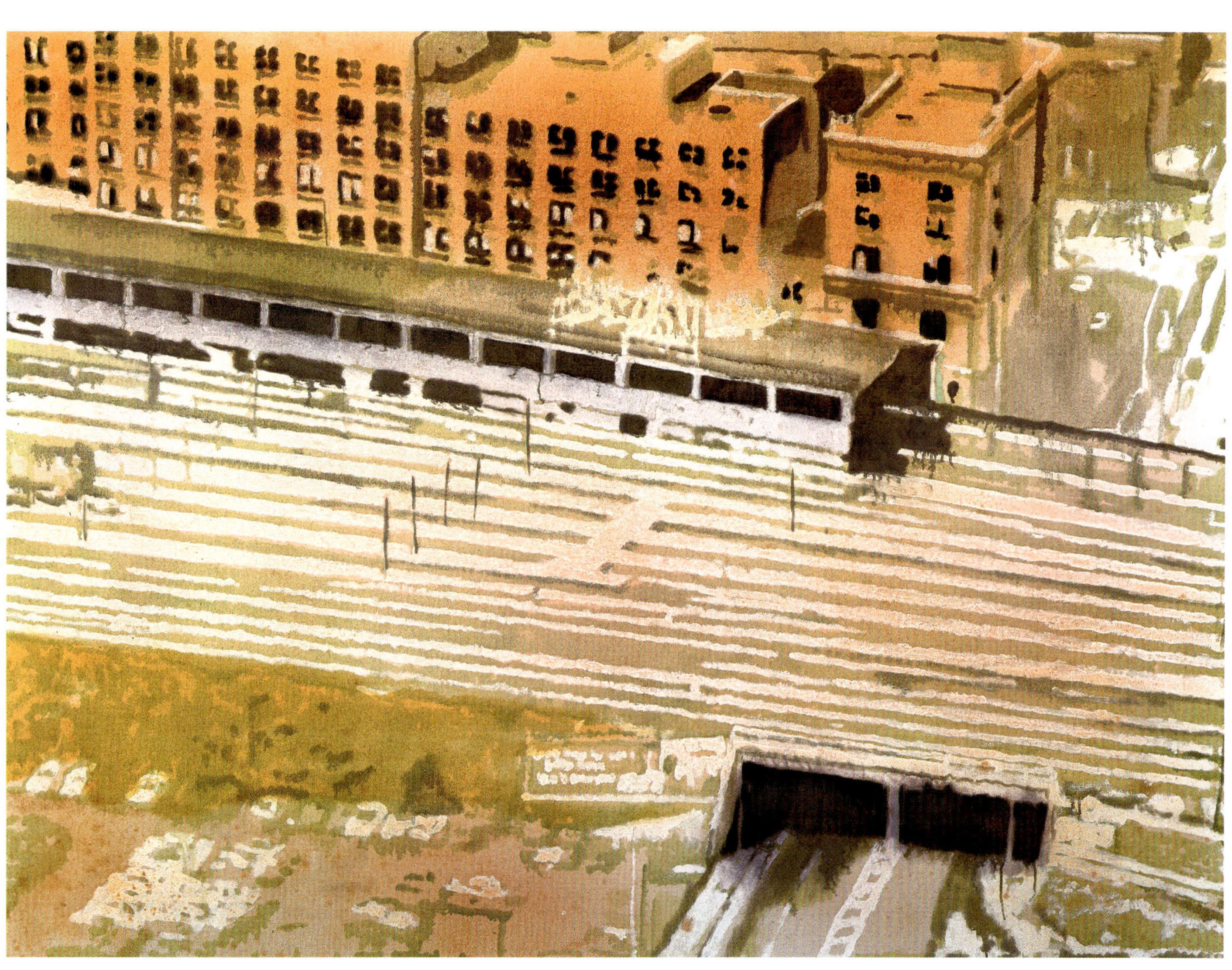

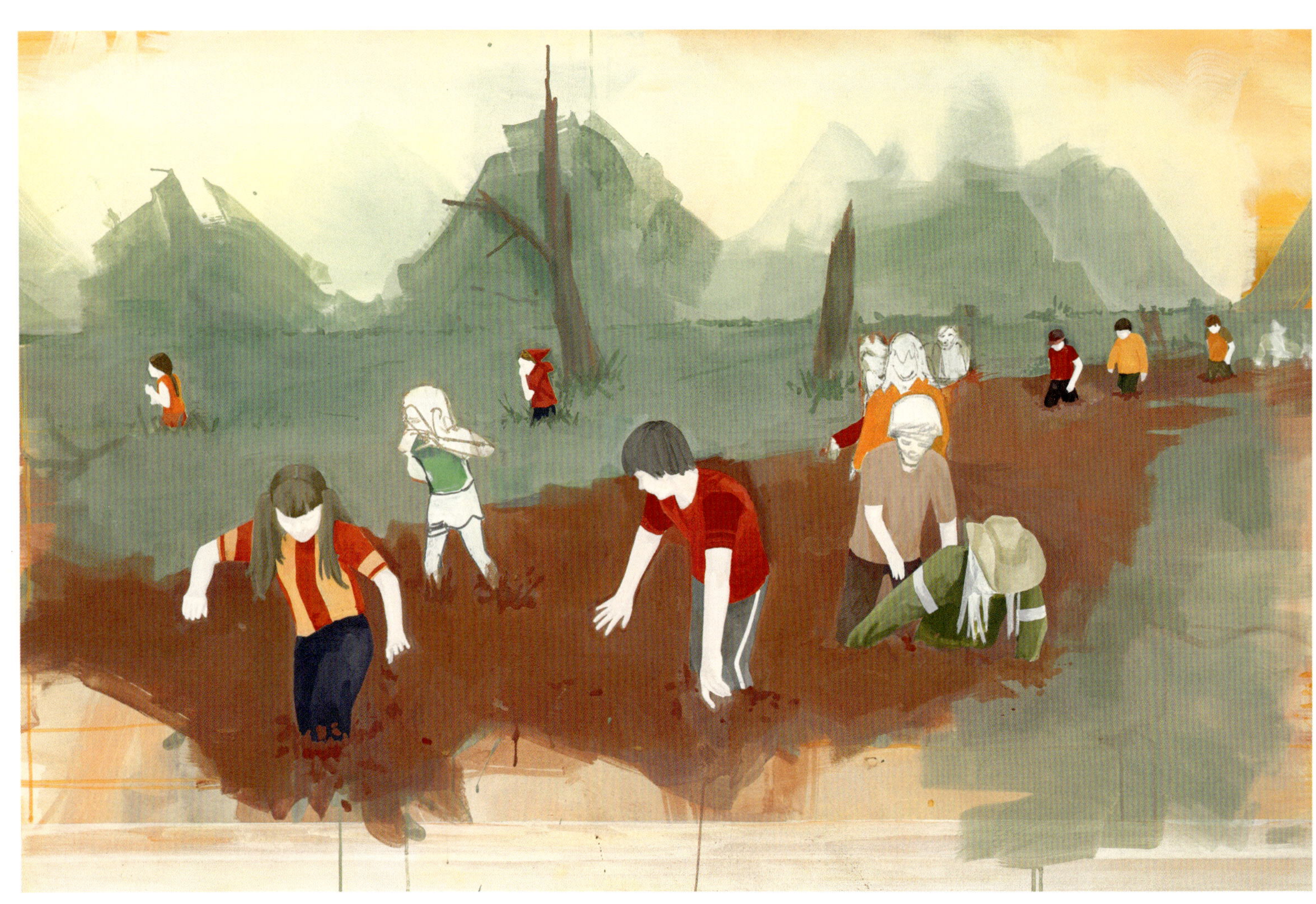

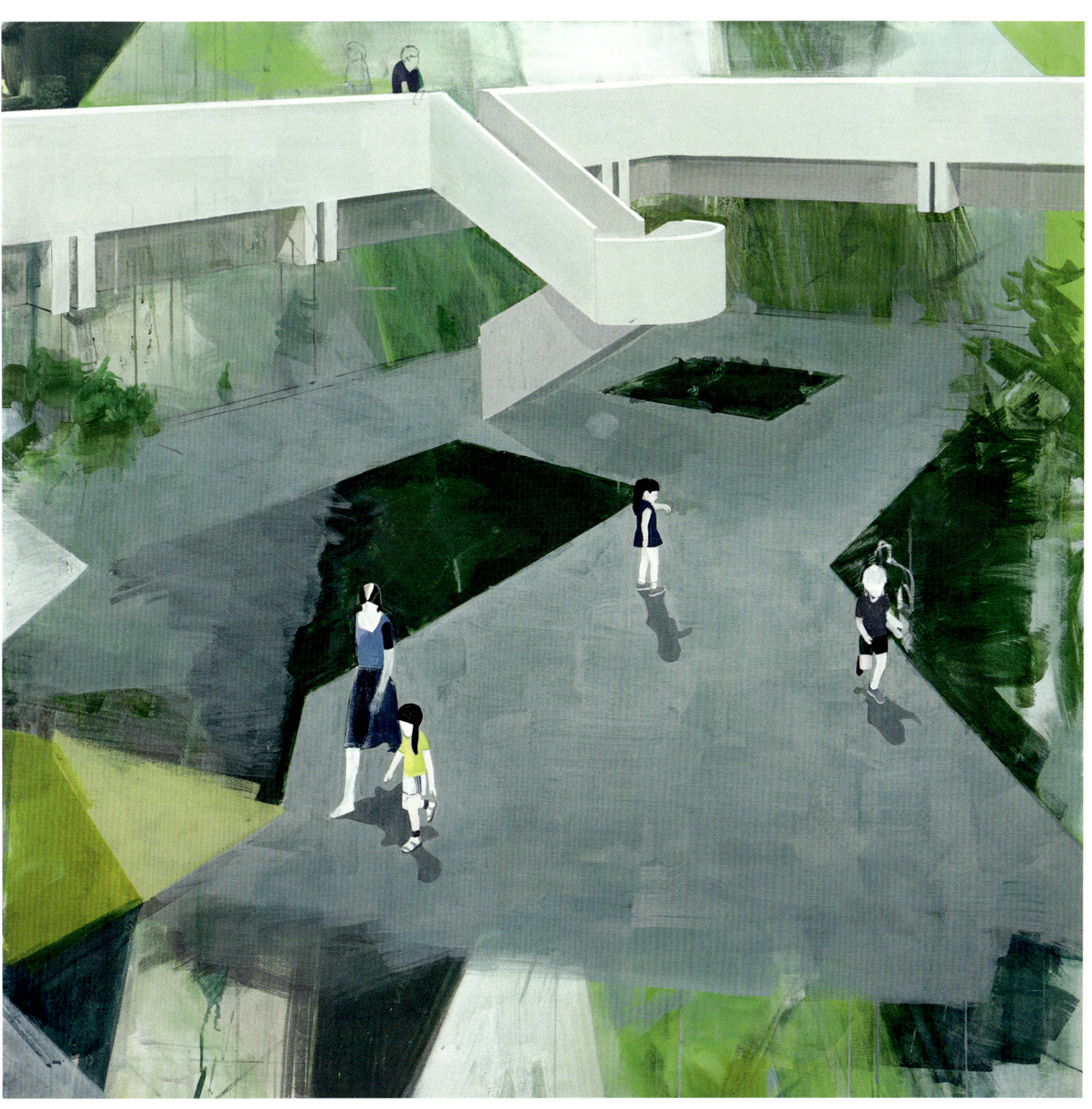

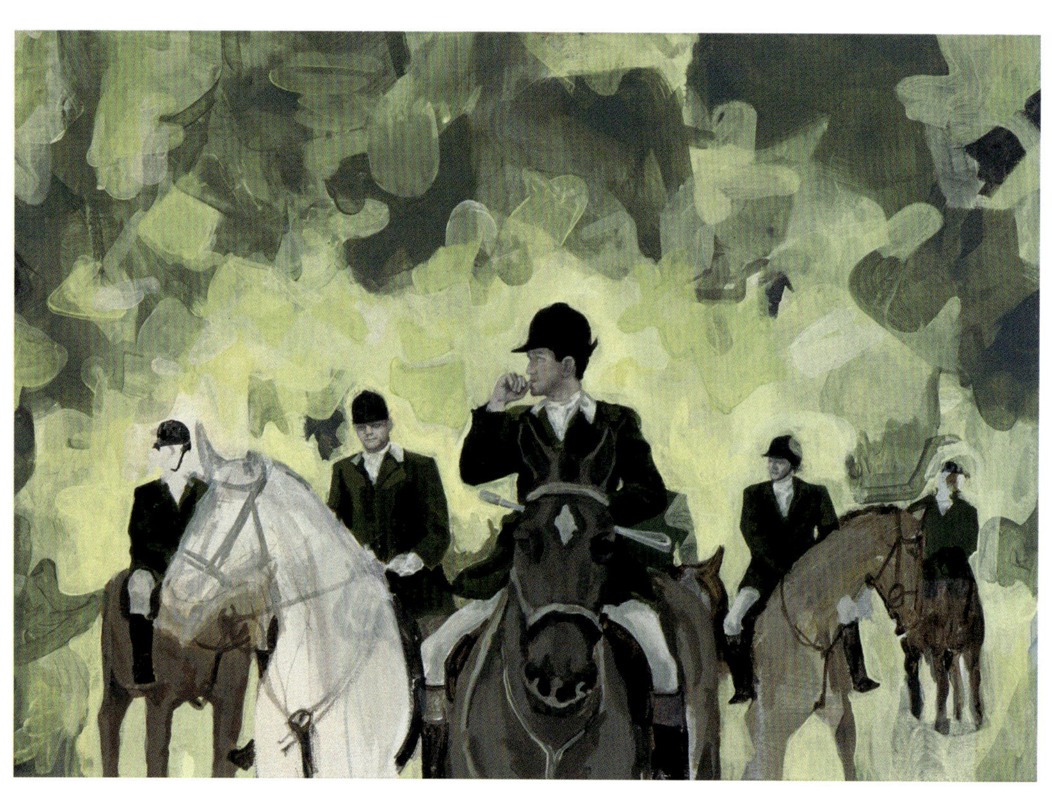

If anything, the relationship in formal terms is even more complex, the social allegory notwithstanding. The ground rejects the figure no more than the figure rejects the ground, and neither rejects the other more than they embrace each other. It is precisely the difficulty of establishing such relationships with any sense of finality that enables the paintings to remain in a kind of constantly shifting movement. They are palimpsests, constantly overwritten and overpainted, and thus insistent on the passage of time, not only in the making of the paintings but also in the experience of them, their flickering back and forth between solidity and dissolution. They lead the viewer out from the starting point of central control to the instability of the edges. As Diedrich Diederichsen wrote, "It is not what the pictures show that eludes theory, what the pictures show actually formulates the theory in the first place. The picture produces the theory."[91]

Thomas Eggerer
Sweet Valley High, 1998

Eggerer compulsively and mistrustfully tests his painting against itself. Even his use of acrylic paint, applied thinly, suggests his arm's-length, even hostile relationship to any potential grandiosity. He resists representation from within, interrupting it with painterly abstraction that soaks through the image like slow-burning acid, only to re-form the picture in new ways. His compositions emerge tentatively, yet he is also clearly obsessed with the way that each stroke of color relates to every other. The color relationships impose another order over the apparent architecture of the painting.

The apparently tentative, unresolved rendering that began with Impressionism has become one of the major paradigms of contemporary painting. Its capacity for monumentality now coexists with a protean instability. Compositional strategies can now simultaneously embrace complex structure and apparent spatial incoherence. For Perez, the abstract ideas of architectural modernism become part of the dialectic

91 Diederichsen, "Crownless Kings and Class Trips," in *Thomas Eggerer: Atrium* (Braunschweig: Kunstverein, 2003), 45.

of his painting, flickering in and out of registration. Otto-Knapp has said of her work that "the architectural elements often become almost invisible, yet a dense, almost claustrophobic space emerges that refers to an interior space. I am much more interested in this shifting perception of space."[92] This ambivalent space can be traced back to the late work of Cézanne, in which drawing is all but eliminated. Edges and surfaces are both articulated by dabs of paint, and the distinction between the two is elided. A brushstroke that represents can easily become a brushstroke that does not.

This shifting quality contributes to painting's capacity to use ambiguity constructively, to engage viewers in active response. For Tuymans, "a good painting to me denounces its own ties so that you are unable to remember it correctly. Thus it generates other images."[93] In *Backyard*, the image at first seems straightforward, as does the way in which it is painted. Yet even as we are conscious of each single brushstroke, we are letting the content suggest a potential narrative. The aerial view and the depopulated landscape have the quality of a surveillance photograph or a TV image of a crime scene. This psychological ambiguity connects with the ambiguity of the roughly painted image to create precisely the unstable image to which Tuymans refers. Even in a more smoothly painted work, such as Duwenhögger's *Perusal of Ill-Begotten Treasures* (2003), the mysterious (and, again, presumptively criminal) scene is given an additional degree of instability through the subtle discontinuities of the pictorial space. As Jan Verwoert has written, "This sense of displacement prevails throughout the work. It is a universe of queer codes transferred to another time and place. The time is the imaginary historicity of literature, the past tense of storytelling."[94]

Lukas Duwenhögger
Perusal of Ill-Begotten Treasures,
2003

92 Otto-Knapp, in "Azalea Gardens," 11.

93 Tuymans, in *The Fascinating Faces of Flanders* (Lisbon: Centro Cultural de Belém, 1998), 126.

94 Verwoert, "Lukas Duwenhögger," *Frieze* no. 84 (June–August 2004): 126.

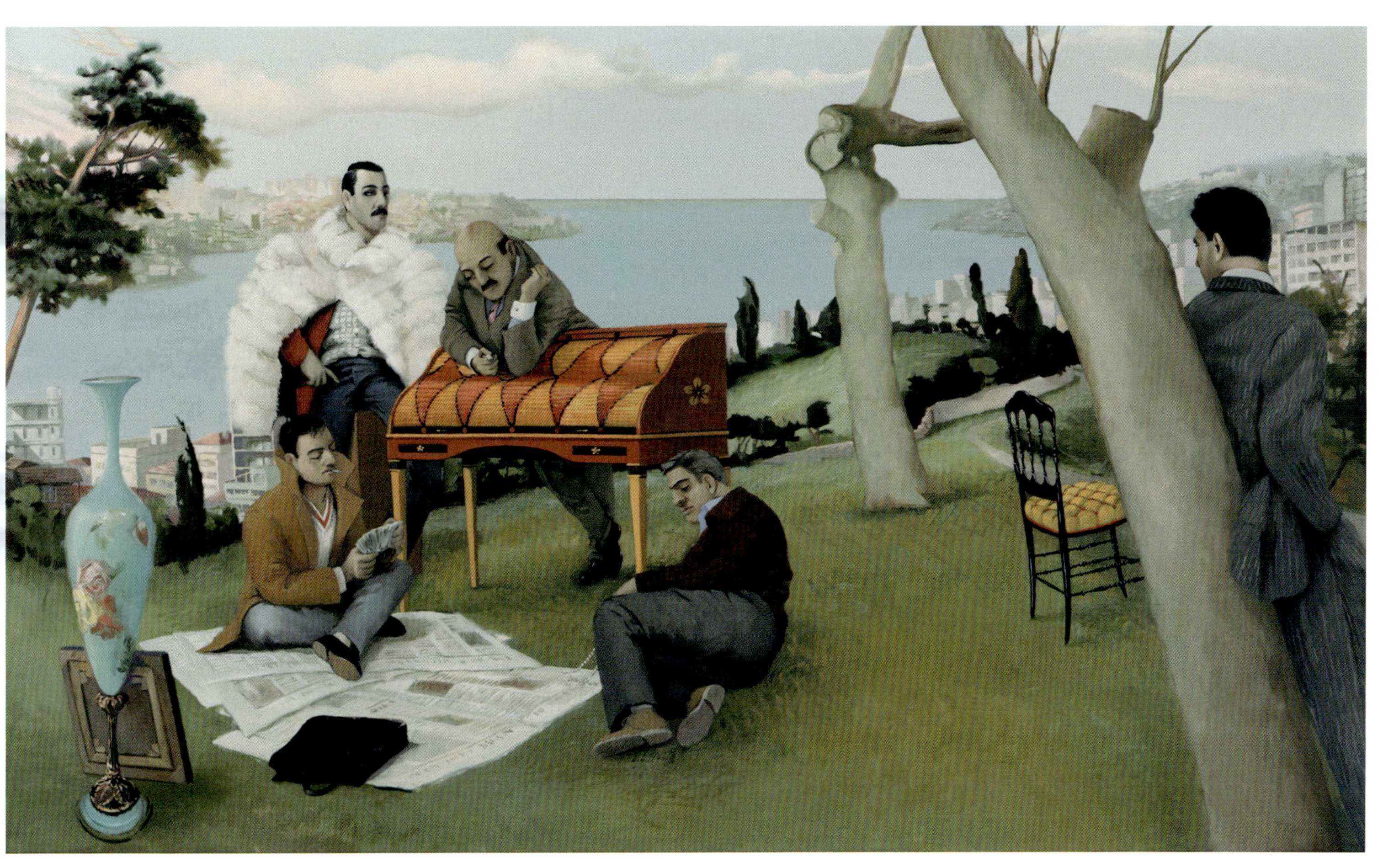

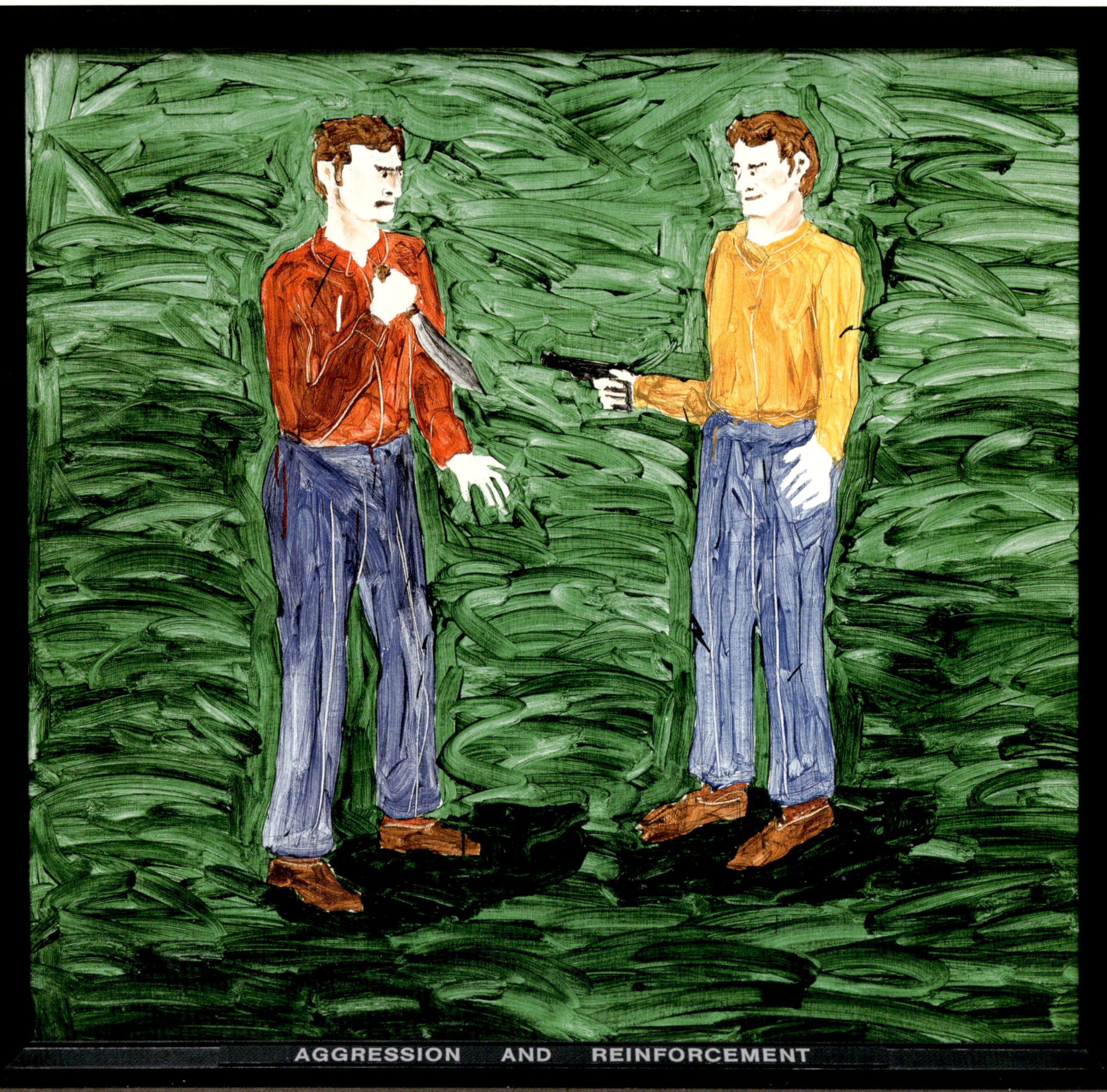
AGGRESSION AND REINFORCEMENT

The narrative element itself is by no means exempt from the instability. While Jenney, for example, can state unequivocally that he is "not interested in a narrative,"[95] *implied* narratives, or fragments of stories, hover around most of the works in this exhibition, including Jenney's. Part of the exchange between the image and the viewer lies in all that is implied before, around, and after the moment represented. Even Lawson now sees narrative in paintings that he had originally thought of in a quite different way:

Neil Jenney
Agression and Reinforcement, 1969

Thomas Lawson
Joy For Baby Jody, 1981

> *At the time it was all reductive painting and media representation, and I still think those are important parts of the work. But I now also think there is a weird relationship to narrative, and particularly the stories one tells about a city in order to inhabit it. This is odd because I always took painting to be an anti-narrative form, at least in its 20th century version. So these paintings are about the difficulty of telling stories about life in New York at that time, in a medium chosen for its resistance to the idea of telling stories of any kind.*[96]

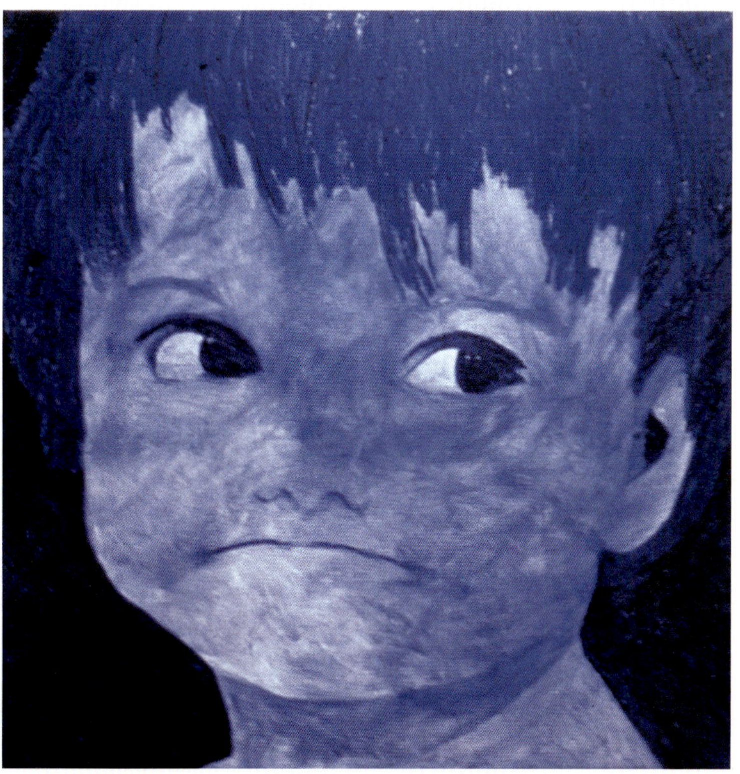

95 Jenney, in *New Image Painting*, 38.

96 Lawson, e-mail to the author, 29 April 2004.

As Lawson indicated, although the painting is always in the most literal sense static, the effects are not.

Painting can combine representation with the tactile and the formal in ways still unavailable to other media. Perhaps to succeed in doing this, however, it is necessary to embrace the kind of self-consciousness that can see painting with a cold objectivity from outside, even while committing oneself to it unreservedly. "Surely," Richter has said, "you don't think that a stupid demonstration of brushwork, or of the rhetoric of painting and its elements, could ever achieve anything, say anything, express any longing."[97] Yet at the same time, the unfashionable seriousness that Richter and others still bring to painting, the element of self-willed faith in the medium's capacity to contribute something, anything, to the way we experience the world, still comes close to convincing. Damisch has pointed out "the essentially performative nature" of painting, "a practice that has no existence, in contradiction to language, save in the act, the exercise."[98] The word "painting" implies both a finished object and an ongoing activity. It continues.

97 Richter, interview with Buchloh (1986), in *The Daily Practice of Painting*, 156.

98 Damisch, *The Origin of Perspective*, 263.

CHECKLIST OF THE EXHIBITION

MAMMA ANDERSSON
Fatherland, 1997–2004
Oil on panel
24 x $96\frac{1}{2}$ in. (61 x 245.1 cm)
The Museum of Contemporary Art,
Los Angeles; Purchased with funds provided
by The Buddy Taub Foundation,
Jill and Dennis Roach, Directors
pages 88–89

We Do Boring Things Together, 2003
Oil, acrylic, and varnish on board
Two panels: 24 x 25 in. each (61 x 63.5 cm)
Ovitz Family Collection, Los Angeles
pages 86–87

JOHN BALDESSARI
A Picture to Treasure, 1966–67
Acrylic and photoemulsion on canvas
12 x 12 in. (30.5 x 30.5 cm)
Collection of Paul Brach and
Miriam Schapiro
page 64

A Painting by Hildegard Reiner, 1969
Oil and acrylic on canvas
$59\frac{1}{4}$ x $45\frac{1}{2}$ in. (150.5 x 115.6 cm)
Courtesy of the artist and
Marian Goodman Gallery, New York
page 59

A Painting by Pat Perdue, 1969
Oil and acrylic on canvas
$59\frac{1}{4}$ x $45\frac{1}{2}$ in. (150.5 x 115.6 cm)
Courtesy of the artist and
Marian Goodman Gallery, New York
page 60

A Painting by William Bowne, 1969
Oil and acrylic on canvas
$59\frac{1}{4}$ x $45\frac{1}{2}$ in. (150.5 x 115.6 cm)
Courtesy of the artist and
Marian Goodman Gallery, New York
page 61

EDGAR BRYAN
Night in the Alte Pinakothek, 2002
Oil on canvas
108 x 78 in. (274.3 x 198.1 cm)
Collection of Dean Valentine
and Amy Adelson, Los Angeles
page 92

The Ledge, 2004
Acrylic, watercolor, and oil on canvas
46 x 54 in. (116.8 x 137.2 cm)
Private Collection
page 91

VIJA CELMINS
Hand Holding a Firing Gun, 1964
Oil on canvas
$24\frac{1}{4}$ x 35 in. (61.6 x 88.9 cm)
Collection of Jack and Joan Quinn,
Beverly Hills
page 57

Lamp #1, 1964
Oil on canvas
$24\frac{1}{2}$ x 35 in. (62.2 x 88.9 cm)
Collection of the artist
page 55

PETER DOIG
City Entrance, 1998–99
Oil on canvas
$47\frac{1}{4}$ x $65\frac{1}{16}$ in. (120 x 165.3 cm)
Collection of Stanley and Gail Hollander
page 105

Figure in Mountain Landscape (I love you big dummy), 1999
Oil on canvas
106 x 77 in. (269.2 x 195.6 cm)
Collection of Dean Valentine
and Amy Adelson, Los Angeles
page 31

LUKAS DUWENHÖGGER
Choreographie für 3 Männer, 2 Besen und Signalband (Choreography for three men,
two brooms, and warning tape), 1994
Oil on canvas
$37\frac{3}{8}$ x $51\frac{3}{16}$ in. (95 x 130 cm)
Collection of Alan Hergott and Curt Shepard
page 37

Roman Holiday, 1999
Oil on canvas
$67\frac{3}{4}$ x $95\frac{1}{4}$ in. (172.1 x 241.9 cm)
Collection of Dean Valentine
and Amy Adelson, Los Angeles
page 136

Perusal of Ill-Begotten Treasures, 2003
Oil on canvas
$44\frac{1}{2}$ x $75\frac{5}{8}$ in. (113 x 192.1 cm)
Collection of Dean Valentine
and Amy Adelson, Los Angeles
page 111

MARI EASTMAN
Marlboro Man, 2003
Acrylic, airbrush, and glitter on canvas
33 x 34 in. (83.8 x 86.4 cm)
Collection of Craig and Lynn Jacobson
page 81

U.S. Soldiers Dismantling the Bust of Saddam Hussein, 2003
Flashe, glitter, and oil on canvas
40 x 60 in. (101.6 x 152.4 cm)
Courtesy of the artist and Karyn Lovegrove Gallery, Los Angeles
page 83

Evening Landscape, 2004
Flashe and spray paint
40 x 60 in. (101.6 x 152.4 cm)
Courtesy of the artist and Karyn Lovegrove Gallery, Los Angeles
page 94

Porcelain Bowl with Dragon Design and Red Glaze, 2004
Spray paint, acrylic, pencil, and glitter on canvas
22 x 26 in. (55.9 x 66 cm)
Courtesy of the artist and Karyn Lovegrove Gallery, Los Angeles
page 82

THOMAS EGGERER
Sweet Valley High, 1998
Acrylic on cotton
27½ x 39 in. (69.9 x 99.1 cm)
Collection of Janice and Mickey Cartin
page 108

Atrium, 2003
Acrylic on cotton
60 x 63 in. (152.4 x 160 cm)
The Museum of Contemporary Art, Los Angeles; Purchased with funds provided by the Acquisition and Collection Committee
page 107

Outdoors, 2003
Acrylic on cotton
41 x 61 in. (104.1 x 154.9 cm)
Collection of Tracy and Gary Mezzatesta
page 106

KIRSTEN EVERBERG
Bar, 2003
Oil and enamel on canvas over panel
72 x 96 in. (182.9 x 243.9 cm)
Collection of Brian Biel
page 97

Lobby, 2003
Oil and enamel on canvas over panel
72 x 96 in. (182.9 x 243.9 cm)
Collection of Jose Noe Suro, Guadalajara; Courtesy of 1301PE, Los Angeles
page 96

PHILIP GUSTON
Untitled, 1975
Oil on canvas
66½ x 78½ in. (168.9 x 199.4 cm)
Collection University of California, Los Angeles, Hammer Museum; Bequest of Musa Guston
page 27

RICHARD HAMILTON
Soft Pink Landscape, 1971–72
Oil on canvas
48 x 64 in. (121.9 x 162.6 cm)
Ludwig Museum Budapest—Museum of Contemporary Art
page 71

Mother and Child, 1984–85
Oil on canvas
59½ x 59½ in. (151.1 x 151.1 cm)
Collection of Keith and Kathy Sachs
page 69

Countdown, 1989
Humbrol enamel on cibachrome on canvas
39½ x 39⅝ in. (100.3 x 100.7 cm)
Hirshhorn Museum and Sculpture Garden, Smithsonian Institution, Holenia Purchase Fund, in memory of Joseph H. Hirshhorn, 1991
page 44

NEIL JENNEY
Aggression and Reinforcement, 1969
Acrylic on canvas with painted wood frame
54 x 64 in. (137.2 x 162.6 cm)
The Eli and Edythe L. Broad Collection, Los Angeles
page 112

Tools and Task, 1969
Acrylic and graphite on canvas with painted wood frame
52¾ x 92½ in. (133 x 234 cm)
The Eli and Edythe L. Broad Collection, Los Angeles
page 52

JOCHEN KLEIN
#39, 1996
Oil and collage on canvas
19½ x 15¾ in. (49.5 x 40 cm)
Collection of Thomas Eggerer
page 12

#53, 1997
Oil and collage on canvas
30 x 39¾ in. (76.2 x 101 cm)
Collection of David and Monica Zwirner
page 72

#57, 1997
Oil on canvas
40⅛ x 57⅞ in. (102 x 147 cm)
Collection of Charles Asprey, London
page 73

THOMAS LAWSON
Don't Hit Her Again, 1981
Oil on canvas
48 x 48 in. (122 x 122 cm)
Collection of Melva Bucksbaum and Raymond Learsy
page 66

Inches From Death, 1981
Oil on canvas
48 x 48 in. (122 x 122 cm)
Collection of the artist
page 67

Joy For Baby Jody, 1981
Oil on canvas
48 x 48 in. (122 x 122 cm)
QCC Art Gallery/The City University of New York
page 113

Happy to Be Alive, 1982
Oil on canvas
48 x 96 in. (122 x 244 cm)
Collection of the artist
page 65

KERRY JAMES MARSHALL
Destiny Is a Rose, 1990
Acrylic and collage on canvas
33½ x 34 in. (85 x 86.4 cm)
Collections of Eileen Harris-Norton and Peter Norton, Santa Monica
page 84

Souvenir 1, 1997
Acrylic and glitter on canvas banner
108 x 156 in. (274 x 396 cm)
Museum of Contemporary Art, Chicago; Bernice and Kenneth Newberger Fund
page 45

LUCY MCKENZIE
They Are Lying on Their CVs, 2000
Acrylic on canvas
46 x 72 in. (117 x 183 cm)
Collection of Stanley and Gail Hollander
page 95

Untitled, 2002
Acrylic and oil on canvas
118⅛ x 78¾ in. (300 x 200 cm)
Galerie Daniel Buchholz, Cologne
page 78

Untitled, 2002
Acrylic and oil on canvas
78¾ x 118⅛ in. (200 x 300 cm)
Cabinet Gallery, London
page 79

SILKE OTTO-KNAPP
Grey Garden, 2003
Watercolor on canvas
31½ x 37½ in. (80 x 95.3 cm)
Rubell Family Collection, Miami
page 102

Mandalay Bay (Night), 2003
Watercolor on canvas
31½ x 41¼ in. (80 x 104.8 cm)
Private Collection, Hamburg
page 103

LAURA OWENS
Untitled, 2004
Oil and acrylic on linen
66 x 66 in. (167.6 x 167.6 cm)
Collection of the artist. Courtesy of Gavin Brown's enterprise, New York
page 85

ENOC PEREZ
El Conquistador, Fajardo, Puerto Rico, 2003
Oil on canvas
72 x 90 in. (182.9 x 228.6 cm)
Collection of Tony Shafrazi, New York
page 100

Normandie, 2003
Oil on canvas
72¼ x 60⅛ in. (183.5 x 152.7 cm)
Courtesy The Brant Foundation, Greenwich, Connecticut
page 101

Ponce Inter-Continental Hotel, Ponce, Puerto Rico, 2003
Oil on canvas
72 x 102 in. (183 x 259 cm)
Courtesy The Brant Foundation, Greenwich, Connecticut
page 98

FAIRFIELD PORTER

Six O'Clock, 1964
Oil on canvas
$71\frac{1}{4}$ x $59\frac{1}{2}$ in. (181 x 151 cm)
Saint Louis Art Museum; Gift of Mr. and Mrs. R. Crosby Kemper, Jr. through the Crosby Kemper Foundation
page 19

Self-Portrait, 1968
Oil on canvas
59 x $45\frac{3}{8}$ in. (150 x 115 cm)
The Dayton Art Institute; Museum purchase with funds provided by the National Endowment for the Arts and matched with funds provided by Mrs. T. Lawrence Saunders, The Honorable Jefferson Patterson and his late mother Mrs. Harrie G. Carnell and the late Mr. Brainerd B. Thresher, and the General Operating Fund, 1973.55
page 22

Amherst Campus No. 1, 1969
Oil on canvas
62 x 46 in. (158 x 117.5 cm)
The Parrish Art Museum, Southampton, N.Y., Gift of the Estate of Fairfield Porter
page 21

RICHARD PRINCE

Nurses' Dormitory, 2002
Inkjet print and acrylic on canvas
58 x 36 in. (147.3 x 91.4 cm)
Private Collection
page 74

Holiday for a Nurse, 2003
Inkjet print and acrylic on canvas
70 x 50 in. (178 x 127 cm)
Collection of Jamie and Steve Tisch
page 76

GERHARD RICHTER

Untitled, 1964
Oil on printed paper mounted on board
$4\frac{5}{8}$ x $4\frac{5}{8}$ in. (11.8 x 11.8 cm)
Elisabeth Cunnick and Peter Freeman, New York
page 14

Waterfall, 1997
Oil on linen
$64\frac{7}{8}$ x $43\frac{3}{8}$ in. (165 x 110 cm)
Hirshhorn Museum and Sculpture Garden, Smithsonian Institution, Joseph H. Hirshhorn Purchase Fund, 1998.
page 30

LUC TUYMANS

Cheese, 1995
Oil on canvas
$31\frac{1}{2}$ x 31 in. (80 x 78.7 cm)
Hort Family Collection, New York; Courtesy David Zwirner, New York
page 4

Chalk, 2000
Oil on canvas
$28\frac{1}{2}$ x $24\frac{1}{4}$ in. (72.4 x 61.6 cm)
Private Collection, San Francisco
page 40

The Mission, 2000
Oil on canvas
33 x $51\frac{1}{4}$ in. (83.8 x 130.2 cm)
Private Collection, Philadelphia; Courtesy David Zwirner, New York
page 41

Backyard, 2002
Oil on canvas
$54\frac{3}{4}$ x $44\frac{7}{8}$ in. (139.1 x 114 cm)
The Museum of Contemporary Art, Los Angeles; Purchased with funds provided by The Buddy Taub Foundation, Jill and Dennis Roach, Directors
page 24

Egypt, 2003
Oil on canvas
$56\frac{1}{8}$ x $34\frac{5}{8}$ in. (142.5 x 88 cm)
Private Collection; Courtesy of Tanya Bonakdar Gallery, New York
page 42

ILLUSTRATION CHECKLIST

EDGAR BRYAN
Illustration for *AirScoop News,* USAFE, 1992
Watercolor on paper
page 90

VIJA CELMINS
Heater, 1964
Oil on canvas
47 7/16 x 48 in. (120.5 x 121.9 cm)
Whitney Museum of American Art, New York; Purchase, with funds from the Contemporary Painting and Sculpture Committee
page 54

PAUL CÉZANNE
Boy Resting, 1887
Oil on canvas
21 1/4 x 25 11/16 in. (54 x 65.3 cm)
Hammer Museum; The Armand Hammer Collection, Gift of the Armand Hammer Foundation
page 47

JEAN-BAPTISTE-CAMILLE COROT
Study of Medieval Ruins, 1829–34
Oil on canvas on board
9 15/16 x 12 5/8 in. (23.7 x 32.1 cm)
Hammer Museum; The Armand Hammer Collection, Gift of the Armand Hammer Foundation
page 17

JACQUES-LOUIS DAVID
The Oath of the Horatii, c. 1784
Oil on canvas
128 11/16 x 165 3/4 in. (330 x 425 cm)
Réunion des Musées Nationaux, Louvre, Paris
page 38

EDGAR DEGAS
Three Dancers in Yellow Skirts, c. 1891
Oil on canvas
32 x 25 5/8 in. (81.28 x 65.1 cm)
Hammer Museum; The Armand Hammer Collection, Gift of the Armand Hammer Foundation
page 25

WILLEM DE KOONING
Woman IV, 1952–53
Oil, enamel, and charcoal on canvas
59 x 46 1/4 in. (149.9 x 117.5 cm)
The Nelson-Atkins Museum of Art, Kansas City, Missouri (Gift of William Inge)
page 49

MARCEL DUCHAMP
Tu m', 1918
Oil on canvas with bottle brush, three safety pins, and one bolt
27 1/4 x 123 in. (69.8 x 313 cm)
Yale University Art Gallery; Gift of the Estate of Katherine S. Dreier
page 58

MARI EASTMAN
July, 2003
Acrylic, spray paint, oil, glitter on canvas
24 x 24 in. (61 x 61 cm)
Destroyed
page 80

PHILIP GUSTON
White Painting I, 1951
Oil on canvas
57 7/8 x 61 7/8 in. (147 x 157 cm)
San Francisco Museum of Modern Art; T. B. Walker Foundation Fund purchase, © Estate of Philip Guston
page 26

RICHARD HAMILTON
Towards a definitive statement on the coming trends in men's wear and accessories (c) Adonis in Y-fronts, 1962
Oil and collage on panel
23 13/16 x 31 9/16 in. (61 x 81 cm)
The Art Institute of Chicago; Restricted Gift of Muriel Newman in honor of Emese and James N. Wood, Walter Aitken Endowment, 1997-545
page 68

The Citizen, 1982–83
Oil on canvas
80 5/8 x 82 in. (207 x 210 cm)
Tate Gallery, London
page 43

MARTIN KIPPENBERGER
Untitled, 1981
Acrylic on canvas
$93\frac{5}{8}$ x 117 in. (240 x 300 cm)
Estate of Martin Kippenberger,
Galerie Gisela Capitain, Cologne
page 62

JOCHEN KLEIN
#38, 1996
Oil and collage on canvas
$29\frac{15}{16}$ x $39\frac{3}{4}$ in. (76 x 101 cm)
Courtesy Galerie Dainel Buchholz, Cologne
page 70

#51, 1997
Oil and collage on canvas
24 x 18 in. (61 x 46 cm)
Courtesy Galerie Dainel Buchholz, Cologne
page 124

GIORGIO MORANDI
Still Life, 1946
Oil on canvas
$14\frac{5}{8}$ x $17\frac{13}{16}$ in. (37.5 x 45.7 cm)
Tate Gallery, London
page 54

RICHARD PRINCE
Untitled (Cowboy), 1992
Ektacolor photograph
20 x 24 in. (50.8 x 61 cm)
Walker Art Center, Minneapolis;
Gift of Barbara Gladstone, 2001
page 80

AD REINHARDT
Abstract Painting, Blue, 1952
Oil on canvas
75 x 28 in. (190.5 x 71.2 cm)
Carnegie Museum of Art, Pittsburgh;
Purchase, gift of the Women's Committee
page 48

GERHARD RICHTER
Annunciation After Titian, 1973
Oil on linen
$49\frac{3}{8}$ x $78\frac{7}{8}$ in. (125 x 200 cm)
Hirshhorn Museum and Sculpture Garden,
Smithsonian Institution; Joseph H. Hirshhorn
Purchase Fund, 1994
page 29

Eight Student Nurses, 1966
Oil on canvas
8 paintings: $36\frac{3}{8}$ x $27\frac{9}{16}$ in.
(95 x 70 cm) each
Hans and Brigitte Wyss Collection,
Zurich
page 77

Uncle Rudi, 1965
Oil on canvas
$34\frac{1}{4}$ x $19\frac{11}{16}$ in. (86 x 50 cm)
The Czech Museum of Fine Arts, Prague;
Lidice Collection
page 35

Record Player [Plattenspieler] from
October 18, 1977, 1988
Oil on canvas
$24\frac{5}{8}$ x $32\frac{3}{4}$ in. (62.6 x 83.2 cm)
The Museum of Modern Art, New York;
The Sidney and Harriet Janis Collection,
gift of Philip Johnson, and acquired through
the Lillie P. Bliss Bequest (all by exchange);
Enid A. Haupt Fund; Nina and Gordon
Bunshaft Bequest Fund; and gift of Emily
Rauh Pulitizer
page 38

LUC TUYMANS
Gas Chamber, 1986
Oil on canvas
$19\frac{1}{2}$ x $27\frac{5}{16}$ in. (50 x 70 cm)
The Over Holland Collection
page 39

JAMES ABBOTT MCNEILL WHISTLER
Nocturne in Black and Gold, the Falling Rocket,
c. 1875
Oil on panel
$23\frac{3}{4}$ x $18\frac{1}{4}$ in. (60.3 x 46.4 cm)
The Detroit Institute of Arts;
Gift of Dexter M. Ferry, Jr.
page 18

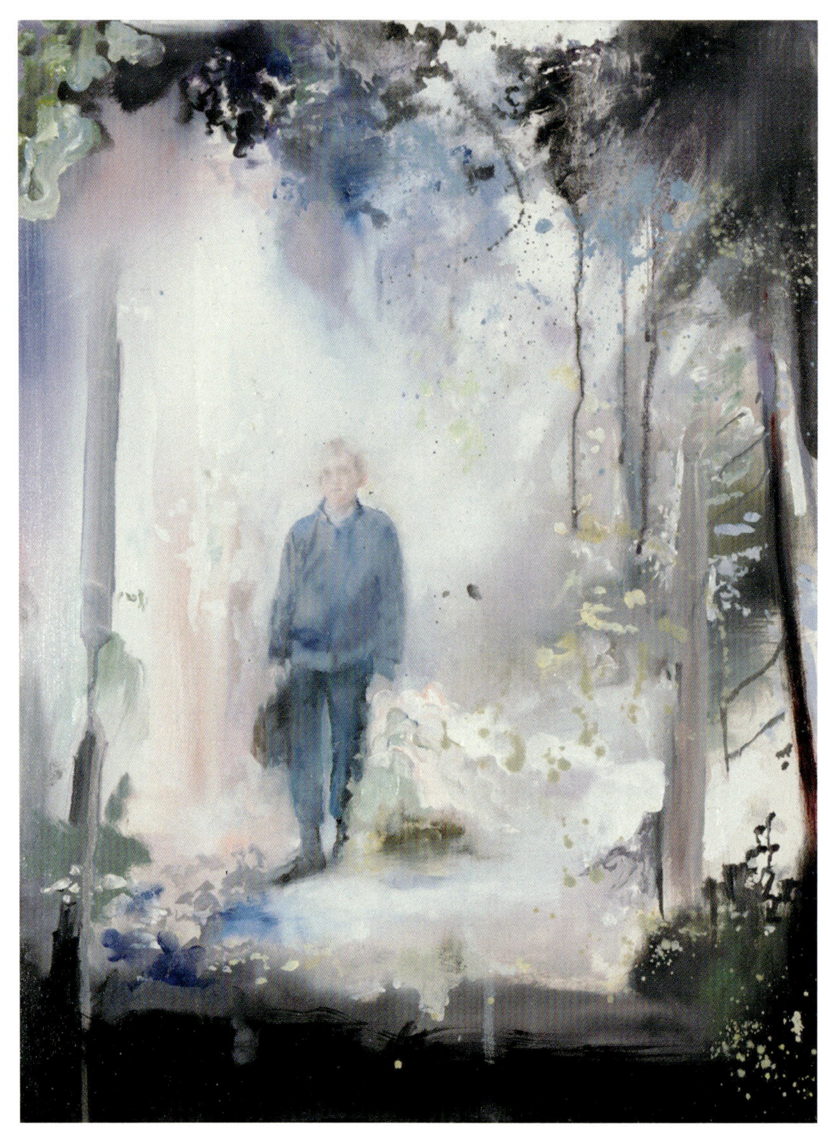

Jochen Klein
#51, 1997

SELECTED EXHIBITIONS AND BIBLIOGRAPHIES

MAMMA ANDERSSON

Born 1962 in Luleå, Sweden
Lives in Stockholm

Solo exhibitions

2004

Galleri Magnus Karlsson, Stockholm

2002

Stephen Friedman Gallery, London

2001

Konstens Hus, Luleå, Sweden
Galleri 1, Gothenburg, Sweden

Group exhibitions

2003

"Devil-may-care," Nordic Pavilion at the 50th Venice Biennale, Venice. Exh. cat.

2002

"Blir du lonesome lille vän," Konstnärshuset, Stockholm

1999

"Aptitretare," Kungliga Akademien för De Fria Konsterna, Stockholm
"X: et 100," Konsthall, Botkyrka, Sweden

Bibliography

Higgie, Jennifer. "Morning Stands on Tiptoe." *Frieze*, no. 68 (June–August 2002): 68–71.

Jortveit, Anne Karin, and Andrea Kroksnes, eds. *Devil-may-care*. Exh. cat. Oslo: Office for Contemporary Art Norway; and Ostfildern-Ruit, Germany: Hatje Cantz Verlag, 2003. Texts by Mieke Bal, Sonia Hedstrand, Jortveit, Kroksnes, Siri Meyer, Toril Moi, Irit Rogoff, and Leena-Maija Rossi.

Morton, Tom. "Mamma Andersson at Stephen Friedman Gallery." *Contemporary*, no. 46 (December 2002): 91.

JOHN BALDESSARI

Born 1931 in National City, California
Lives in Los Angeles

Solo exhibitions

2004

"John Baldessari: Somewhere Between Almost Right and Not Quite (With Orange)," Deutsche Guggenheim, Berlin. Exh. cat.

2001

"Baldessari: While Something Is Happening Here, Something Else Is Happening There, Works 1965–2001," Reykjavik Art Museum, Reykjavik. Exh. cat.

2000

Museo d'Arte Moderna e Contemporanea di Trento e Rovereto, Trento, Italy. Exh. cat.

1999

"Baldessari: While Something Is Happening Here, Something Else Is Happening There: Works 1988–1999," Sprengel Museum, Hannover, Germany. Traveled to Staatlich Kunstammlungen, Dresden, Germany. Exh. cat.

1998

"Baldessari—RMS W VU: Wallpaper, Lamps, and Plants. new," Museum für Gegenwartskunst, Zürich, Switzerland. Exh. cat.

1996

"John Baldessari: National City," Museum of Contemporary Art, San Diego. Exh. cat.

"This Not That: John Baldessari, A Retrospective," Cornerhouse, Manchester, England. Traveled to Serpentine Gallery, London; Württembergischer Kunstverein, Stuttgart, Germany; Modern Galerija, Ljubljana; Museet for Samtidskunst, Oslo; and Fundação Calouste Gulbenkian, Lisbon. Exh. cat.

1990

"John Baldessari," The Museum of Contemporary Art, Los Angeles. Traveled to San Francisco Museum of Modern Art, San Francisco; Hirshhorn Museum and Sculpture Garden, Washington, D.C.; Walker Art Center, Minneapolis; Whitney Museum of American Art, New York; and Musée d'art contemporain, Montréal, Canada. Exh. cat.

Bibliography

Baldessari—RMS WVU: Wallpaper, Lamps, and Plants (new). Exh. cat. Zürich, Switzerland: Museum für Gegenwartskunst, 1998. Texts by Jeremy Gilbert-Rolfe, Bartomeu Marí, and Rein Wolfs.

Baldessari: While Something Is Happening Here, Something Else Is Happening There: Works 1988–1999. Exh. cat. Hannover, Germany: Sprengel Museum, 1999. Texts by Meg Cranston, Diedrich Diederichsen, and Thomas Weski.

Baldessari: While Something Is Happening Here, Something Else Is Happening There: Works 1965–2001. Exh. cat. Reykjavik: Reykjavik Art Museum, 2001. Texts by Dave Hickey, Eirikur Thorlaksson, Thorvaldur Thorsteinsson, and Thomas Weski.

John Baldessari. Exh. cat. New York: The New Museum, 1981. Texts by Robert Pincus-Witten and Marcia Tucker, interview by Nancy Drew.

John Baldessari. Exh. cat. Milan: Skira, 2000. Texts by Gabriella Belli, Meg Cranston, Diedrich Diederichsen, and Thomas Weski.

John Baldessari: National City. Exh. cat. San Diego: Museum of Contemporary Art, 1996. Texts by David Antin, Jan Avgikos, Bice Curiger, Hugh M. Davies, Andrea Hales, Dave Hickey, Anne Rorimer, and Abigail Solomon-Godeau.

John Baldessari: Ni por ésas/Not Even So. Exh. cat. Madrid: Centro Nacional de Exposiciones; and Valencia, Spain: Generalitat Valenciana, Instituto Valenciano de Arte Moderno, 1989. Texts by Baldessari, Guadalupe Echevarría and Vicente Todolí, Thomas Lawson, and John Miller.

John Baldessari: Somewhere Between Almost Right and Not Quite (With Orange). Exh. cat. New York: The Solomon R. Guggenheim Foundation, 2004. Texts by Tracey Bashkoff, Russell Ferguson, John Hanhardt, and Frederic Tuten.

Snoddy, Stephen. *This Not That*. Exh. cat. Manchester, England: Cornerhouse, 1995. Texts by Alexandre Melo, Uta Nusser, Snoddy, and Igor Zabel.

Van Bruggen, Coosje. *John Baldessari*. Exh. cat. Los Angeles: The Museum of Contemporary Art; and New York: Rizzoli, 1990.

EDGAR BRYAN

Born 1970 in Birmingham, Alabama
Lives in Los Angeles

Solo exhibitions

2004

Ruzicska, Salzburg

2002

China Art Objects, Los Angeles

Group exhibitions

2004

"Likeness: Portraits of Artists by Other Artists," CCA Wattis Institute for Contemporary Arts, San Francisco. Exh. cat.

"100 Artists see God," Organized by John Baldessari and Meg Cranston for Independent Curators International, New York. Traveled to The Jewish Museum San Francisco; Laguna Art Museum, Laguna Beach, California; Contemporary Art Center of Virginia, Virginia Beach. Exh. cat.

2002

"Hello, My Name Is...," Carnegie Museum of Art, Pittsburgh

2001

"Snapshot: New Art from Los Angeles," UCLA Hammer Museum, Los Angeles. Exh. cat.

Bibliography

Likeness: Portraits of Artists by Other Artists. Exh. cat. San Francisco: CCA Wattis Institute; and New York: Independent Curators International, 2004.

McDevitt, Siobhan. "Edgar Bryan at China Art Objects." *Frieze*, no. 67 (May 2002): 97–98.

100 Artists see God. Exh. cat. New York: Independent Curators International, 2004.

Snapshot: New Art from Los Angeles. Exh. cat. Los Angeles: UCLA Hammer Museum, 2001.

VIJA CELMINS

Born 1938 in Riga, Latvia
Lives in New York City

Solo exhibitions

2002

"The Prints of Vija Celmins," The Metropolitan Museum of Art, New York. Exh. cat.

2001

"Vija Celmins, New Paintings," McKee Gallery, New York. Exh. cat.

1996

"Vija Celmins: Works 1964–1996," Institute of Contemporary Arts, London. Traveled to Museo Nacional Centro de Arte Reina Sofía, Madrid; Kunstmuseum, Winterthur, Switzerland; and Museum für Moderne Kunst, Frankfurt, Germany. Exh. cat.

1995

"Vija Celmins," Fondation Cartier pour l'art contemporain, Paris. Exh. cat.

1992

"Vija Celmins," Institute of Contemporary Art, Philadelphia. Traveled to Henry Art Gallery, University of Washington, Seattle; Walker Art Center, Minneapolis; Whitney Museum of American Art, New York; and the Museum of Contemporary Art, Los Angeles. Exh. cat.

Bibliography

Bartman, William, ed. *Vija Celmins.* Los Angeles: A.R.T. Press, 1992.

Vija Celmins. London: Phaidon Press. 2004. Texts by Jorge Luis Borges, Celmins, Briony Fer, Robert Gober, and Lane Relyea.

Parkett, no. 44 (July 1995). Includes Vija Celmins and Jeanne Silverthorne, "Vija Celmins in Conversation with Jeanne Silverthorne"; Jim Lewis, "Night, Sleep, Death and the Stars: Twelve Exercises in Honor of Vija Celmins"; Nancy Princenthal, "Vija Celmins: Material Fictions"; and Richard Shiff, "Vija Celmins's Play of Imitation."

Lingwood, James, ed. *Vija Celmins Works 1964–96.* Exh. cat. London: Institute of Contemporary Arts, 1996.

Rippner, Samantha. *The Prints of Vija Celmins.* Exh. cat. New York: The Metropolitan Museum of American Art; and New Haven: Yale University Press, 2002.

Tannenbaum, Judith, ed. *Vija Celmins.* Exh. cat. Philadelphia: Institute of Contemporary Art, University of Pennsylvania, 1992. Texts by Douglas Blau and Dave Hickey.

Vija Celmins. Exh. cat. New York: McKee Gallery, 2001. Text by Bill Berkson.

PETER DOIG

Born 1959 in Edinburgh
Lives in Trinidad

Solo Exhibitions

2004

"Peter Doig—Metropolitain," Pinakothek der Moderne, Munich, and Kestnergesellschaft, Hannover. Exh. cat.

2003

"Charley's Space," Bonnefanten Museum, Maastricht, The Netherlands. Traveled to Carré d'art—Musée d'art contemporain, Nîmes, France; and The Arts Club of Chicago. Exh. cat.

2002

"Peter Doig: 100 Years Ago," Victoria Miro Gallery, London. Exh. cat.

2001

"Peter Doig," Morris and Helen Belkin Art Gallery, University of British Columbia, Vancouver. Traveled to National Gallery of Canada, Ottawa; and The Power Plant, Toronto. Exh. cat.

2000

"Peter Doig: Matrix 183/ Echo Lake," Berkeley Art Museum, University of California, Berkeley. Traveled to Museum of Contemporary Art, North Miami; Saint Louis Art Museum, Saint Louis.

1998

"Peter Doig: Blizzard Seventy-Seven," Kunsthalle, Kiel, Germany. Traveled to Kunsthalle, Nürnberg, Germany; and Whitechapel Art Gallery, London. Exh. cat.

Group exhibitions

2002

"Cavepainting: Peter Doig, Chris Ofili, and Laura Owens," Santa Monica Museum of Art, Santa Monica. Exh. cat.

"Dear Painter, Paint Me...: Painting the Figure Since Late Picabia," Centre Georges Pompidou, Paris; Schirn Kunsthalle, Frankfurt, Germany; and Kunsthalle, Vienna. Exh. cat.

2000

"Twisted: Urban and Visionary Landscapes in Contemporary Painting," Stedelijk Van Abbemuseum, Eindhoven, The Netherlands. Exh. cat.

Bibliography

100 Years Ago. Exh. cat. London: Victoria Miro Gallery, 2002.

Cavepainting. Exh. cat. Santa Monica, California: Santa Monica Museum of Art, 2002. Text by Jonathan Jones, interview by Lane Relyea.

Charley's Space. Exh. cat. Maastricht: Bonnefanten Museum, 2003. Texts by Paula van den Bosch and Catherine Grenier.

Gingeras, Alison M., ed. *Dear Painter, Paint Me...: Painting the Figure Since Late Picabia*. Exh. cat. Paris: Centre Georges Pompidou, 2002.

Metropolitain. Exh. cat. Cologne: Walther König, 2004. Texts by Bernhart Schwenk and Hilke Wagner.

Parkett, no. 67 (May 2003). Includes Paul Bonaventura, "Peter Doig: A Partial Record"; Rudi Fuchs, "Contemporary Fragility"; and Beatrix Ruf, "Peter Doig's 'Now.'"

Peter Doig. Exh. cat. Vancouver: Morris and Helen Belkin Art Gallery, University of British Columbia, 2001. Texts by Matthew Higgs, Kitty Scott, and Johanne Sloan.

Peter Doig: Blizzard Seventy-Seven. Exh. cat. Kiel, Germany: Kunsthalle; and London: Whitechapel Art Gallery, 1998. Texts by Felicity Lunn, Eva Meyer-Hermann, Terry R. Myers, and Hans-Werner Schmidt.

LUKAS DUWENHÖGGER

Born 1956 in Munich
Lives in Istanbul

Solo exhibitions

2004

"Prinzenbad," Kunstverein, Hamburg

2002

"Figures in a Carpet," Galerie Daniel Buchholz, Cologne

2000

"Down Via Uppia," Emily Tsingou Gallery, London

1997

"Innuendo," Galerie Neu, Berlin
Malmö Museet, Sweden

1995

Künstlerhaus, Stuttgart

Group exhibitions

2004

"Atomkrieg," Kunsthaus, Dresden

2003

"I and My Chimney: Lukas Duwenhögger, Lucy McKenzie, Lari Pittman," Galerie Daniel Buchholz, Cologne

"Organized Conflict," Proje4L—Istanbul Museum of Contemporary Art, Istanbul. Exh. cat.

2000

"Rocaille," Shedhalle, Zürich, Switzerland

1999

"The Passion and the Wave," 6th International Istanbul Biennale, Istanbul

1998

"From the Corner of the Eye," Stedelijk Museum, Amsterdam

1994

"Oh Boy, It's a Girl: Feminismen in der Kunst," Kunstverein, Munich, Germany. Exh. cat.

Bibliography

Organized Conflict. Exh. cat. Istanbul: Proje4L—Istanbul Museum of Contemporary Art, 2003.

Rebentisch, Juliane. "Innuendo." *Texte zur Kunst*, no. 28 (November 1997): 145–47.

Schorr, Collier. "Men Without Women." *Frieze*, no. 49 (November–December 1999): 82–87.

Verwoert, Jan. "Lukas Duwenhögger at Kunstverein Hamburg." *Frieze* (July–August 2004):126–127.

Wege, Astrid. "Lukas Duwenhögger at Galerie Daniel Buchholz." *Artforum* 41, no. 3 (November 2002): 196.

MARI EASTMAN

Born 1970 in Berkeley, California
Lives in Los Angeles

Solo exhibitions

2004
Sies + Höke Galerie, Düsseldorf, Germany

2001
Galleri Nicolai Wallner, Copenhagen
"Hello, Goodbye," Los Angeles Contemporary Exhibitions

2000
"Summertime," Bronwyn Keenan Gallery, New York

Group Exhibitions

2004
"Mary Weatherford, Mari Eastman, Liz Arnold," Daniel Hug Gallery, Los Angeles

2003
"Girls Gone Wild," Bronwyn Keenan Gallery, New York
"The Cat Show," Acme, Los Angeles

2002
"Painting and Illustration," Luckman Gallery, California State University, Los Angeles

2001
"Snapshot: New Art from Los Angeles," UCLA Hammer Museum, Los Angeles. Exh. cat.
"Painting 2001: Artists from Berlin, Los Angeles, and New York," Victoria Miro Gallery, London

Bibliography

Belden, Kris. "Mari Eastman, The Suburban." *Ten by Ten* (Chicago) 2, no. 1 (2002).
Smith, Roberta. "Art in Review: Girls Gone Wild." *The New York Times*, 4 July 2003, E31.
Snapshot: New Art from Los Angeles. Exh. cat. Los Angeles: UCLA Hammer Museum, 2001.

THOMAS EGGERER

Born 1963 in Munich
Lives in Los Angeles

Solo exhibitions

2004
Friedrich Petzel Gallery, New York

2003
Richard Telles Fine Art, Los Angeles
"Thomas Eggerer: Atrium," Kunstverein, Braunschweig, Germany. Exh. cat.
Galerie Daniel Buchholz, Cologne

2002
Wadsworth Atheneum Museum of Art, Hartford, Connecticut. Exh. brochure

1999
Galerie Daniel Buchholz, Cologne

Group exhibitions

2003
"deutschemalereizweitausenddrei," Kunstverein, Frankfurt, Germany. Exh. cat.

2002
"Painting on the Move," Kunsthalle, Basel, Switzerland

2001
"Snapshot: New Art from Los Angeles," UCLA Hammer Museum, Los Angeles. Exh. cat.

1999
"Malerei," INIT Kunsthalle, Berlin

1994
"Oh Boy, It's a Girl: Feminismen in der Kunst," Kunstverein, Munich, Germany. Exh. cat.

Bibliography

Grässlin, Karola, ed. *Thomas Eggerer: Atrium*. Exh. cat. Braunschweig, Germany: Kunstverein, 2003. Texts by Diedrich Diederichsen and David Joselit.
Anxious Pleasures. Exh. brochure. Hartford, Connecticut: Wadsworth Atheneum Museum of Art, 2002. Text by Nicholas Baume.

KIRSTEN EVERBERG

Born 1965 in Los Angeles
Lives in London

Solo exhibitions

2004
1301PE, Los Angeles

Group exhibitions

2004
"Supersonic," Art Center College of Design, Pasadena, California

2003
Anna Helwing Gallery, Los Angeles

2002
"...with pleasure, wickedness and finesse," The Basement, Los Angeles

Bibliography

Sorkin, Jenni. "Kirsten Everberg." *Frieze*, no. 84 (July–August 2004): 131.

PHILIP GUSTON

Born 1913 in Montreal
Died 1980 in Woodstock, New York

Solo exhibitions

2003

"Philip Guston: Retrospective," Modern Art Museum of Fort Worth, Forth Worth, Texas. Traveled to San Francisco Museum of Modern Art, San Francisco; The Metropolitan Museum of Art, New York; and Royal Academy of Arts, London. Exh. cat.

2001

"Poor Richard by Philip Guston," McKee Gallery, New York. Traveled to Mass MOCA, North Adams, Massachusetts; and Fine Arts Museum of San Francisco, Legion of Honor, San Francisco. Exh. cat.

1999

"Philip Guston: Gemälde 1947–1979," Kunstmuseum, Bonn, Germany. Traveled to Württembergischer Kunstverein, Stuttgart, Germany; and National Gallery of Canada, Ottawa. Exh. cat.

1994

"Philip Guston's Poem Pictures," Addison Gallery of American Art, Andover, Massachusetts. Traveled to The Drawing Center, New York. Exh. cat.

Bibliography

Auping, Michael, ed. *Philip Guston: Retrospective*. Exh. cat. Forth Worth, Texas: Modern Art Museum of Fort Worth; and New York: Thames and Hudson, 2003. Texts by Dore Ashton, Auping, Bill Berkson, Guston, Andrew Graham-Dixon, Joseph Rishel, and Michael E. Shapiro.

Balken, Debra Bricker. *Philip Guston's Poem-Pictures*. Exh. cat. Andover, Massachusetts: Addison Gallery of American Art, Phillips Academy; and Seattle: University of Washington Press, 1994. Texts by Balken, Bill Berkson, Clark Coolidge, William Corbett, Stanley Kunitz, and Jock Reynolds.

——— *Philip Guston's Poor Richard*. Exh. cat. Chicago: The University of Chicago Press, 2001.

Corbett, William. *Philip Guston's Late Work: A Memoir*. Boston: Zoland Books, 1994.

Mayer, Musa. *Night Studio: A Memoir of Philip Guston*. London: Thames and Hudson, 1991.

Philip Guston: Gemälde 1947–1979. Exh. cat. Bonn, Germany: Kunstmuseum, 1999. Texts by Michael Auping, Martin Hentschel, and Christoph Schreier.

RICHARD HAMILTON

Born 1922 in London
Lives in Oxfordshire, England

Solo exhibitions

2003

"Richard Hamilton: Introspective," Museu d'Art Contemporani, Barcelona, Spain. Traveled to Museum Ludwig, Cologne, Germany. Exh. cat.

"Richard Hamilton: Products," Gagosian Gallery, London. Exh. cat.

2002

"Imaging Ulysses." The British Museum, London. Traveled to Irish Museum of Modern Art, Dublin; and Museum Boijmans Van Beuningen, Rotterdam. Exh. cat.

"Richard Hamilton: Prints and Multiples, 1939–2002," Kunstmuseum, Winterthur, Switzerland. Traveled to Yale Center for British Art, Yale University, New Haven, Connecticut. Exh. cat.

1998

"Richard Hamilton: Subject to an Impression," Kunsthalle, Bremen, Germany. Exh. cat.

1992

"Richard Hamilton," Tate Gallery, London. Traveled to Irish Museum of Modern Art, Dublin. Exh. cat.

1974

Nationalgalerie, Berlin

1973

Solomon R. Guggenheim, Museum, New York

Bibliography

Hamilton, Richard. *Collected Words*. London: Thames and Hudson, 1983.

Morphet, Richard, ed. *Richard Hamilton*. Exh. cat. London: The Tate Gallery, 1992.

Richard Hamilton: Retrospective/Introspective. Exh. cat. 2 vols. Cologne, Germany: Verlag der Buchhandlung Walther König, 2003. Texts by Laszlo Glozer, Hal Foster, and Hamilton.

Richard Hamilton: Prints and Multiples 1939–2002. Exh. cat. Düsseldorf, Germany: Richter Verlag, 2004. Texts by Stephen Coppel, Etienne Lullin, and Dieter Schwarz.

Richard Hamilton: Products. London: Gagosian Gallery, 2003.

Richard Hamilton: Subject to an Impression. Exh. cat. Bremen: Kunsthalle, 1998.

NEIL JENNEY

Born 1945 in Torrington, Connecticut
Lives in New York

Solo exhibitions

2001

"Neil Jenney: The Bad Years, 1969–70," Gagosian Gallery, New York. Exh. cat.

1981

"Neil Jenney: Paintings and Sculpture 1967–1980," University of California Art Museum, Berkeley. Traveled to Contemporary Arts Museum, Houston; Corcoran Gallery of Art, Washington, D.C.; Stedelijk Museum, Amsterdam; Louisiana Museum, Humlebaek, Denmark; Kunsthalle, Basel, Switzerland. Exh. cat.

Bibliography

Marshall, Richard. *New Image Painting*. Exh. cat. New York: Whitney Museum of American Art, 1978.

Rosenthal, Mark. *Neil Jenney: Paintings and Sculpture 1967–1980*. Exh. cat. Berkeley, California: University of California Art Museum, 1981.

Neil Jenney: The Bad Years 1969–70. Exh. cat. New York: Gagosian Gallery, 2001. Text by Paul Gardner.

JOCHEN KLEIN

Born 1967 in Giengen a.d. Brenz, Germany
Died 1997 in Munich

Solo exhibitions

2004

Maureen Paley/Interim Art, London

1998

Kunstraum, Munich. Traveled to Cubitt, London. Exh. cat.

1998

Feature, New York

1997

Galerie Daniel Buchholz, Cologne

Group exhibitions

1998

"From the Corner of the Eye," Stedelijk Museum, Amsterdam

1994

"Oh Boy, It's a Girl: Feminismen in der Kunst," Kunstverein, Munich, Germany. Exh. cat.

Bibliography

Dziewior, Yilmaz. "Jochen Klein at Galerie Daniel Buchholz." *Artforum* 36, no. 5 (January 1998): 111.

Nieuwenhuyzen, Martijn van "Jochen Klein" in *From the Corner of the Eye* (Amsterdam: Stedelijk Museum, 1998).

Tillmans, Wolfgang, ed. *Jochen Klein*. Exh. cat. Cologne: Walther König, 1998. Texts by Doug Ashford and Helmut Draxler.

Time Out. Exh. cat. Nürnberg, Germany: Kunsthalle, 1997. Texts by Stefan Schmidt-Wulffen and Raimar Stange.

THOMAS LAWSON

Born 1951 in Glasgow
Lives in Los Angeles

Solo exhibitions

2001

Sleeper, Edinburgh

1995

Anthony Reynolds Gallery, London

1990

"Thomas Lawson," Third Eye Centre, Glasgow. Traveled to Anthony Reynolds Gallery, London; and Battersea Arts Centre, London.

1989

Metro Pictures, New York

Bibliography

A Forest of Signs: Art in the Crisis of Representation. Exh. cat. Los Angeles: The Museum of Contemporary Art; and Cambridge, Massachusetts: The MIT Press, 1989. Texts by Ann Goldstein, Mary Jane Jacob, Anne Rorimer, and Howard Singerman.

The Heroic Figure. Exh. cat. Houston: Contemporary Arts Museum, 1984. Texts by Linda L. Cathcart and Craig Owens.

Lawson, Thomas. *Mining for Gold: Selected Writings (1979–1996)*. Zurich: JRP/Ringier, and Dijon: Les presses du réel, 2004.

Thomas Lawson. Exh. cat. Glasgow: Third Eye Centre, 1990. Text by Jeanne Silverthorne.

KERRY JAMES MARSHALL

Born 1955 in Birmingham, Alabama
Lives in Chicago

Solo exhibitions

2003

"Kerry James Marshall: One True Thing, Meditations on Black Aesthetics," Museum of Contemporary Art, Chicago. Traveled to Miami Art Museum, Miami; Baltimore Museum of Art, Baltimore; Studio Museum in Harlem, New York; and Birmingham Museum of Art, Birmingham. Exh. cat.

1998

"Kerry James Marshall: Mementos," The Renaissance Society, University of Chicago, Chicago. Exh. cat.

Bibliography

Walker, Hamza, ed. *Kerry James Marshall: Mementos*. Exh. cat. Chicago: The Renaissance Society, University of Chicago, 2000. Texts by Will Alexander, Cheryl I. Harris, and Richard J. Powell.

Kerry James Marshall. New York: Harry N. Abrams, 2000. Texts by Arthur Jafa, Marshall, and Terrie Sultan.

Kerry James Marshall: One True Thing, Meditations on Black Aesthetics. Exh. cat. Chicago: Museum of Contemporary Art, 2003. Texts by Jeff Donaldson, Nathaniel McLin, Charles Mills, and Helen Molesworth.

LUCY MCKENZIE

Born 1977 in Glasgow
Lives in Glasgow

Solo exhibitions

2004

"Bi-Curious," Cabinet Gallery, London

"Deathwatch," Van Abbemuseum, Eindhoven, The Netherlands

2003

"Brian Eno," Neuer Aachener Kunstverein, Aachen, Germany. Exh. cat.

"MMIV," Tate Britain, London

2002

"If It Moves, Kiss It," Galerie Christian Nagel, Berlin

2001

"Global Joy," Galerie Daniel Buchholz, Cologne. Exh. cat.

Group exhibitions

2003

"I and My Chimney: Lukas Duwenhögger, Lucy McKenzie, Lari Pittman," Galerie Daniel Buchholz, Cologne, Germany

2002

"Painting on the Move," Öffentliche Kunstsammlung, Museum für Gegenwartskunst, and Kunsthalle, Basel, Switzerland. Exh. cat.

2001

"Painting at the Edge of the World," Walker Art Center, Minneapolis.

Bibliography

Archer, Michael. "Opening: Lucy McKenzie." *Artforum* 40, no. 1 (September 2001): 184–85.

The Best Book About Pessimism I Ever Read. Exh. cat. Braunschweig, Germany: Kunstverein, 2002.

Fogle, Douglas, ed. *Painting at the Edge of the World.* Exh. cat. Minneapolis: Walker Art Center, 2001.

Lucy McKenzie: Brian Eno. Exh. cat. Frankfurt, Germany: Revolver, Archiv für Aktuelle Kunst, 2004.

Lucy McKenzie: Global Joy. Exh. cat. Cologne, Germany: Galerie Daniel Buchholz, 2001.

Slyce, John. "London: Last Exit Painting." *Flash Art,* no. 226 (October 2002): 66–69.

SILKE OTTO-KNAPP

Born 1970 in Osnabrück, Germany
Lives in London

Solo exhibitions

2004

Greengrassi, London

2003

"Orange View," Kunstverein für die Rheinlande und Westfalen, Düsseldorf, Germany. Exh. cat.

"25th Floor," Galerie Daniel Buchholz, Cologne, Germany

2002

Galerie Karin Guenther, Hamburg, Germany

Group exhibitions

2004

"Étrangement proche/Seltsam vertraut," Saarland Museum, Saarbrücken, Germany

2003

"deutschemalereizweitausenddrei," Kunstverein, Frankfurt, Germany

"Creeping Revolution 2," Rooseum Center for Contemporary Art, Malmö, Sweden

2002

"Imagining L.A.: Ed Ruscha and Silke Otto-Knapp," Kunstverein, Wolfsburg, Germany

Bibliography

Esche, Charles. "Silke Otto-Knapp." In *Cream 3: Contemporary Art in Culture,* 268–72. London: Phaidon Press, 2003.

Heiser, Jörg. "Ed Ruscha and Silke Otto-Knapp." *Frieze,* no. 68 (June–August 2002): 103–04.

Higgie, Jennifer. "Vanishing Act." *Frieze,* no. 79 (November–December 2003): 82–85.

Silke Otto-Knapp: Orange View. Exh. cat. Düsseldorf: Kunstverein für die Rheinlande und Westfalen, 2003. Texts by Andreas Spiegl and Jan Verwoert.

LAURA OWENS

Born 1970 in Euclid, Ohio
Lives in Los Angeles

Solo Exhibitions

2004

Gavin Brown's enterprise, New York

2003

"Laura Owens," The Museum of Contemporary Art, Los Angeles. Traveled to Aspen Art Museum, Aspen, Colorado; Milwaukee Art Museum; Museum of Contemporary Art, North Miami. Exh. cat.

2001

"Laura Owens," Isabella Stewart Gardner Museum, Boston. Exh. cat.

2000

Inverleith House, Royal Botanic Garden Edinburgh. Exh. cat.

Group exhibitions

2002

"Painting on the Move," Öffentliche Kunstsammlung, Museum für Gegenwartskunst, and Kunsthalle, Basel, Switzerland. Exh. cat.

"Cavepainting: Peter Doig, Chris Ofili, and Laura Owens," Santa Monica Museum of Art, California. Exh. cat.

2001

"Painting at the Edge of the World," Walker Art Center, Minneapolis

1999

"Examining Pictures," Whitechapel Art Gallery, London, and Museum of Contemporary Art, Chicago. Traveled to UCLA Hammer Museum, Los Angeles. Exh. cat.

Bibliography

Examining Pictures. Exh. cat. London: Whitechapel Art Gallery; and Chicago: Museum of Contemporary Art, Chicago, 1999. Texts by Francesco Bonami and Judith Nesbitt.

Cavepainting. Exh. cat. Santa Monica, California: Santa Monica Museum of Art, 2002. Text by Jonathan Jones, interview by Lane Relyea.

Fogle, Douglas, ed. *Painting at the Edge of the World*. Exh. cat. Minneapolis: Walker Art Center, 2001.

Laura Owens. Exh. cat. Boston: Isabella Stewart Gardner Museum; and Milan: Edizione Charta, 2001. Texts by Russell Ferguson and Jennifer R. Gross.

Laura Owens. Exh. cat. Los Angeles: The Museum of Contemporary Art, 2003. Texts by Thomas Lawson and Paul Schimmel.

New Work by Laura Owens (1999–2000) and John Hutton Balfour's Botanical Teaching Diagrams (1840–1879). Exh. cat. Edinburgh: Inverleith House, Royal Botanic Garden, 2000. Texts by Susan Morgan and Henry Noltie.

Parkett, no. 65 (September 2002). Includes Russell Ferguson, "Laura Owens Paints a Picture"; Mungo Thomson, "From my Junkyard to Yours"; and Benjamin Weissman, "Monkey Man Killer."

ENOC PEREZ

Born 1967 in San Juan, Puerto Rico
Lives in New York

Solo exhibitions

2004
The Happy Lion, Los Angeles

2003
"Enoc Perez: Monuments," Elizabeth Dee Gallery, New York

2002
"Enoc Perez: Holiday," Kunstverein, Heilbronn, Germany

1993
White Columns, New York

Group exhibitions

2002
"Dear Painter, Paint Me… : Painting the Figure since late Picabia," Centre Pompidou, Paris. Traveled to Schirn Kunsthalle, Frankfurt, and Kunsthalle, Vienna. Exh. cat.

1998
"Message to Pretty," Thread Waxing Space. Exh. cat.

Bibliography

Message to Pretty. Exh. cat. New York: Thread Waxing Space, 1998. Texts by Lia Gangitano and Eileen Myles.

Gingeras, Alison M., ed. *Dear Painter, Paint Me… : Painting the Figure since late Picabia*. Exh. cat. Paris: Centre Pompidou, 2002.

FAIRFIELD PORTER

Born 1907 in Winnetka, Illinois
Died 1975 in Southampton, New York

Solo exhibitions

2000
"Fairfield Porter: A Life in Art," AXA Gallery, New York. Exh. cat.

1997
"Fairfield Porter Paintings, 1950–1975," Tibor de Nagy Gallery, New York

1993
"Fairfield Porter: An American Painter," The Parrish Art Museum, Southampton, New York

Bibliography

Ludman, Joan. *Fairfield Porter: A Catalogue Raisonné of the Paintings, Watercolors, and Pastels*. New York: Hudson Hills Press, 2001. Texts by William C. Agee, Rackstraw Downes, and John T. Spike.

Spike, John T. *Fairfield Porter: An American Classic*. New York: Abrams, 1992.

Spring, Justin. *Fairfield Porter: A Life in Art*. New Haven, Connecticut: Yale University Press, 2000.

RICHARD PRINCE

Born 1949 in the Panama Canal Zone
Lives in upstate New York

Solo exhibitions

2004

"Man," Galerie Eva Presenhuber, Zürich
"Women," Regen Projects, Los Angeles

2003

"Richard Prince: Nurse Paintings," Barbara Gladstone Gallery, New York. Exh. cat.

2002

"Richard Prince: Paintings," Kunsthalle, Zürich. Exh. cat.
"Richard Prince: Photographs," Museum für Gegenwartskunst, Basel. Exh. cat.
"Richard Prince: Principal Gemälde und Fotografien 1977–2001," Kunstmuseum, Wolfsburg, Germany. Exh. cat.

1992

"Richard Prince," Whitney Museum of American Art, New York. Traveled to Kunstverein, Düsseldorf; San Francisco Museum of Modern Art, San Francisco; and Museum Boymans-van Beuningen, Rotterdam. Exh. cat.

Bibliography

Phillips, Lisa, ed. *Richard Prince*. Exh. cat. New York: Whitney Museum of American Art, 1992.
Prince, Richard. *Adult Comedy Action Drama*. Zürich: Scalo, 1995.
———. *Why I Go to the Movies Alone*. New York: Tanam Press, 1983.
Richard Prince. London: Phaidon Press, 2003. Texts by Rosetta Brooks, Jeff Rian, and Luc Sante.
Richard Prince: Nurse Paintings. Exh. cat. New York: Barbara Gladstone Gallery, 2003. Text by Matthew Collings.
Richard Prince, Paintings—Photographs. Exh. cat. Ostfildern-Ruit, Germany: Hatje Cantz, 2002. Text by Bruce Hainley.

GERHARD RICHTER

Born 1932 in Dresden
Lives in Cologne

Solo exhibitions

2002

"Gerhard Richter: Forty Years of Painting," The Museum of Modern Art, New York; Traveled to The Art Institute of Chicago, Chicago; San Francisco Museum of Modern Art, San Francisco; and Hirshhorn Museum and Sculpture Garden, Smithsonian Institution, Washington, D.C. Exh. cat.
"Gerhard Richter: Acht Grau/Eight Gray," Deutsche Guggenheim, Berlin. Exh. cat.
"Gerhard Richter: Landscapes," Sprengel Museum, Hanover.

1995

"Atlas," Dia Center for the Arts, New York. Exh. cat.

1993

"Gerhard Richter," Musée d'Art Moderne de la Ville de Paris, Paris. Traveled to Kunst- und Ausstellungshalle der Bundesrepublik Deutschland, Bonn, Germany; Modern Museet, Stockholm; and Museo Nacional Centro de Arte Reina Sofía, Madrid. Exh. cat. and cat. raisonné.

1991

Tate Gallery, London

1990

"Gerhard Richter: 18. October 1977," St. Louis Art Museum. Traveled to Grey Art Gallery, New York; Musée des Beaux-Arts de Montréal; Lannan Foundation, Los Angeles; Institute of Contemporary Art, Boston.

Bibliography

Elger, Dietmar, (ed.), *Gerhard Richter: Landscapes*. Ostfildern-Ruit: Cantz, 1998. Texts by Elger and Oskar Bätschmann.

Gerhard Richter. Exh. cat. London: Tate Gallery, 1991. Texts by Neal Ascherson, Stefan Germer, and Sean Rainbird.

Gerhard Richter. 3 vols. Bonn, Germany: Kunst- und Ausstellungshalle der Bundesrepublik Deutschland; and Ostfildern-Ruit, Germany: Cantz, 1993. Exh. cat. and cat. raisonné. Texts by Benjamin H. D. Buchloh, Peter Gidal, and Birgit Pelzer.

Gerhard Richter: 18. Oktober 1977. Krefeld: Museum Haus Esters; Frankfurt: Portikus; Cologne: König, 1989. Texts by Benjamin H.D. Buchloh, Gerhard Storck, and Stefan Germer. Trans. London: Institute of Contemporary Art, 1989.

Gerhard Richter: Atlas. Exh. cat. New York: Dia Center for the Arts, 1995.

Obrist, Hans-Ulrich, ed. *Gerhard Richter: The Daily Practice of Painting, Writings and Interviews 1962–1993*. trans. David Britt. Cambridge, Massachusetts: The MIT Press; and London: Anthony D'Offay Gallery, 1995.

Storr, Robert. *Gerhard Richter: Forty Years of Painting*. Exh. cat. New York: The Museum of Modern Art, 2002.

———. *Gerhard Richter: Doubt and Belief in Painting*. New York: The Museum of Modern Art, 2003.

LUC TUYMANS

Born 1958 in Mortsel, Belgium
Lives in Antwerp

Solo exhibitions

2004

Tate Modern, London. Traveled to K21–Kunstsammlung Nordrhein-Westfalen, Düsseldorf, Germany. Exh. cat.

2003

"Luc Tuymans: The Arena," Kunstverein, Hannover. Traveled to Pinakothek der Moderne, Munich; and Kunstmuseum, St. Gallen, Switzerland. Exh. cat.

2001

Belgian Pavilion, Venice Bienniale

1999

Kuntsmuseum Wolfsburg

Bibliography

Berg, Stephan, ed. *Luc Tuymans: The Arena*. Exh. cat. Ostfildern-Ruit, Germany: Hatje Cantz, 2003. Texts by Berg, Konrad Bitterli, and Philippe Pirotte.

Drolet, Owen. "Luc Tuymans: The Truth of the Matter." *Flash Art*, no. 235 (March–April 2004): 76–79.

Garrett, Craig, and Michele Robecchi. "The Dark Places: Interview with Luc Tuymans." *Flash Art*, no. 235 (March–April 2004): 79.

Luc Tuymans. London: Phaidon Press, 2003. Texts by Juan Vicente Aliaga, Ulrich Loock, Andrei Platonov, Hans Rudolf Reust, Nancy Spector, and Tuymans.

Luc Tuymans. Exh. cat. London: Tate Modern, 2004. Texts by Emma Dexter, Jesus Fuenmajor, and Julian Heynen.

Trouble Spot: Painting. Exh. cat. Antwerp: NICC and Museum van Hedendaagse Kunst, 1999.

Tuymans, Luc. "Display." *Flash Art*, no. 235 (March–April 2004): 40.

This publication accompanies the exhibition "**THE UNDISCOVERED COUNTRY**," organized by Russell Ferguson and presented at the Hammer Museum, Los Angeles, 3 October 2004–16 January 2005.

"**THE UNDISCOVERED COUNTRY**" is generously supported by The Andy Warhol Foundation for the Visual Arts, Eileen Harris-Norton and the Peter Norton Family Foundation, Beth Swofford, Maria Hummer and Bob Tuttle, David Teiger, Gail and Stanley Hollander, and The Broad Art Foundation.

PHOTOGRAPHY CREDITS

Courtesy of David Zwirner, New York, photo by Felix Tirry, pp. 4, 40, 41, 42; photo: Joshua White, pp. 12, 64, 65, 67, 91, 92, 95, 105; photo © D. James Dee, p. 14; photograph © 1988 The Detroit Institute of Arts, p. 18; photo: Jim Strong, p. 21; photo: Brian Forrest, pp. 24, 88–89; photo: Robert Wedemeyer, pp. 25, 27; photo: Lee Stalsworth, pp. 29, 30, 44; courtesy of Gavin Brown's enterprise, New York, pp. 31, 85; courtesy Galerie Daniel Buchholz, Cologne, pp. 37, 70, 72–73, 78–79, 102–03, 111, back cover; Réunion des Musées Nationaux / Art Resource, NY, p. 38; digital image © The Museum of Modern Art / Licensed by SCALA / Art Resource, NY, p. 38; Tate Gallery, London / Art Resource, NY © 2004 Artists Rights Society (ARS), New York / DACS, London, p. 43; photograph © Museum of Contemporary Art, Chicago, p. 45; photo: Ed Cornachio, p. 47; photo: Richard Stoner, p. 48; photo: Jamison Miller, p. 49; photo: Douglas M. Parker Studio, pp. 52, 57, 112; Tate Gallery, London / Art Resource, NY © 2004 Artists Tights Society (ARS), New York / SIAE Rome, p. 54; courtesy McKee Gallery, New York, pp. 54, 55; courtesy the artist and Marian Goodman Gallery, New York, pp. 59, 60, 61; courtesy of Metro Pictures, New York, pp. 66, 113; reproduction, The Art Institute of Chicago © 2004 Artists Rights Society (ARS), New York / DACS, London, p. 68; courtesy of the artist, p. 69; photo: József Rosta, p. 71; courtesy Barbara Gladstone, pp. 74, 76; courtesy Karyn Lovegrove Gallery, Los Angeles, p. 80 (photo: Gene Ogami), pp. 81, 82–83, 94 (photo: Robert Wedemeyer); photo: Stephen White, pp. 86–87; courtesy of the artist, p. 90; courtesy the artist and 1301PE, Los Angeles, photo: Fredrik Nilsen, pp. 96–97; courtesy Elizabeth Dee Gallery, New York, photo: Tom Powell, pp. 98, 100–01; and courtesy of Richard Telles Fine Art, Los Angeles, photo: Fredrik Nilsen, pp. 106–07, 108.

Copy editor: Jane Hyun
Design: Lorraine Wild with Stuart Smith
Printer: Dr. Cantz'sche Druckerei, Ostfildern, Germany

Published by the Armand Hammer Museum of Art and Cultural Center, 10899 Wilshire Boulevard, Los Angeles, California 90024-4201.

The Armand Hammer Museum of Art and Cultural Center is operated by the University of California, Los Angeles. Occidental Petroleum Corporation has partially endowed the Museum and constructed the Occidental Petroleum Cultural Center Building, which houses the museum.

ISBN 0-943739-27-6

Available through D.A.P./
Distributed Art Publishers
155 Sixth Avenue, 2nd Floor
New York, NY 10013
Tel: (212) 627-1999
Fax: (212) 627-9484

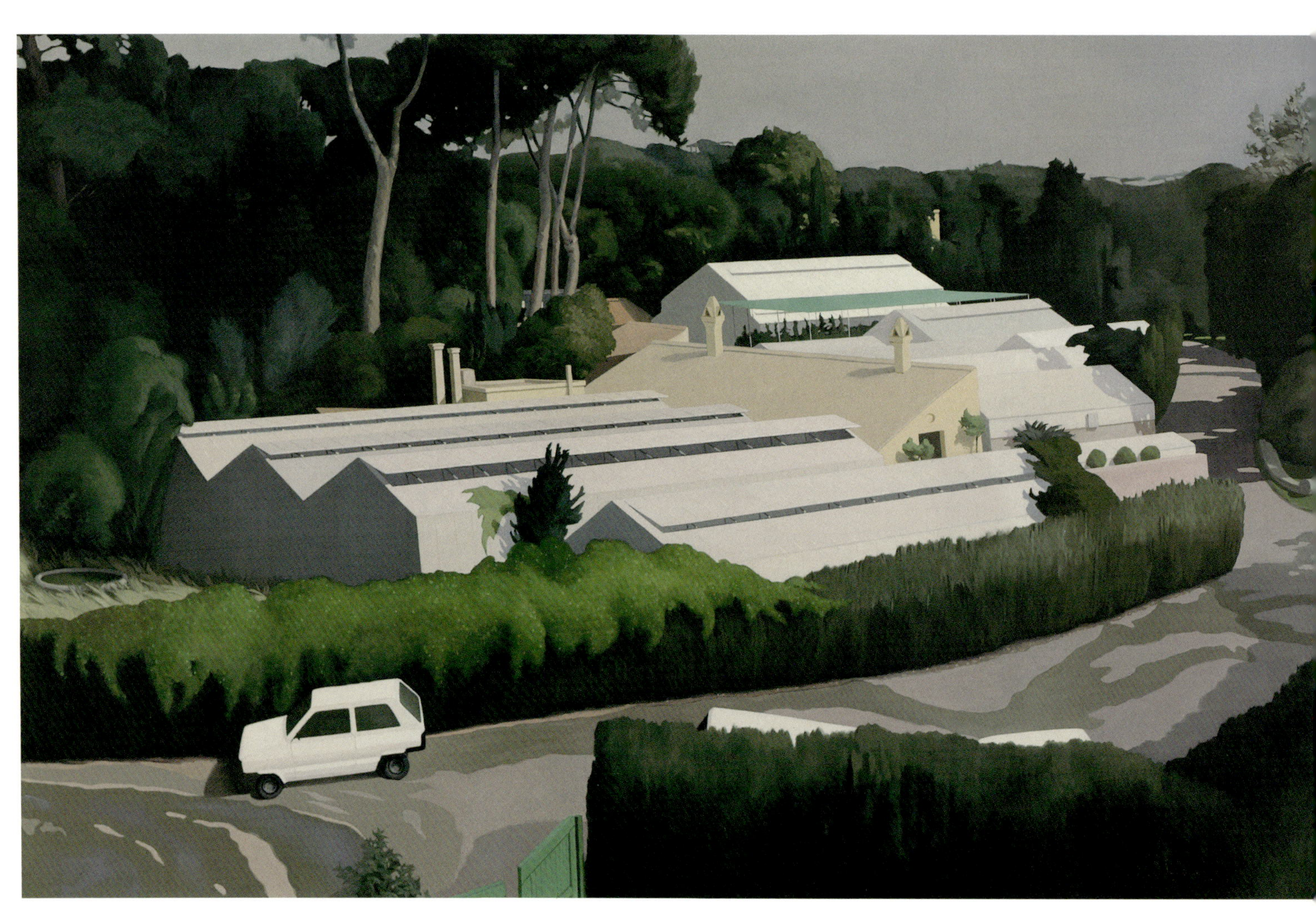

Lukas Duwenhögger
Roman Holiday, 1999